Born with genetic mutations that gave them abilities beyond those of normal humans, mutants are the next stage in evolution. As such, they are feared and hated by humanity. A group of mutants known as the X-Men fight for peaceful coexistence between mutants and humankind. But not all mutants see peaceful coexistence as a reality.

UNCANNY X·MEN

Cyclops is the public face for what he calls "the new mutant revolution." Vowing to protect the mutant race, he's begun to gather and train a new generation of mutants.

When Charles Xavier died at the hands of a phoenix-possessed Scott Summers, the reading of his last will and testament brought to light the existence of a mutant of immense power whom Xavier had kept hidden. With thousands of lives being lost as the mutant lost control of his abilities, Eva Bell traveled back in time and used the help of a younger Xavier to ensure the mutant was never born. In doing this, she erased the deaths caused by the mutant, also changing Xavier's will to now read that all that he owned should be left to Scott Summers. Racked by guilt, Scott was unable to accept his surrogate father's gifts, and relinquished the ownership of the school to Storm, walking away from his father's legacy.

Meanwhile, his brother Alex, a.k.a. Havok, finding that his beliefs no longer fell in line with the Avengers' mission, left the Uncanny Avengers to join his brother.

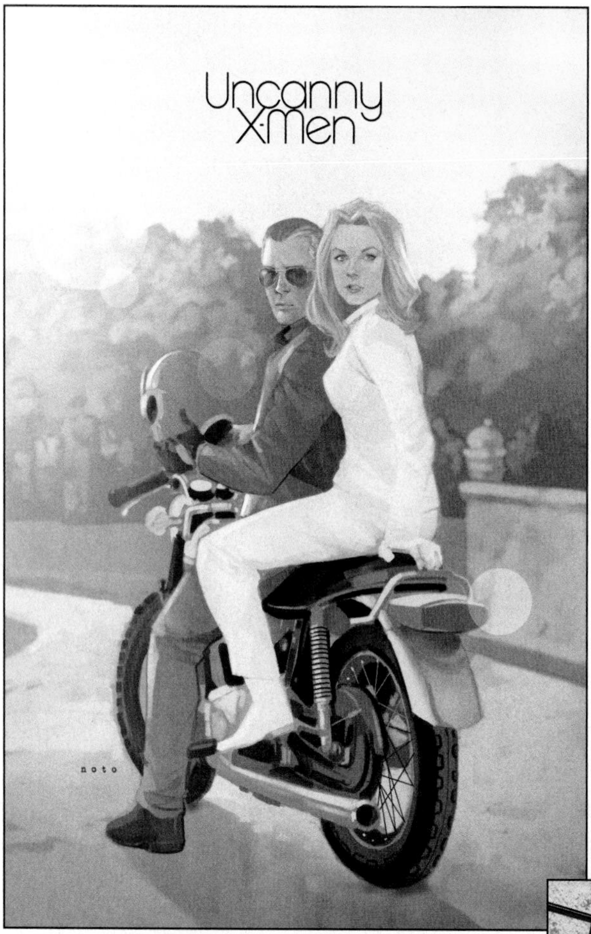
Uncanny
X-Men
noto

UNCANNY X-MEN #32 VARIANT
BY PHIL NOTO

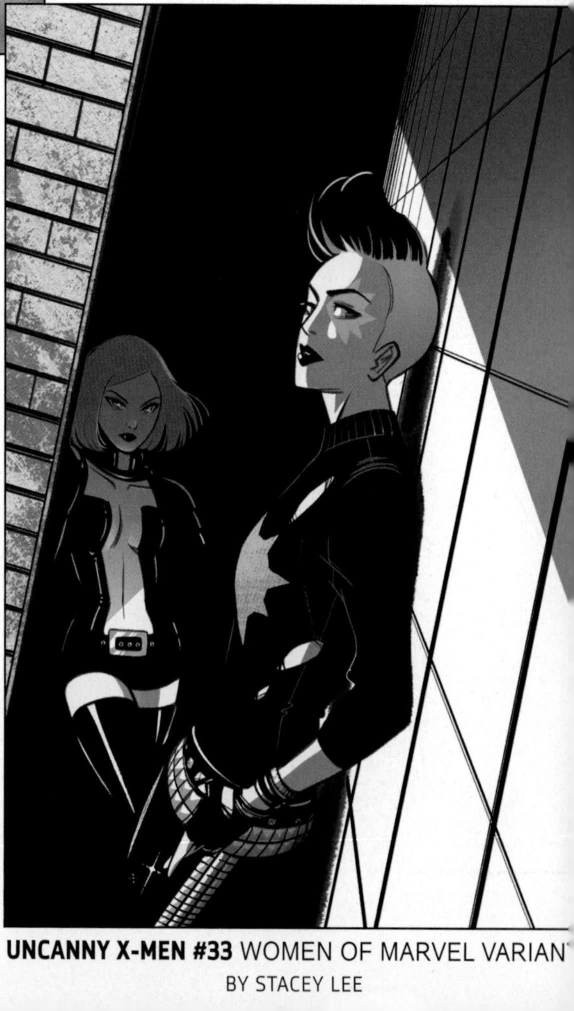

UNCANNY X-MEN #33 WOMEN OF MARVEL VARIAN
BY STACEY LEE

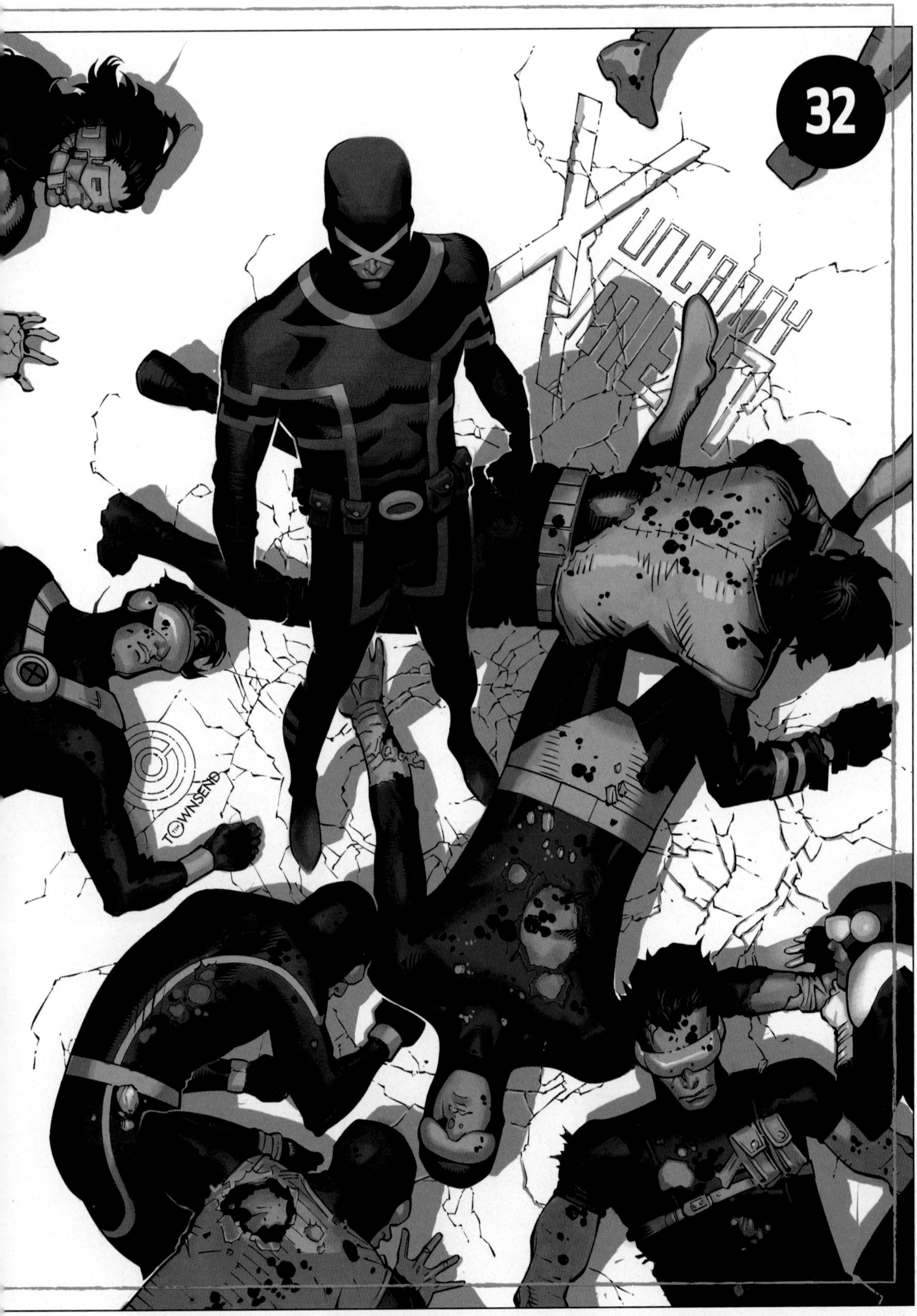

32
UNCANNY X-MEN
TOWNSEND

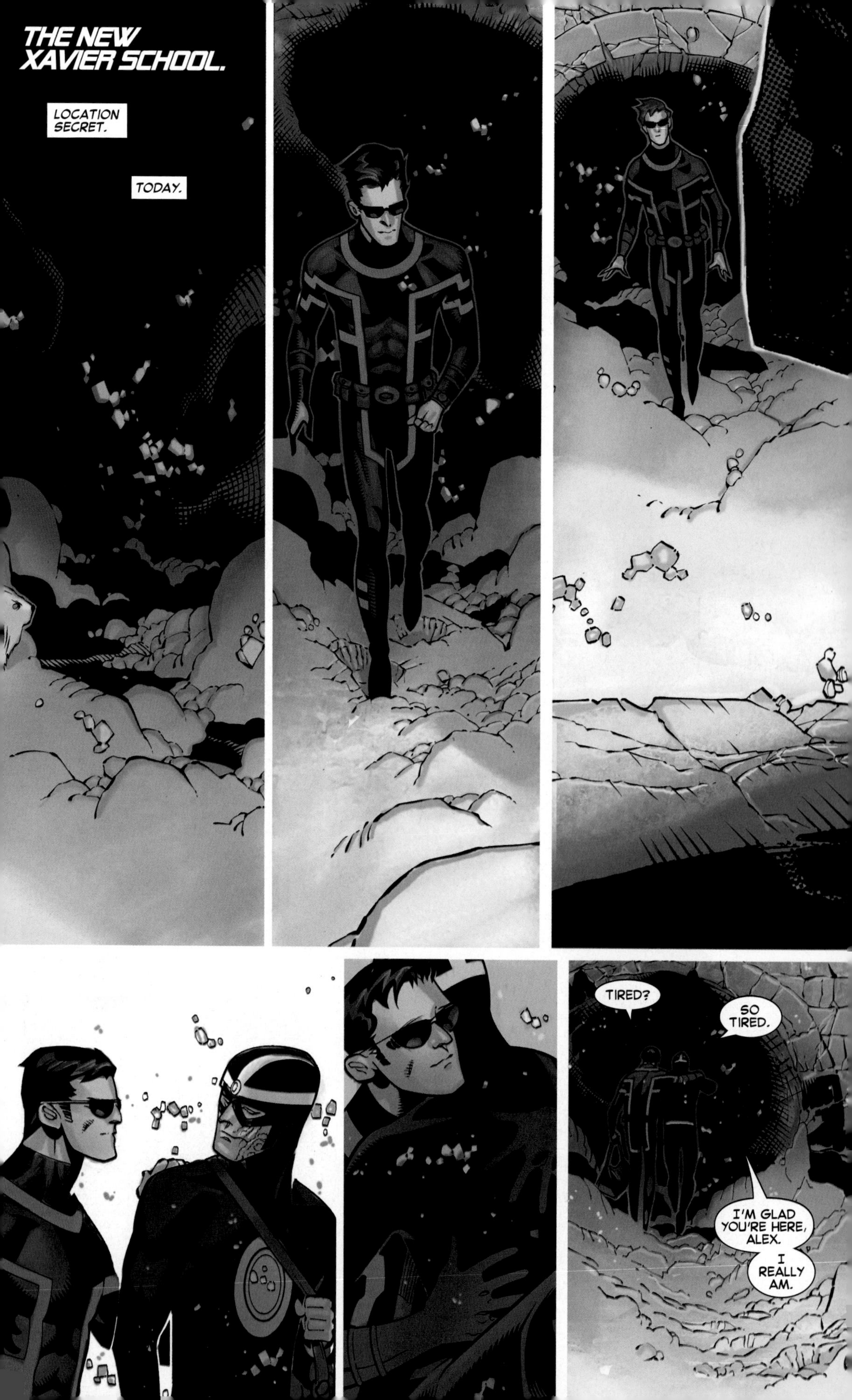
THE NEW XAVIER SCHOOL.
LOCATION SECRET.
TODAY.
TIRED?
SO TIRED.
I'M GLAD YOU'RE HERE, ALEX.
I REALLY AM.

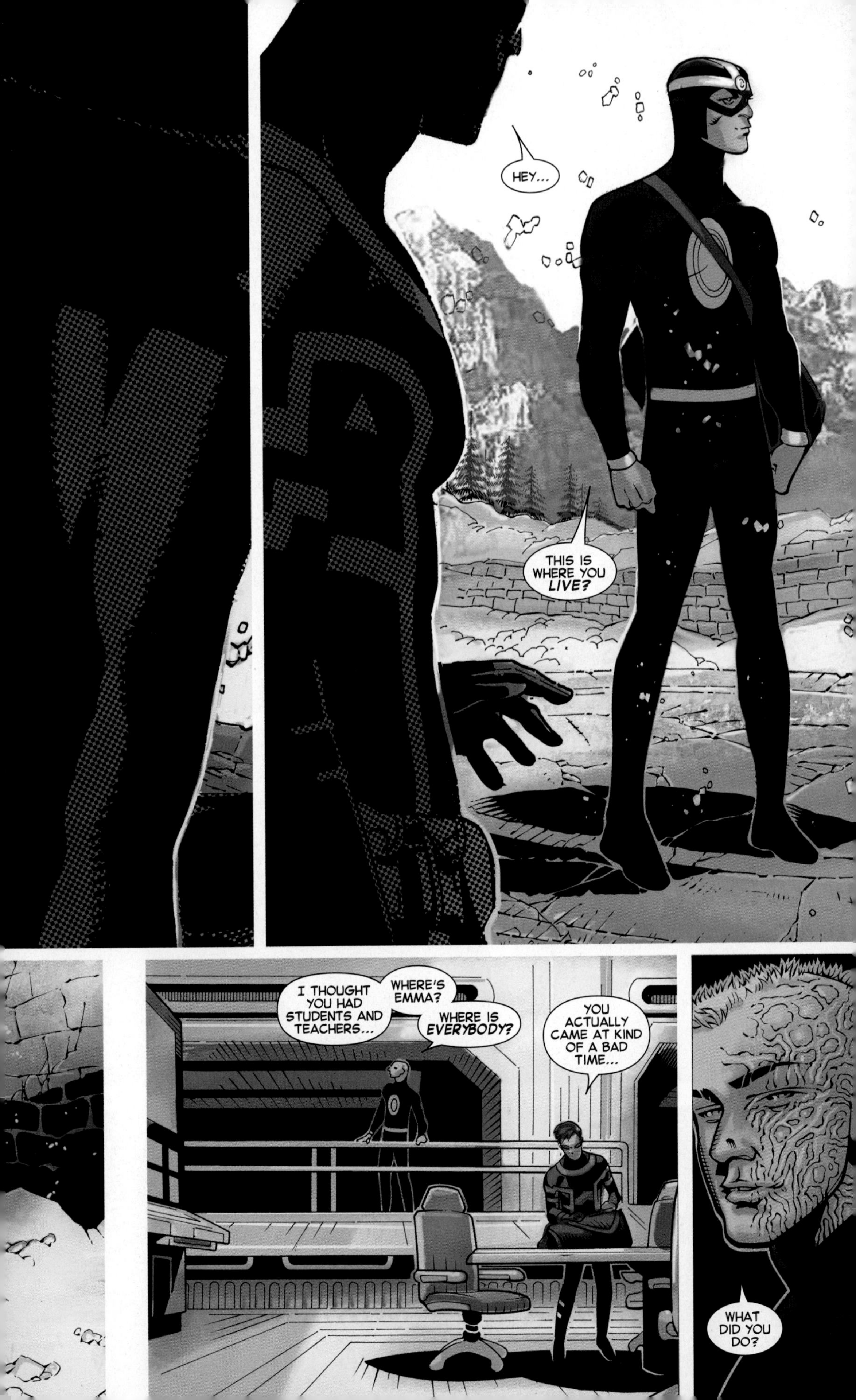
HEY...
THIS IS WHERE YOU *LIVE?*
I THOUGHT YOU HAD STUDENTS AND TEACHERS...
WHERE'S EMMA?
WHERE IS *EVERYBODY?*
YOU ACTUALLY CAME AT KIND OF A BAD TIME...
WHAT DID YOU DO?

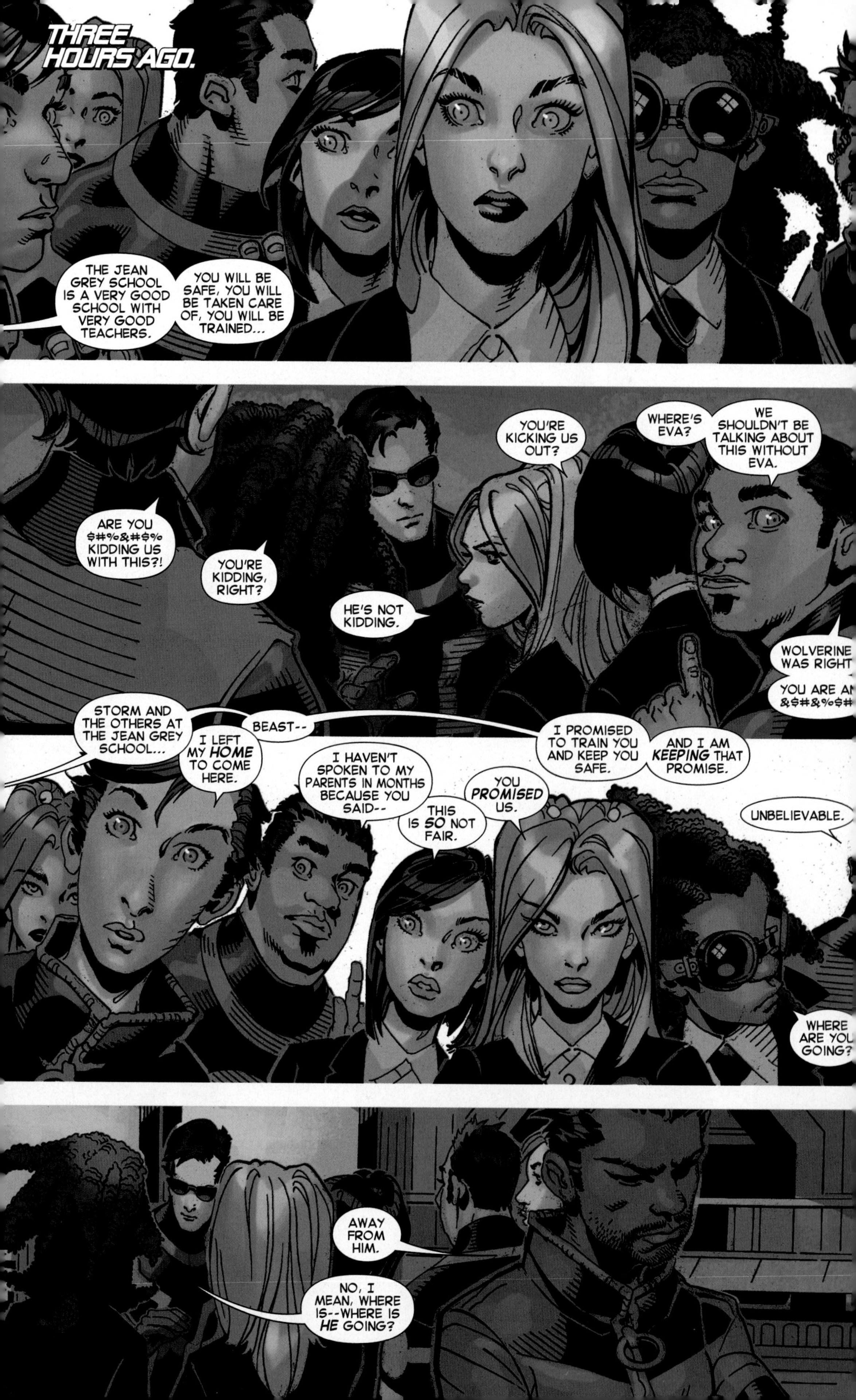
THREE HOURS AGO.
THE JEAN GREY SCHOOL IS A VERY GOOD SCHOOL WITH VERY GOOD TEACHERS.
YOU WILL BE SAFE, YOU WILL BE TAKEN CARE OF, YOU WILL BE TRAINED...
ARE YOU $#%&#$% KIDDING US WITH THIS?!
YOU'RE KIDDING, RIGHT?
HE'S NOT KIDDING.
YOU'RE KICKING US OUT?
WHERE'S EVA?
WE SHOULDN'T BE TALKING ABOUT THIS WITHOUT EVA.
WOLVERINE WAS RIGHT
YOU ARE A
STORM AND THE OTHERS AT THE JEAN GREY SCHOOL...
BEAST--
I LEFT MY HOME TO COME HERE.
I HAVEN'T SPOKEN TO MY PARENTS IN MONTHS BECAUSE YOU SAID--
THIS IS SO NOT FAIR.
YOU PROMISED US.
I PROMISED TO TRAIN YOU AND KEEP YOU SAFE.
AND I AM KEEPING THAT PROMISE.
UNBELIEVABLE.
WHERE ARE YOU GOING?
AWAY FROM HIM.
NO, I MEAN, WHERE IS--WHERE IS HE GOING?

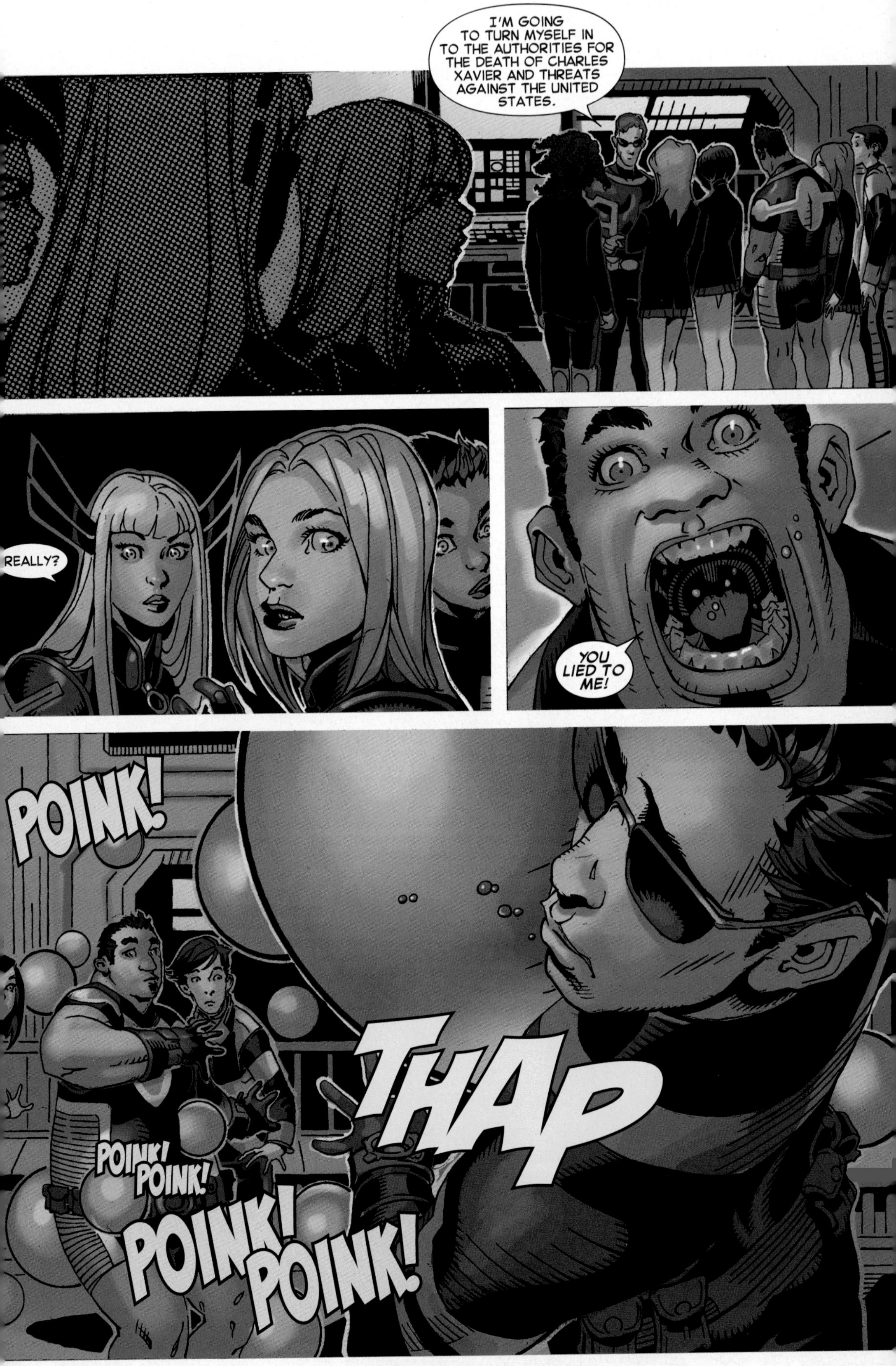
I'M GOING TO TURN MYSELF IN TO THE AUTHORITIES FOR THE DEATH OF CHARLES XAVIER AND THREATS AGAINST THE UNITED STATES.
REALLY?
YOU LIED TO ME!
POINK!
THAP
POINK! POINK!
POINK! POINK!

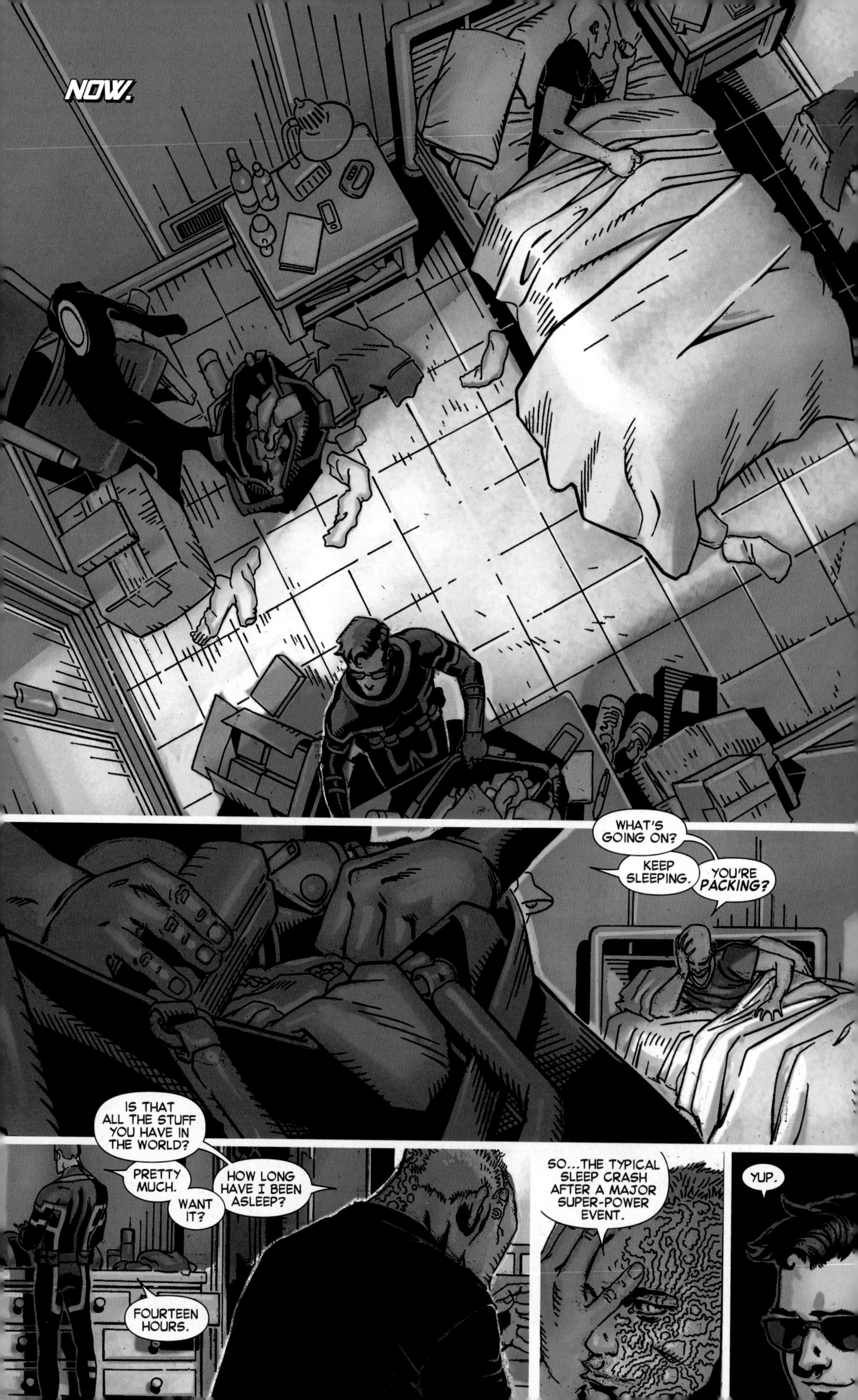
NOW.
WHAT'S GOING ON?
KEEP SLEEPING.
YOU'RE PACKING?
IS THAT ALL THE STUFF YOU HAVE IN THE WORLD?
PRETTY MUCH.
WANT IT?
HOW LONG HAVE I BEEN ASLEEP?
FOURTEEN HOURS.
SO...THE TYPICAL SLEEP CRASH AFTER A MAJOR SUPER-POWER EVENT.
YUP.

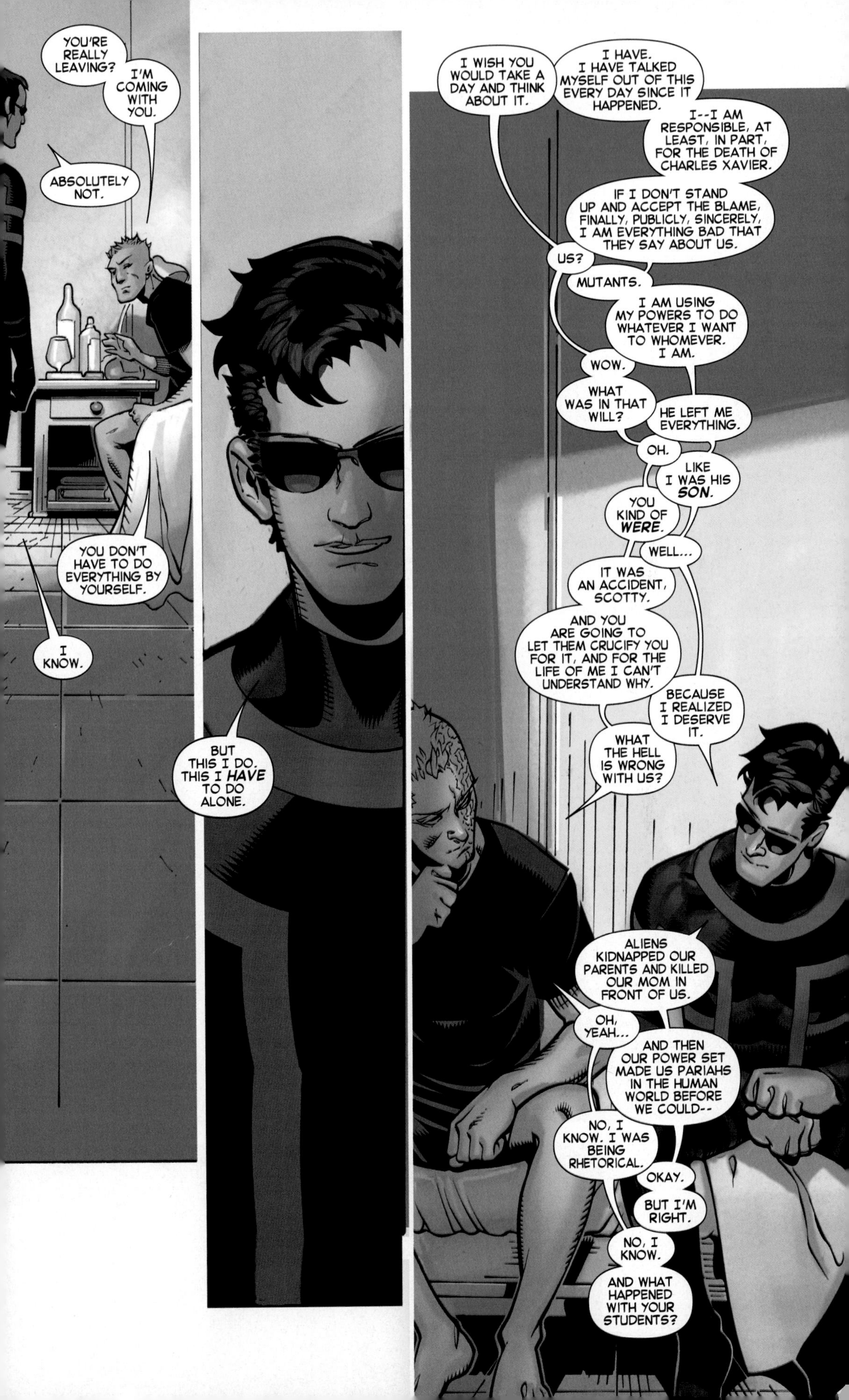
YOU'RE REALLY LEAVING?
I'M COMING WITH YOU.
ABSOLUTELY NOT.
YOU DON'T HAVE TO DO EVERYTHING BY YOURSELF.
I KNOW.
BUT THIS I DO. THIS I *HAVE* TO DO ALONE.
I WISH YOU WOULD TAKE A DAY AND THINK ABOUT IT.
I HAVE. I HAVE TALKED MYSELF OUT OF THIS EVERY DAY SINCE IT HAPPENED.
I--I AM RESPONSIBLE, AT LEAST, IN PART, FOR THE DEATH OF CHARLES XAVIER.
IF I DON'T STAND UP AND ACCEPT THE BLAME, FINALLY, PUBLICLY, SINCERELY, I AM EVERYTHING BAD THAT THEY SAY ABOUT US.
US?
MUTANTS.
I AM USING MY POWERS TO DO WHATEVER I WANT TO WHOMEVER. I AM.
WOW.
WHAT WAS IN THAT WILL?
HE LEFT ME EVERYTHING.
OH.
LIKE I WAS HIS *SON.*
YOU KIND OF *WERE.*
WELL...
IT WAS AN ACCIDENT, SCOTTY.
AND YOU ARE GOING TO LET THEM CRUCIFY YOU FOR IT, AND FOR THE LIFE OF ME I CAN'T UNDERSTAND WHY.
BECAUSE I REALIZED I DESERVE IT.
WHAT THE HELL IS WRONG WITH US?
ALIENS KIDNAPPED OUR PARENTS AND KILLED OUR MOM IN FRONT OF US.
OH, YEAH...
AND THEN OUR POWER SET MADE US PARIAHS IN THE HUMAN WORLD BEFORE WE COULD--
NO, I KNOW. I WAS BEING RHETORICAL.
OKAY.
BUT I'M RIGHT.
NO, I KNOW.
AND WHAT HAPPENED WITH YOUR STUDENTS?

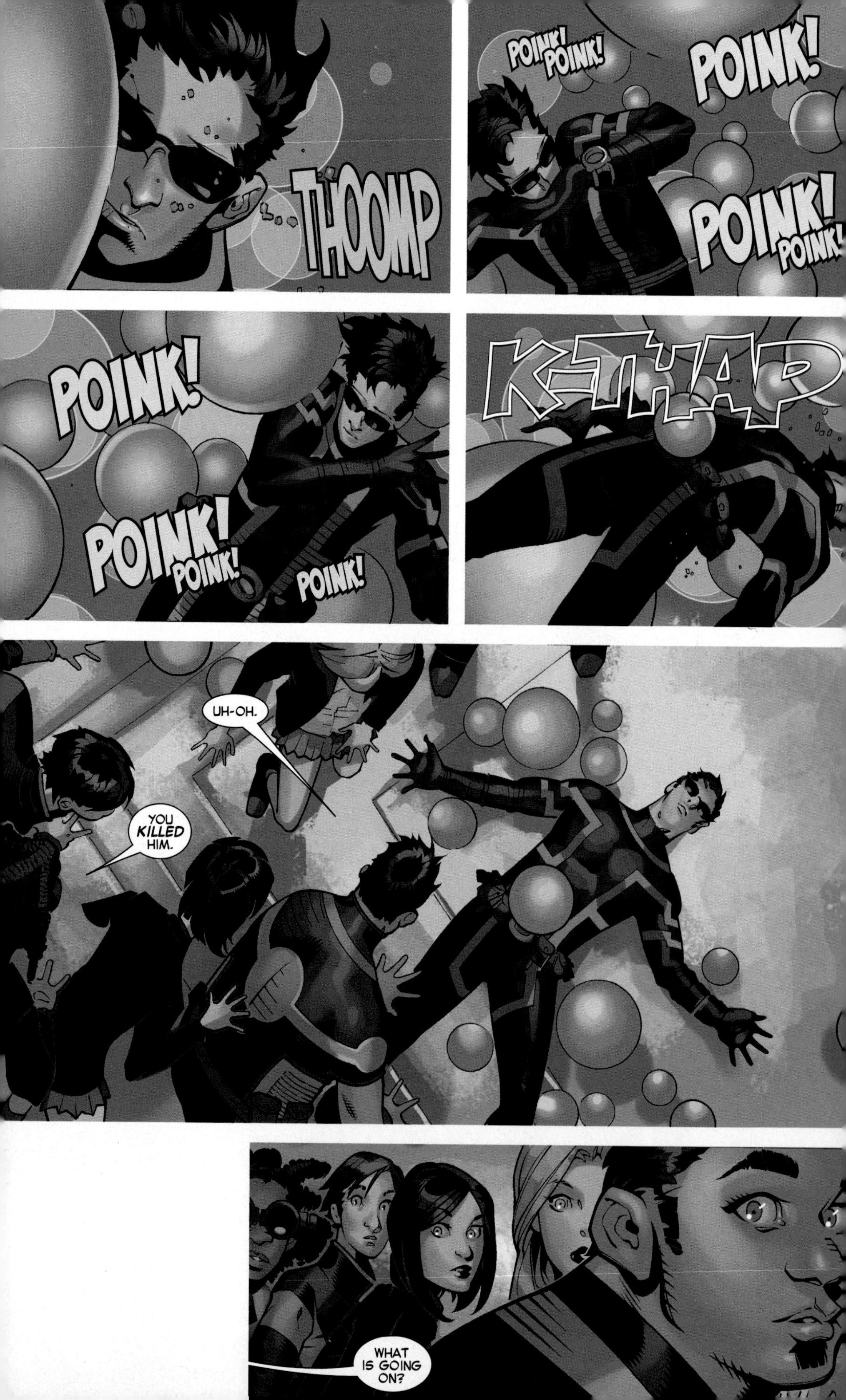
THOOMP
POINK! POINK!
POINK!
POINK! POINK!
POINK!
POINK! POINK!
POINK!
K-THAP
UH-OH.
YOU KILLED HIM.
WHAT IS GOING ON?

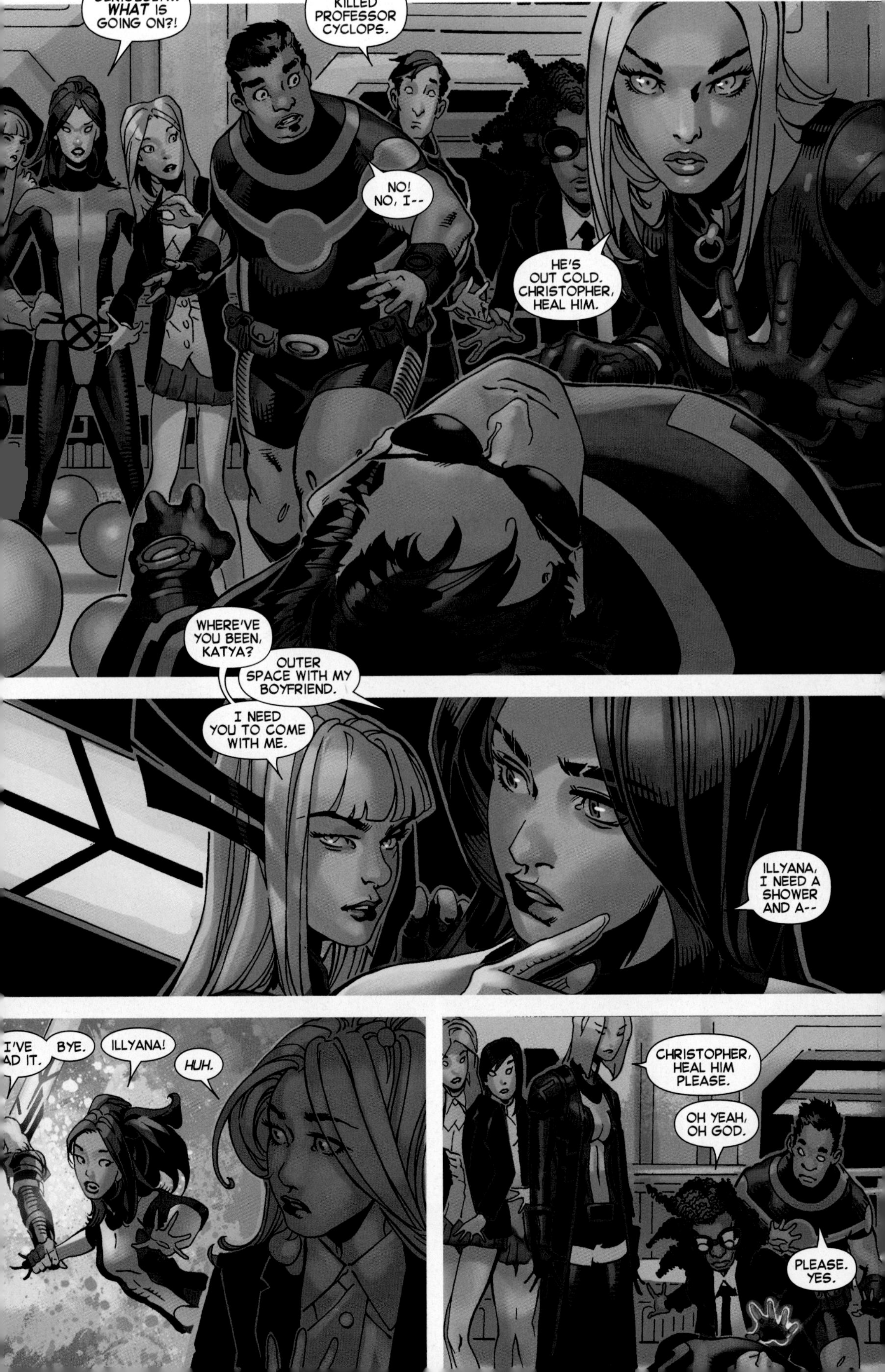
SERIOUSLY... *WHAT* IS GOING ON?!
FABIO KILLED PROFESSOR CYCLOPS.
NO! NO, I--
HE'S OUT COLD. CHRISTOPHER, HEAL HIM.
WHERE'VE YOU BEEN, KATYA?
OUTER SPACE WITH MY BOYFRIEND.
I NEED YOU TO COME WITH ME.
ILLYANA, I NEED A SHOWER AND A--
I'VE AD IT.
BYE.
ILLYANA!
HUH.
CHRISTOPHER, HEAL HIM PLEASE.
OH YEAH, OH GOD.
PLEASE. YES.

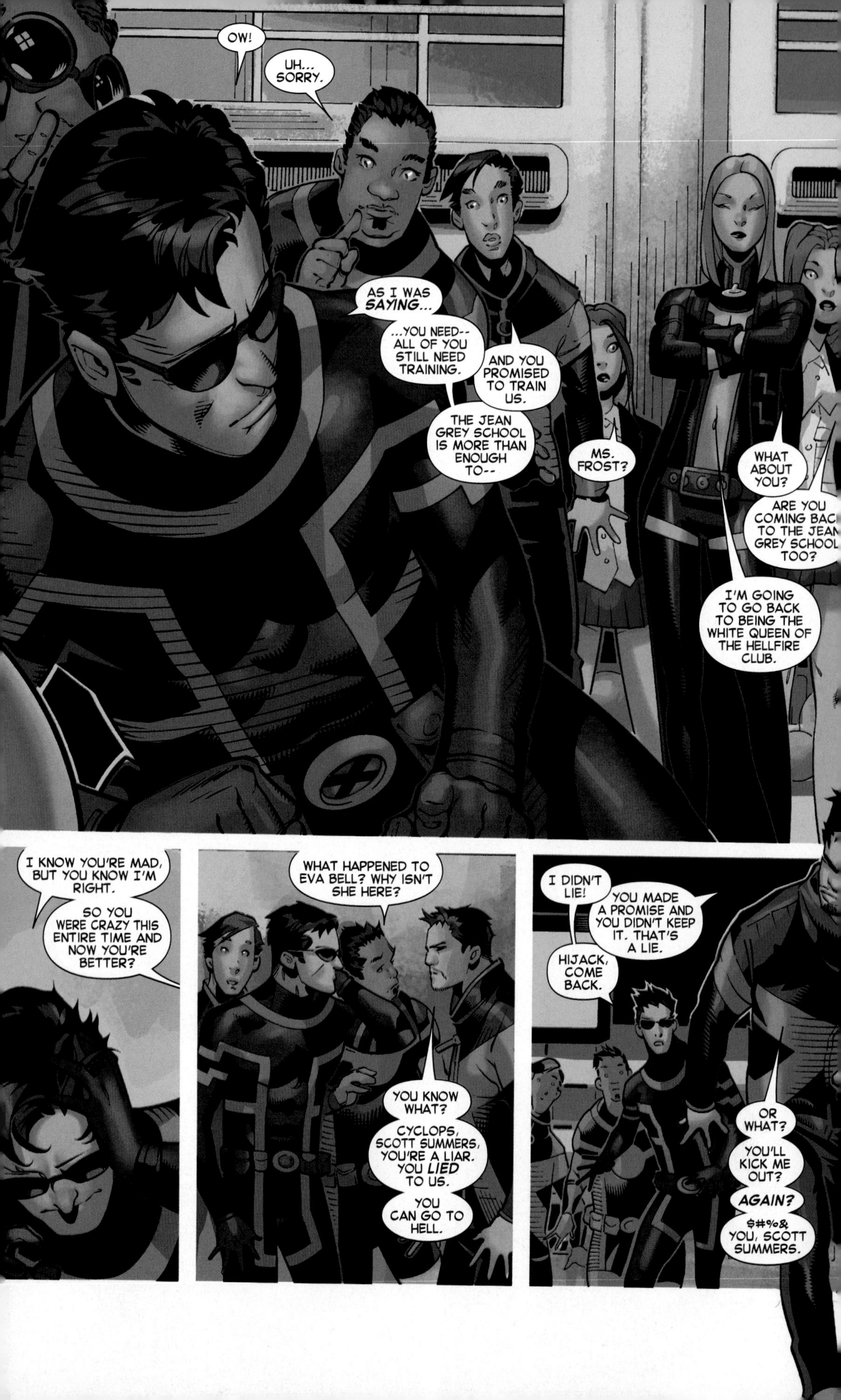
OW!
UH... SORRY.
AS I WAS SAYING...
...YOU NEED-- ALL OF YOU STILL NEED TRAINING.
AND YOU PROMISED TO TRAIN US.
THE JEAN GREY SCHOOL IS MORE THAN ENOUGH TO--
MS. FROST?
WHAT ABOUT YOU?
ARE YOU COMING BAC TO THE JEAN GREY SCHOOL TOO?
I'M GOING TO GO BACK TO BEING THE WHITE QUEEN OF THE HELLFIRE CLUB.
I KNOW YOU'RE MAD, BUT YOU KNOW I'M RIGHT.
SO YOU WERE CRAZY THIS ENTIRE TIME AND NOW YOU'RE BETTER?
WHAT HAPPENED TO EVA BELL? WHY ISN'T SHE HERE?
YOU KNOW WHAT?
CYCLOPS, SCOTT SUMMERS, YOU'RE A LIAR. YOU LIED TO US.
YOU CAN GO TO HELL.
I DIDN'T LIE!
YOU MADE A PROMISE AND YOU DIDN'T KEEP IT. THAT'S A LIE.
HIJACK, COME BACK.
OR WHAT?
YOU'LL KICK ME OUT?
AGAIN?
$#%& YOU, SCOTT SUMMERS.

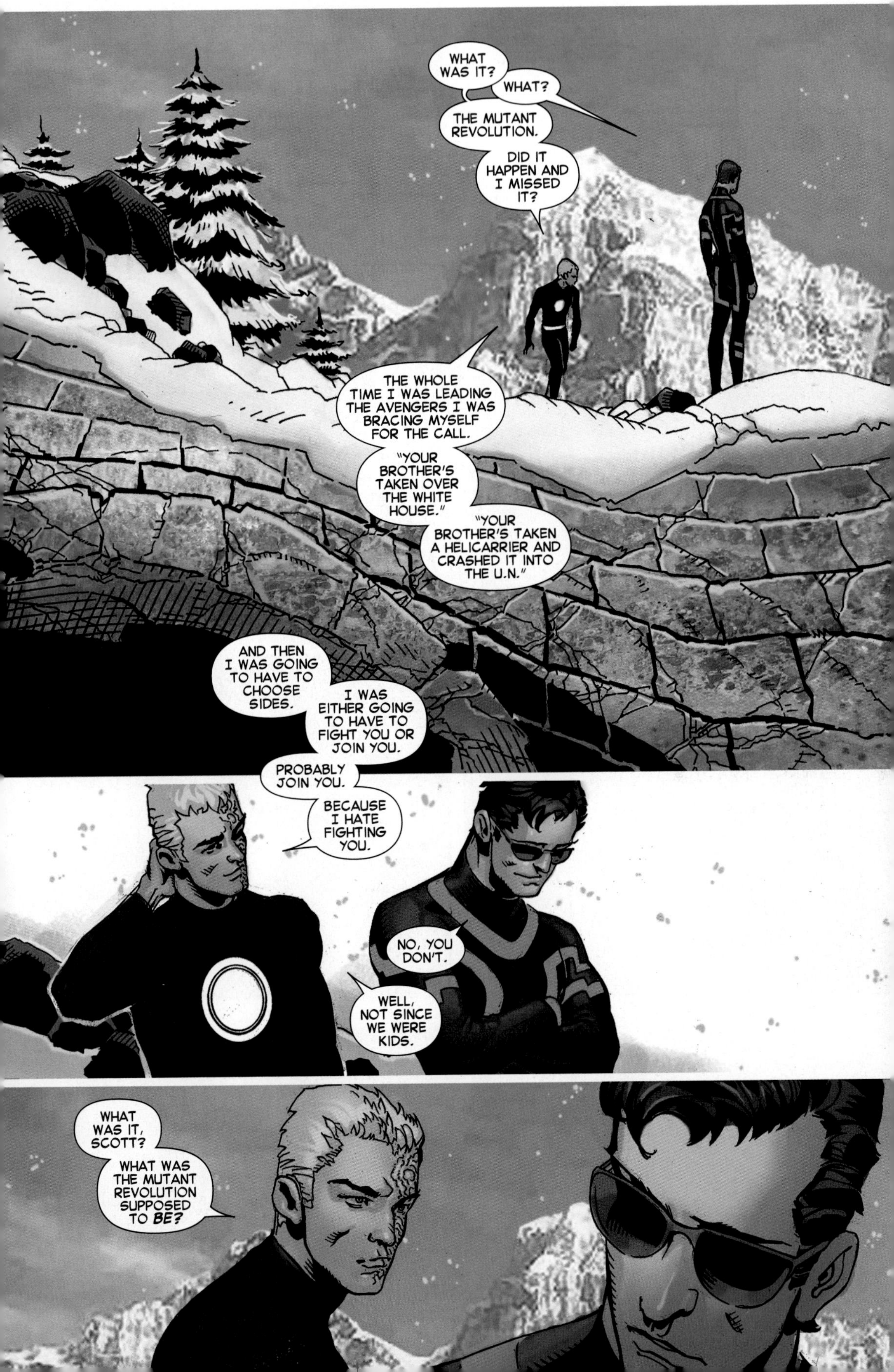
WHAT WAS IT?
WHAT?
THE MUTANT REVOLUTION.
DID IT HAPPEN AND I MISSED IT?
THE WHOLE TIME I WAS LEADING THE AVENGERS I WAS BRACING MYSELF FOR THE CALL.
"YOUR BROTHER'S TAKEN OVER THE WHITE HOUSE."
"YOUR BROTHER'S TAKEN A HELICARRIER AND CRASHED IT INTO THE U.N."
AND THEN I WAS GOING TO HAVE TO CHOOSE SIDES.
I WAS EITHER GOING TO HAVE TO FIGHT YOU OR JOIN YOU.
PROBABLY JOIN YOU.
BECAUSE I HATE FIGHTING YOU.
NO, YOU DON'T.
WELL, NOT SINCE WE WERE KIDS.
WHAT WAS IT, SCOTT?
WHAT WAS THE MUTANT REVOLUTION SUPPOSED TO *BE?*

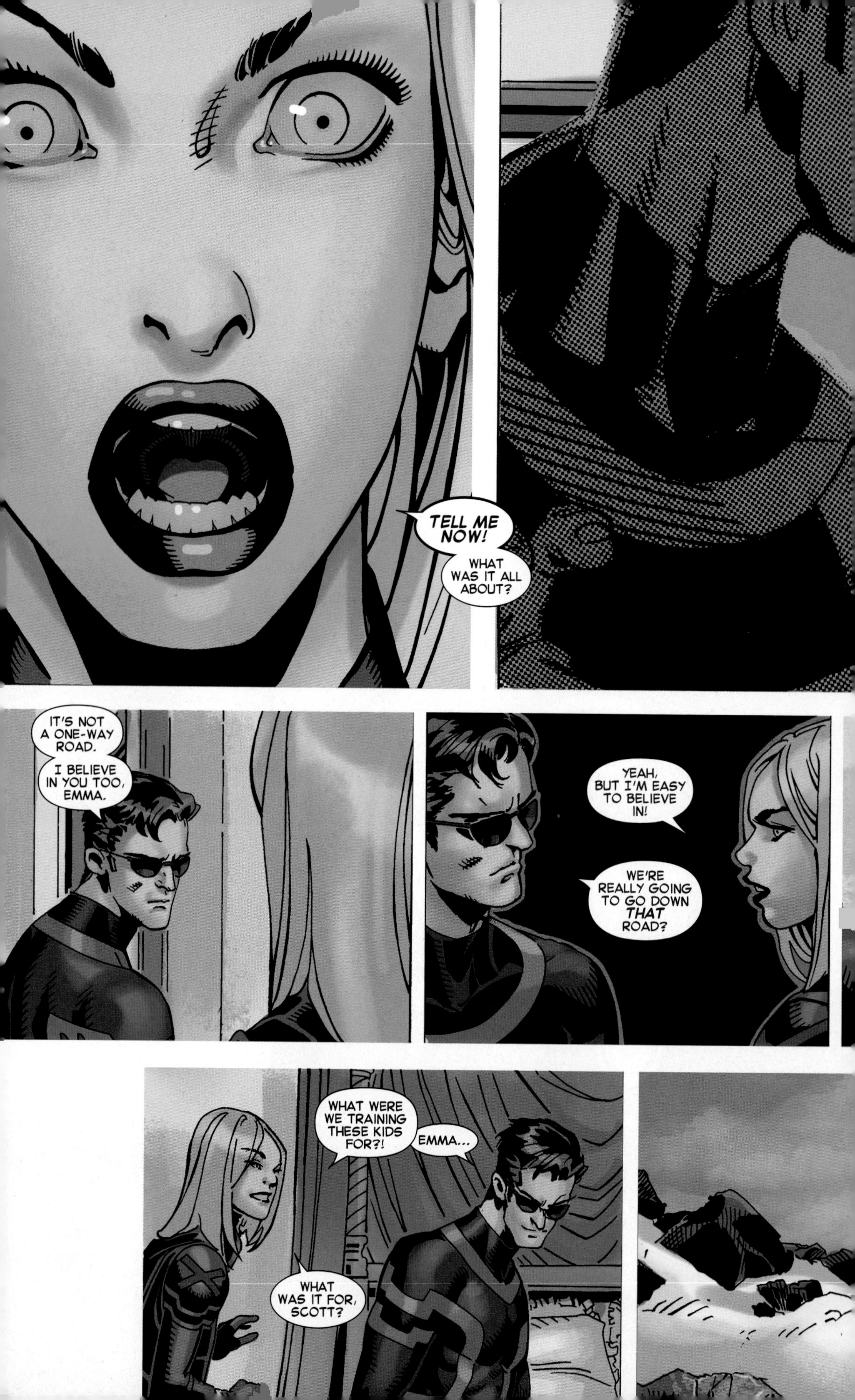
TELL ME NOW!
WHAT WAS IT ALL ABOUT?
IT'S NOT A ONE-WAY ROAD.
I BELIEVE IN YOU TOO, EMMA.
YEAH, BUT I'M EASY TO BELIEVE IN!
WE'RE REALLY GOING TO GO DOWN THAT ROAD?
WHAT WERE WE TRAINING THESE KIDS FOR?!
EMMA...
WHAT WAS IT FOR, SCOTT?

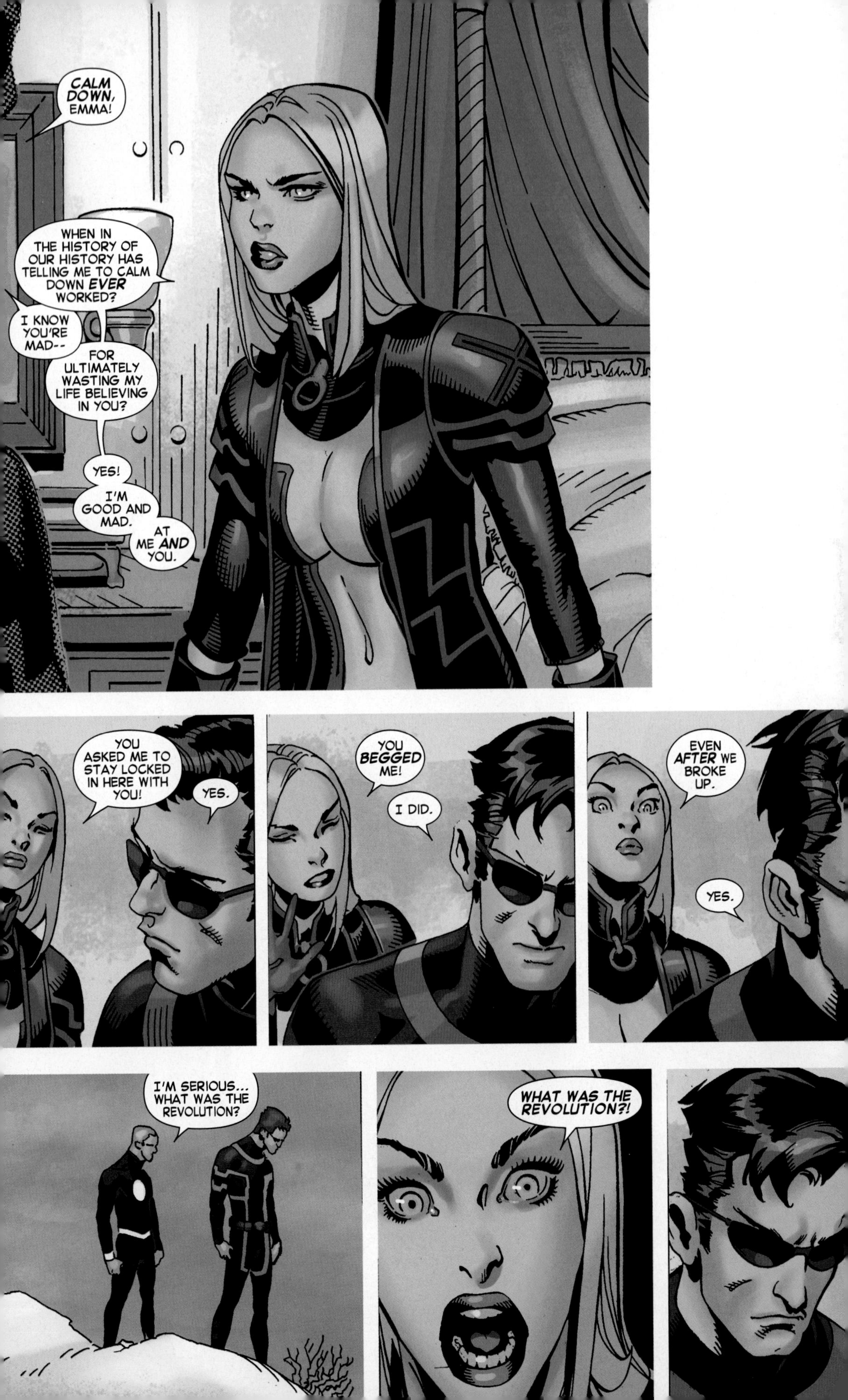

CALM DOWN, EMMA!
WHEN IN THE HISTORY OF OUR HISTORY HAS TELLING ME TO CALM DOWN EVER WORKED?
I KNOW YOU'RE MAD--
FOR ULTIMATELY WASTING MY LIFE BELIEVING IN YOU?
YES!
I'M GOOD AND MAD.
AT ME AND YOU.
YOU ASKED ME TO STAY LOCKED IN HERE WITH YOU!
YES.
YOU BEGGED ME!
I DID.
EVEN AFTER WE BROKE UP.
YES.
I'M SERIOUS... WHAT WAS THE REVOLUTION?
WHAT WAS THE REVOLUTION?!

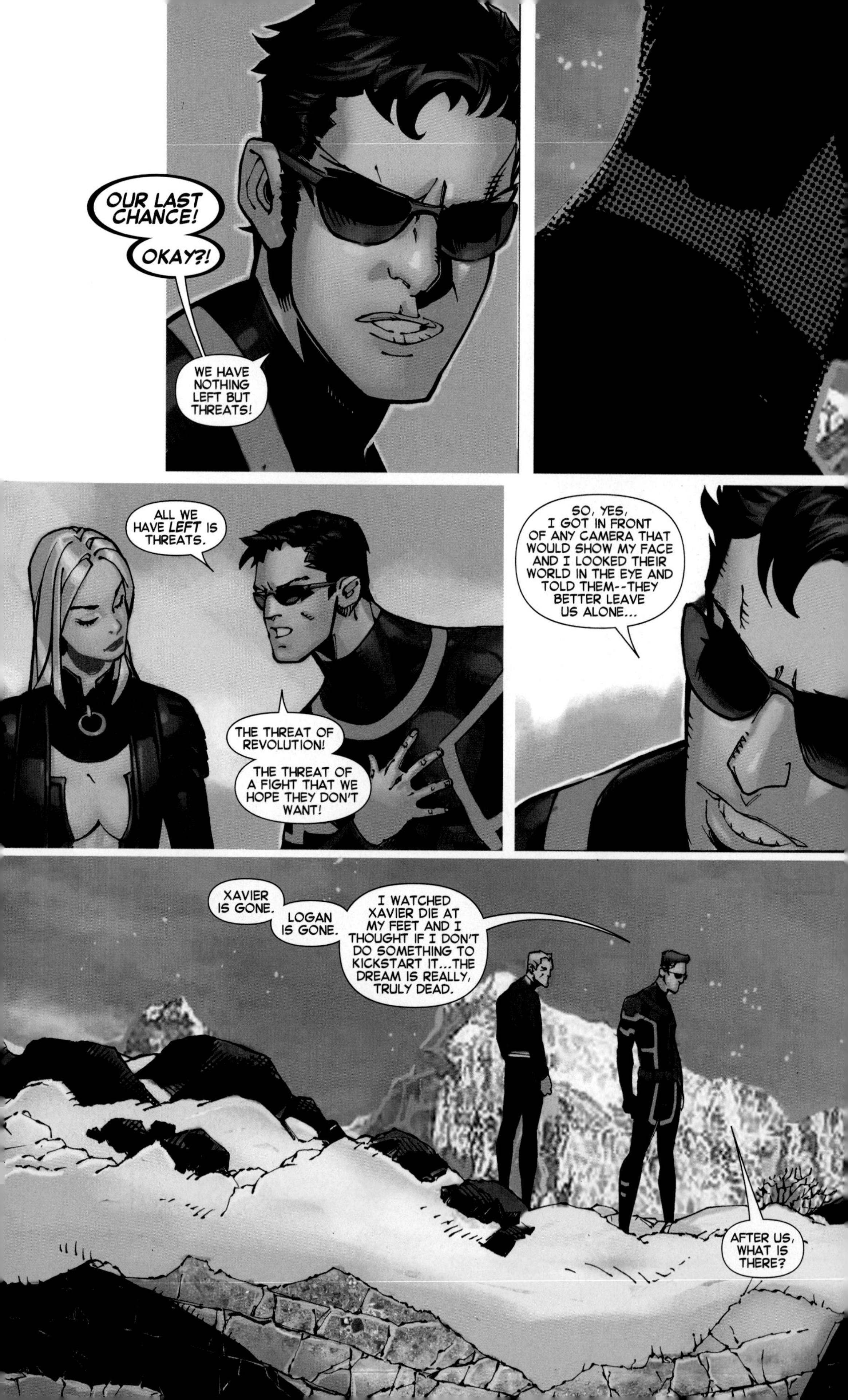
OUR LAST CHANCE!
OKAY?!
WE HAVE NOTHING LEFT BUT THREATS!
ALL WE HAVE LEFT IS THREATS.
THE THREAT OF REVOLUTION!
THE THREAT OF A FIGHT THAT WE HOPE THEY DON'T WANT!
SO, YES, I GOT IN FRONT OF ANY CAMERA THAT WOULD SHOW MY FACE AND I LOOKED THEIR WORLD IN THE EYE AND TOLD THEM--THEY BETTER LEAVE US ALONE...
XAVIER IS GONE.
LOGAN IS GONE.
I WATCHED XAVIER DIE AT MY FEET AND I THOUGHT IF I DON'T DO SOMETHING TO KICKSTART IT...THE DREAM IS REALLY, TRULY DEAD.
AFTER US, WHAT IS THERE?

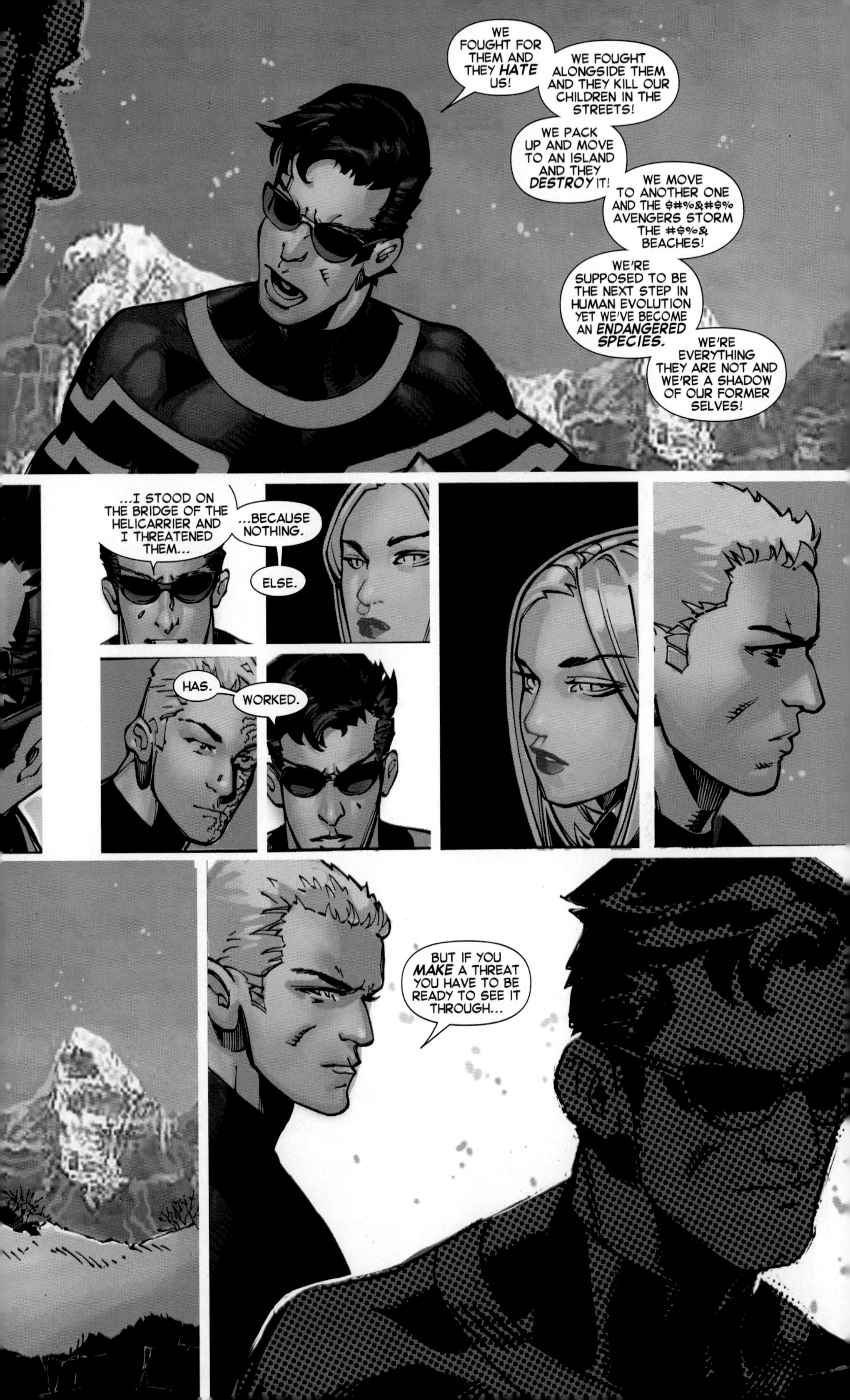
WE FOUGHT FOR THEM AND THEY *HATE* US!
WE FOUGHT ALONGSIDE THEM AND THEY KILL OUR CHILDREN IN THE STREETS!
WE PACK UP AND MOVE TO AN ISLAND AND THEY *DESTROY* IT!
WE MOVE TO ANOTHER ONE AND THE $#%&#$% AVENGERS STORM THE #$%& BEACHES!
WE'RE SUPPOSED TO BE THE NEXT STEP IN HUMAN EVOLUTION YET WE'VE BECOME AN *ENDANGERED SPECIES.*
WE'RE EVERYTHING THEY ARE NOT AND WE'RE A SHADOW OF OUR FORMER SELVES!
...I STOOD ON THE BRIDGE OF THE HELICARRIER AND I THREATENED THEM...
...BECAUSE NOTHING.
ELSE.
HAS.
WORKED.
BUT IF YOU *MAKE* A THREAT YOU HAVE TO BE READY TO SEE IT THROUGH...

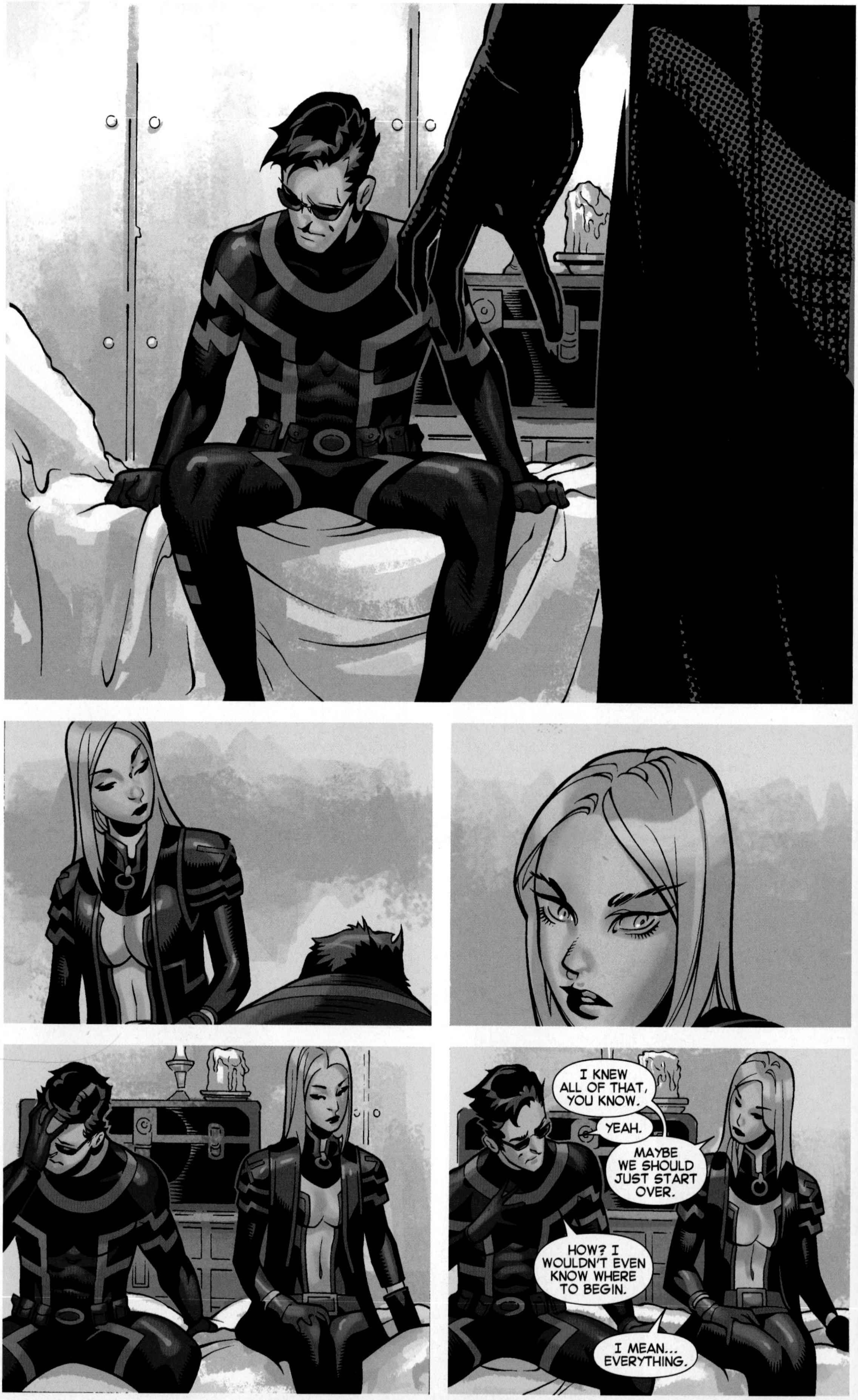
I KNEW ALL OF THAT, YOU KNOW.
YEAH.
MAYBE WE SHOULD JUST START OVER.
HOW? I WOULDN'T EVEN KNOW WHERE TO BEGIN.
I MEAN... EVERYTHING.

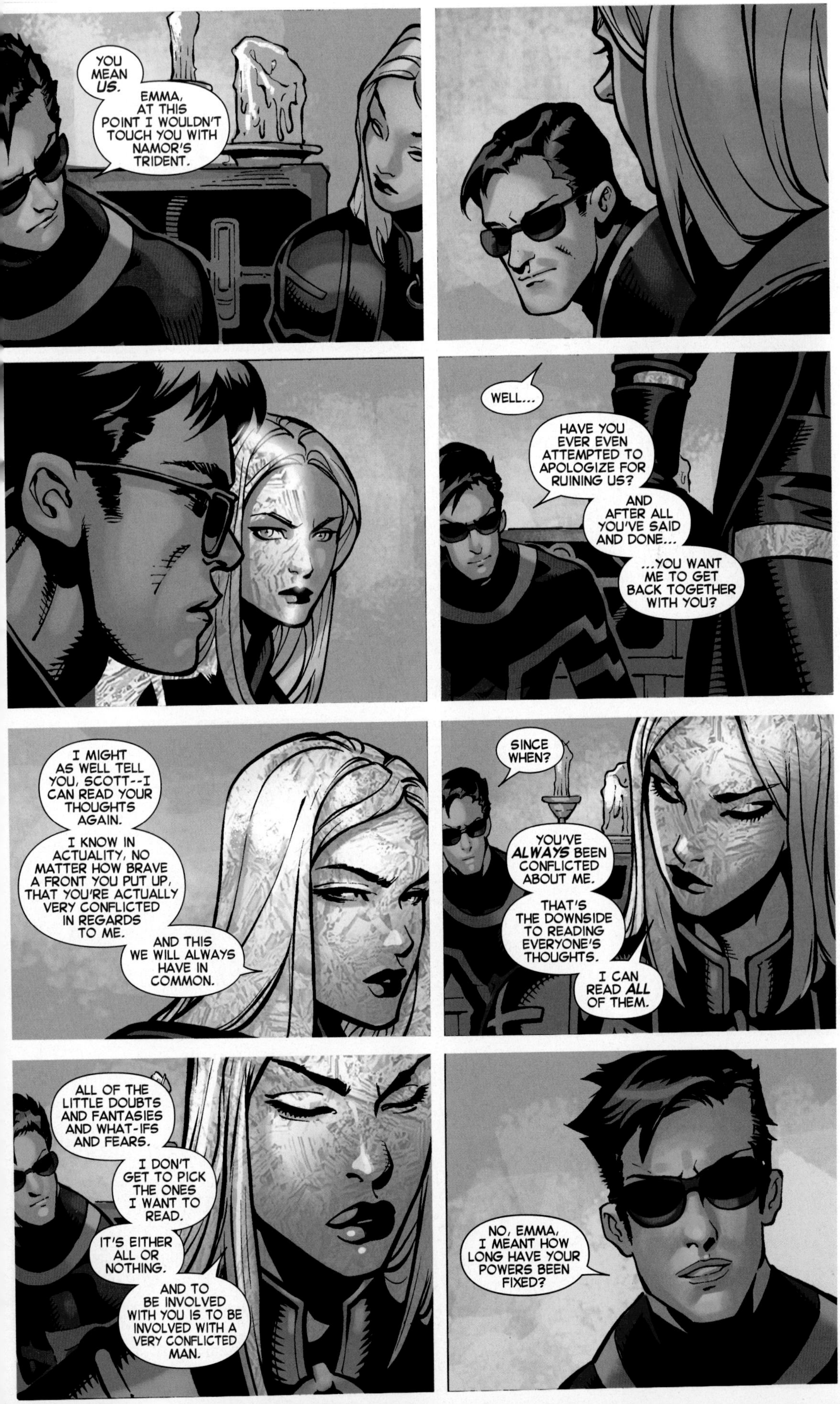
YOU MEAN US.
EMMA, AT THIS POINT I WOULDN'T TOUCH YOU WITH NAMOR'S TRIDENT.
WELL...
HAVE YOU EVER EVEN ATTEMPTED TO APOLOGIZE FOR RUINING US?
AND AFTER ALL YOU'VE SAID AND DONE...
...YOU WANT ME TO GET BACK TOGETHER WITH YOU?
I MIGHT AS WELL TELL YOU, SCOTT--I CAN READ YOUR THOUGHTS AGAIN.
I KNOW IN ACTUALITY, NO MATTER HOW BRAVE A FRONT YOU PUT UP, THAT YOU'RE ACTUALLY VERY CONFLICTED IN REGARDS TO ME.
AND THIS WE WILL ALWAYS HAVE IN COMMON.
SINCE WHEN?
YOU'VE ALWAYS BEEN CONFLICTED ABOUT ME.
THAT'S THE DOWNSIDE TO READING EVERYONE'S THOUGHTS.
I CAN READ ALL OF THEM.
ALL OF THE LITTLE DOUBTS AND FANTASIES AND WHAT-IFS AND FEARS.
I DON'T GET TO PICK THE ONES I WANT TO READ.
IT'S EITHER ALL OR NOTHING.
AND TO BE INVOLVED WITH YOU IS TO BE INVOLVED WITH A VERY CONFLICTED MAN.
NO, EMMA, I MEANT HOW LONG HAVE YOUR POWERS BEEN FIXED?

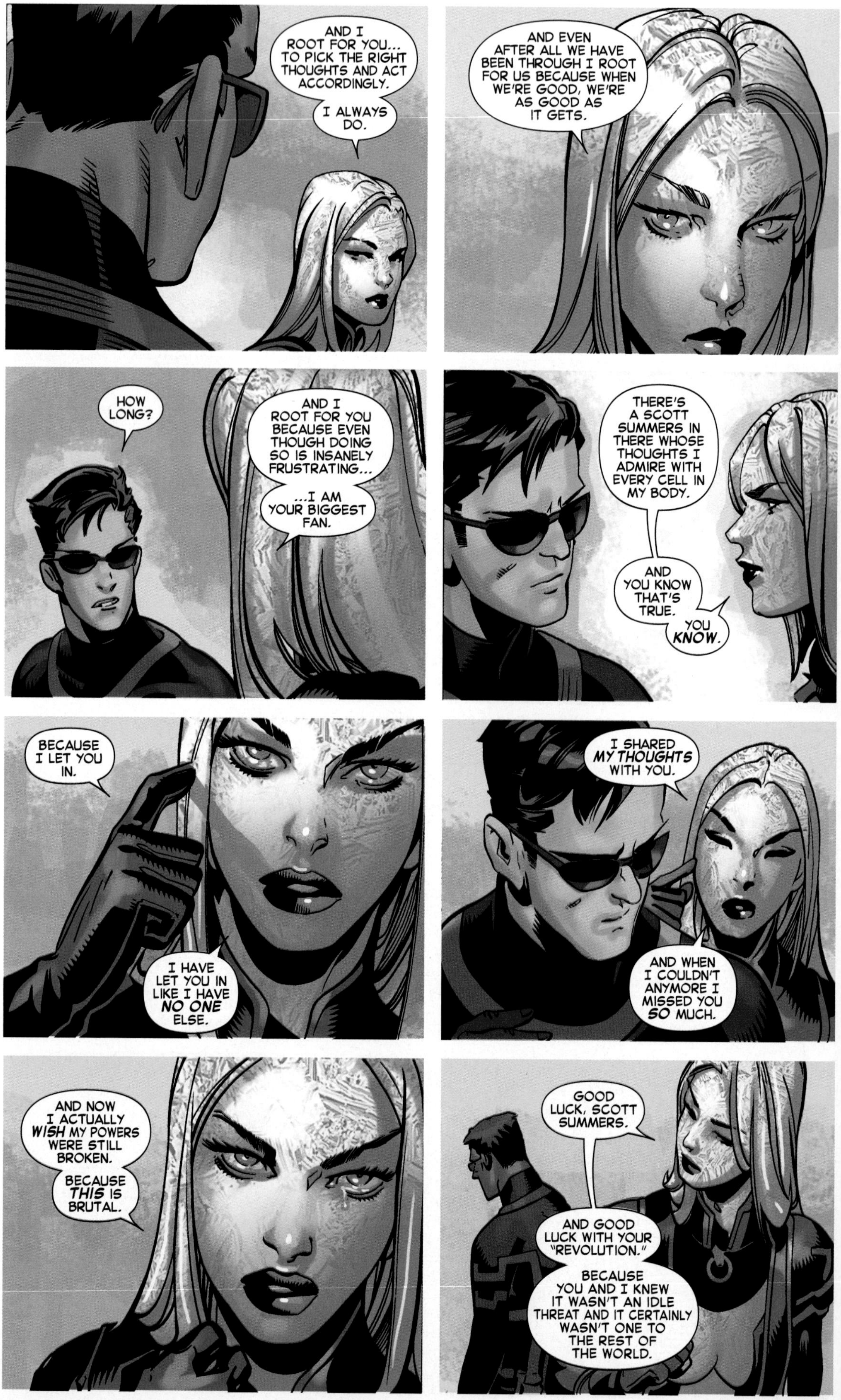
AND I ROOT FOR YOU... TO PICK THE RIGHT THOUGHTS AND ACT ACCORDINGLY.
I ALWAYS DO.
AND EVEN AFTER ALL WE HAVE BEEN THROUGH I ROOT FOR US BECAUSE WHEN WE'RE GOOD, WE'RE AS GOOD AS IT GETS.
HOW LONG?
AND I ROOT FOR YOU BECAUSE EVEN THOUGH DOING SO IS INSANELY FRUSTRATING...
...I AM YOUR BIGGEST FAN.
THERE'S A SCOTT SUMMERS IN THERE WHOSE THOUGHTS I ADMIRE WITH EVERY CELL IN MY BODY.
AND YOU KNOW THAT'S TRUE.
YOU *KNOW*.
BECAUSE I LET YOU IN.
I HAVE LET YOU IN LIKE I HAVE *NO ONE* ELSE.
I SHARED *MY THOUGHTS* WITH YOU.
AND WHEN I COULDN'T ANYMORE I MISSED YOU *SO* MUCH.
AND NOW I ACTUALLY *WISH* MY POWERS WERE STILL BROKEN.
BECAUSE *THIS* IS BRUTAL.
GOOD LUCK, SCOTT SUMMERS.
AND GOOD LUCK WITH YOUR "REVOLUTION."
BECAUSE YOU AND I KNEW IT WASN'T AN IDLE THREAT AND IT CERTAINLY WASN'T ONE TO THE REST OF THE WORLD.

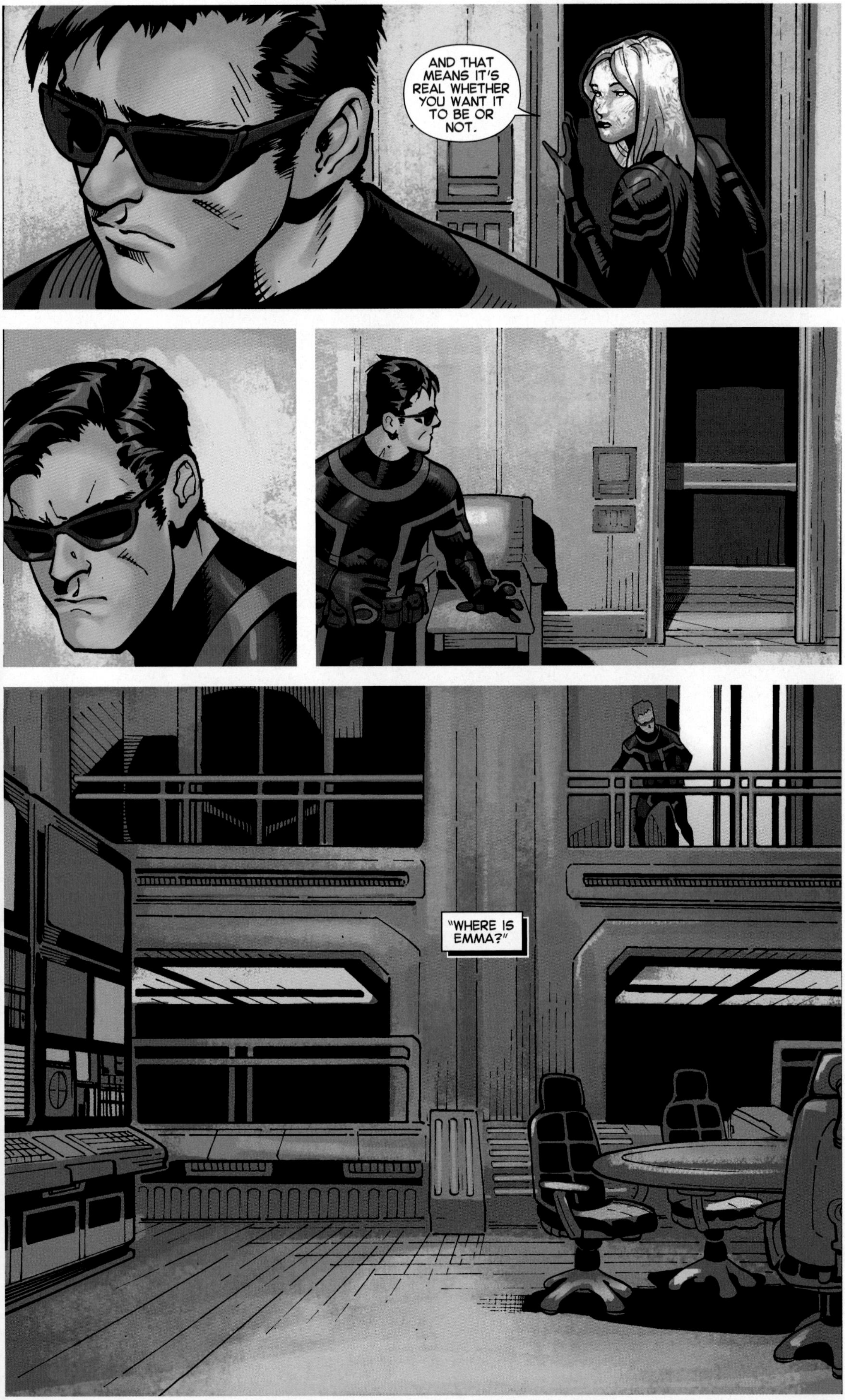
AND THAT MEANS IT'S REAL WHETHER YOU WANT IT TO BE OR NOT.
"WHERE IS EMMA?"

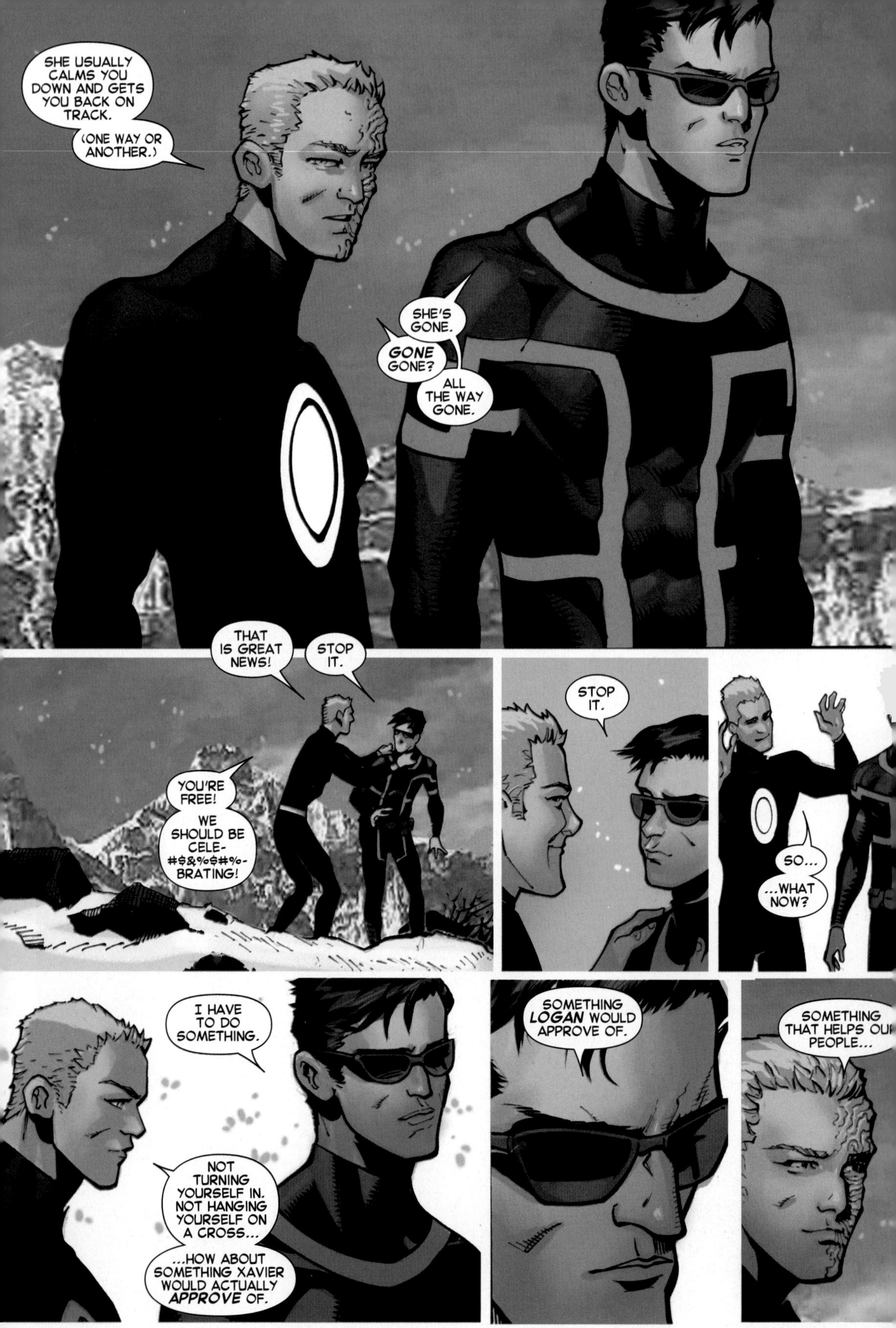
SHE USUALLY CALMS YOU DOWN AND GETS YOU BACK ON TRACK.
(ONE WAY OR ANOTHER.)
SHE'S GONE.
GONE GONE?
ALL THE WAY GONE.
THAT IS GREAT NEWS!
STOP IT.
YOU'RE FREE!
WE SHOULD BE CELE- #$&%$#%- BRATING!
STOP IT.
SO...
...WHAT NOW?
I HAVE TO DO SOMETHING.
NOT TURNING YOURSELF IN. NOT HANGING YOURSELF ON A CROSS...
...HOW ABOUT SOMETHING XAVIER WOULD ACTUALLY *APPROVE* OF.
SOMETHING *LOGAN* WOULD APPROVE OF.
SOMETHING THAT HELPS OUR PEOPLE...

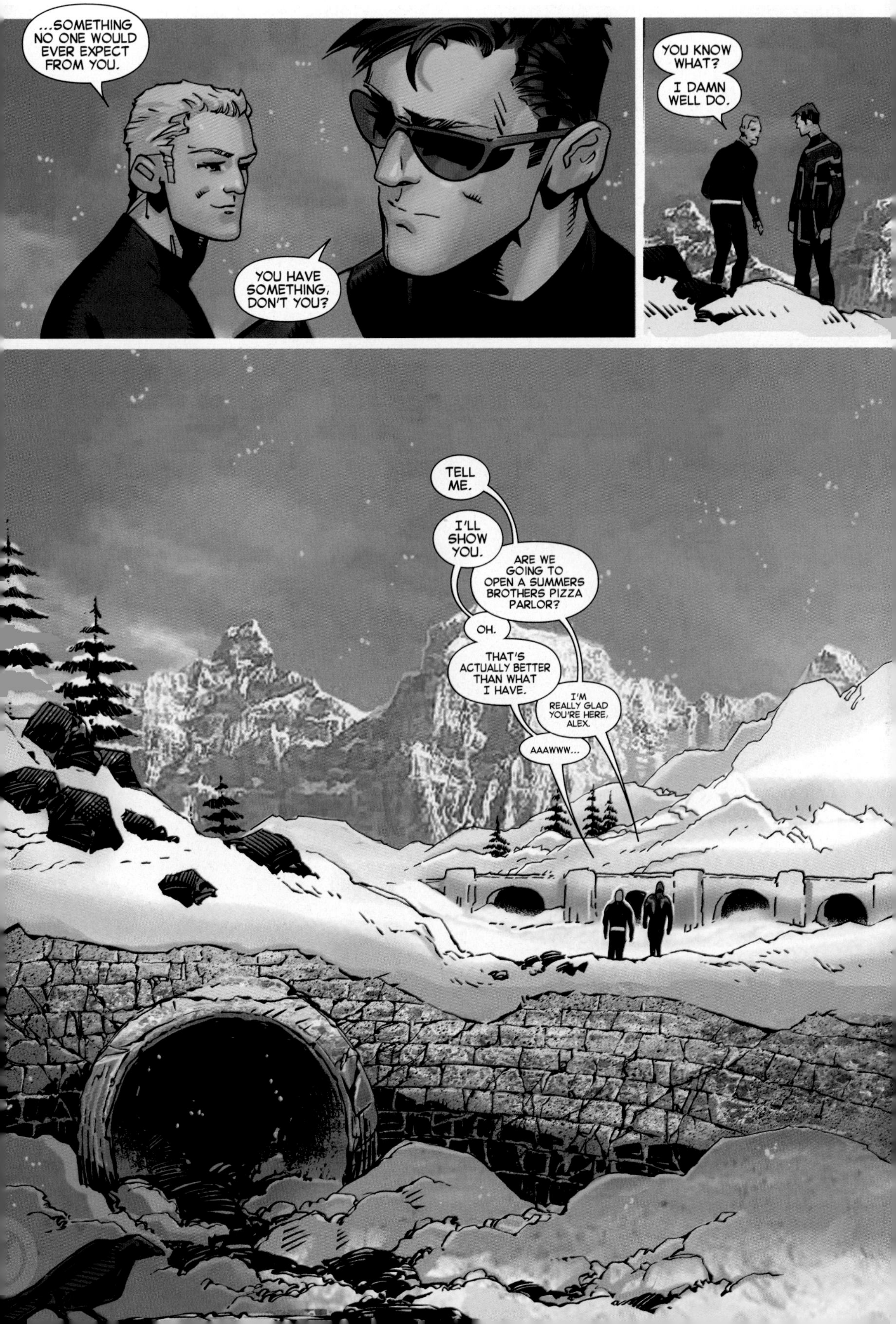
...SOMETHING NO ONE WOULD EVER EXPECT FROM YOU.
YOU HAVE SOMETHING, DON'T YOU?
YOU KNOW WHAT?
I DAMN WELL DO.
TELL ME.
I'LL SHOW YOU.
ARE WE GOING TO OPEN A SUMMERS BROTHERS PIZZA PARLOR?
OH.
THAT'S ACTUALLY BETTER THAN WHAT I HAVE.
I'M REALLY GLAD YOU'RE HERE, ALEX.
AAAWWW...

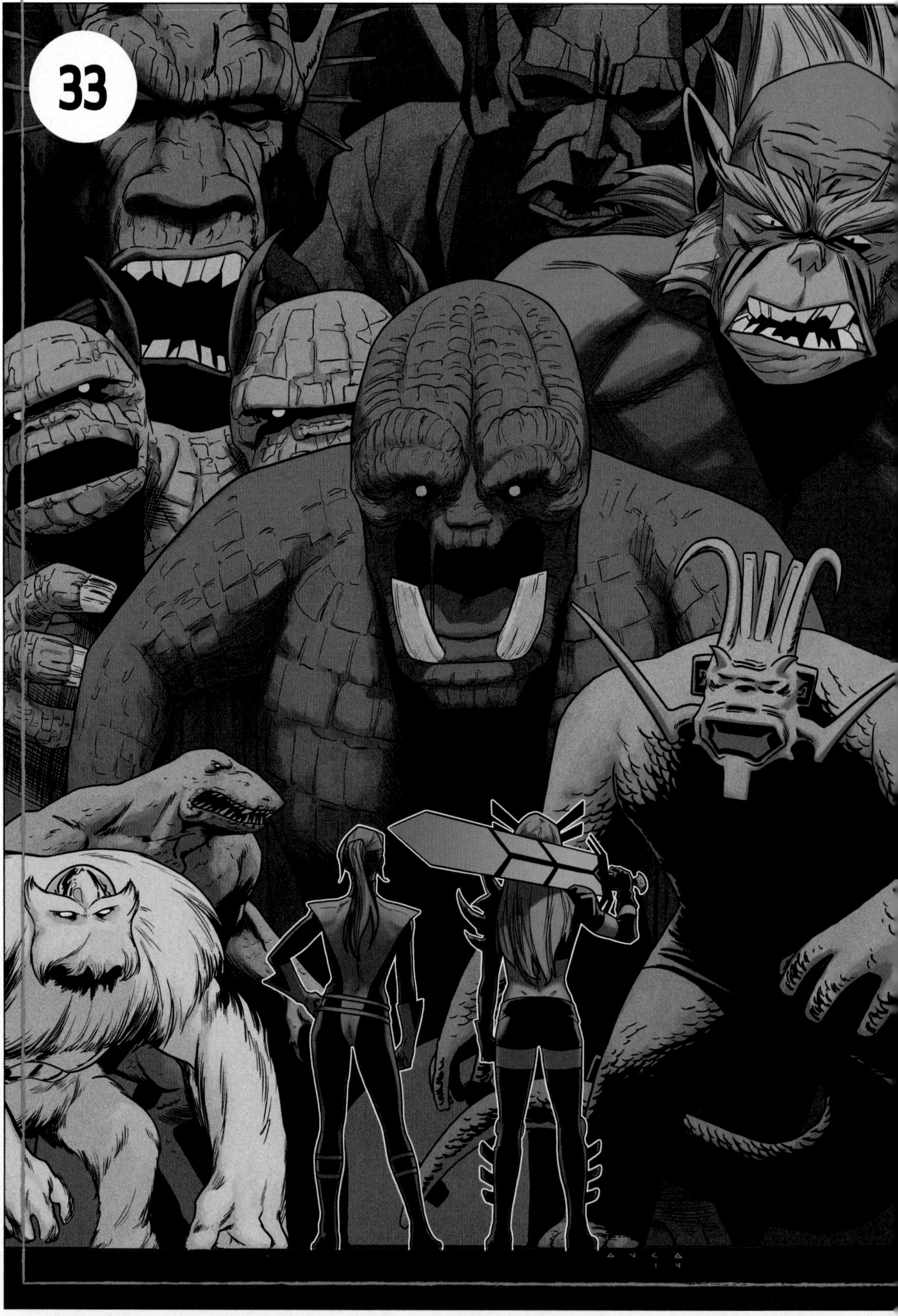
33

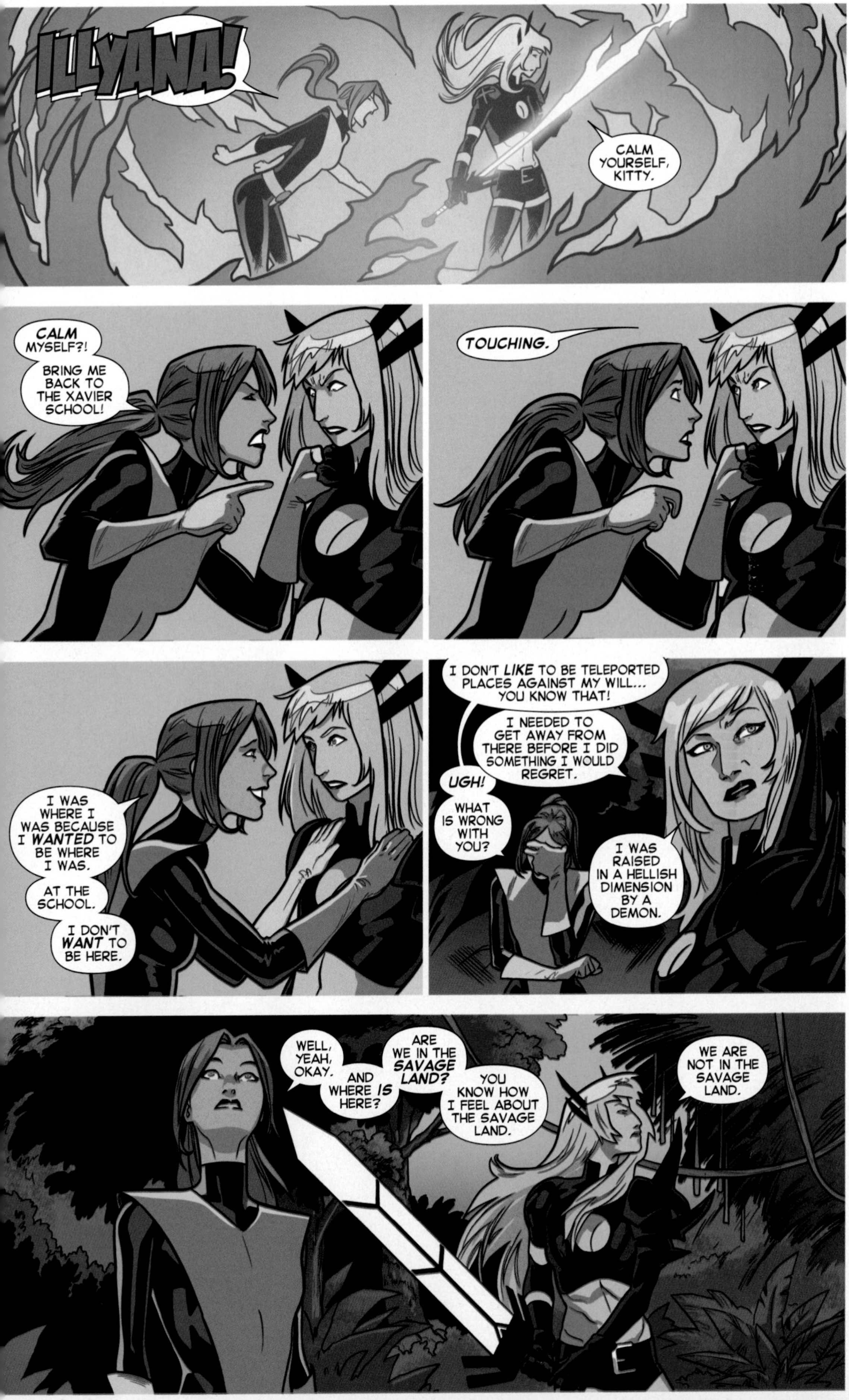
ILLYANA!
CALM YOURSELF, KITTY.
CALM MYSELF?!
BRING ME BACK TO THE XAVIER SCHOOL!
TOUCHING.
I WAS WHERE I WAS BECAUSE I WANTED TO BE WHERE I WAS.
AT THE SCHOOL.
I DON'T WANT TO BE HERE.
I DON'T LIKE TO BE TELEPORTED PLACES AGAINST MY WILL... YOU KNOW THAT!
I NEEDED TO GET AWAY FROM THERE BEFORE I DID SOMETHING I WOULD REGRET.
UGH!
WHAT IS WRONG WITH YOU?
I WAS RAISED IN A HELLISH DIMENSION BY A DEMON.
WELL, YEAH, OKAY.
AND WHERE IS HERE?
ARE WE IN THE SAVAGE LAND?
YOU KNOW HOW I FEEL ABOUT THE SAVAGE LAND.
WE ARE NOT IN THE SAVAGE LAND.

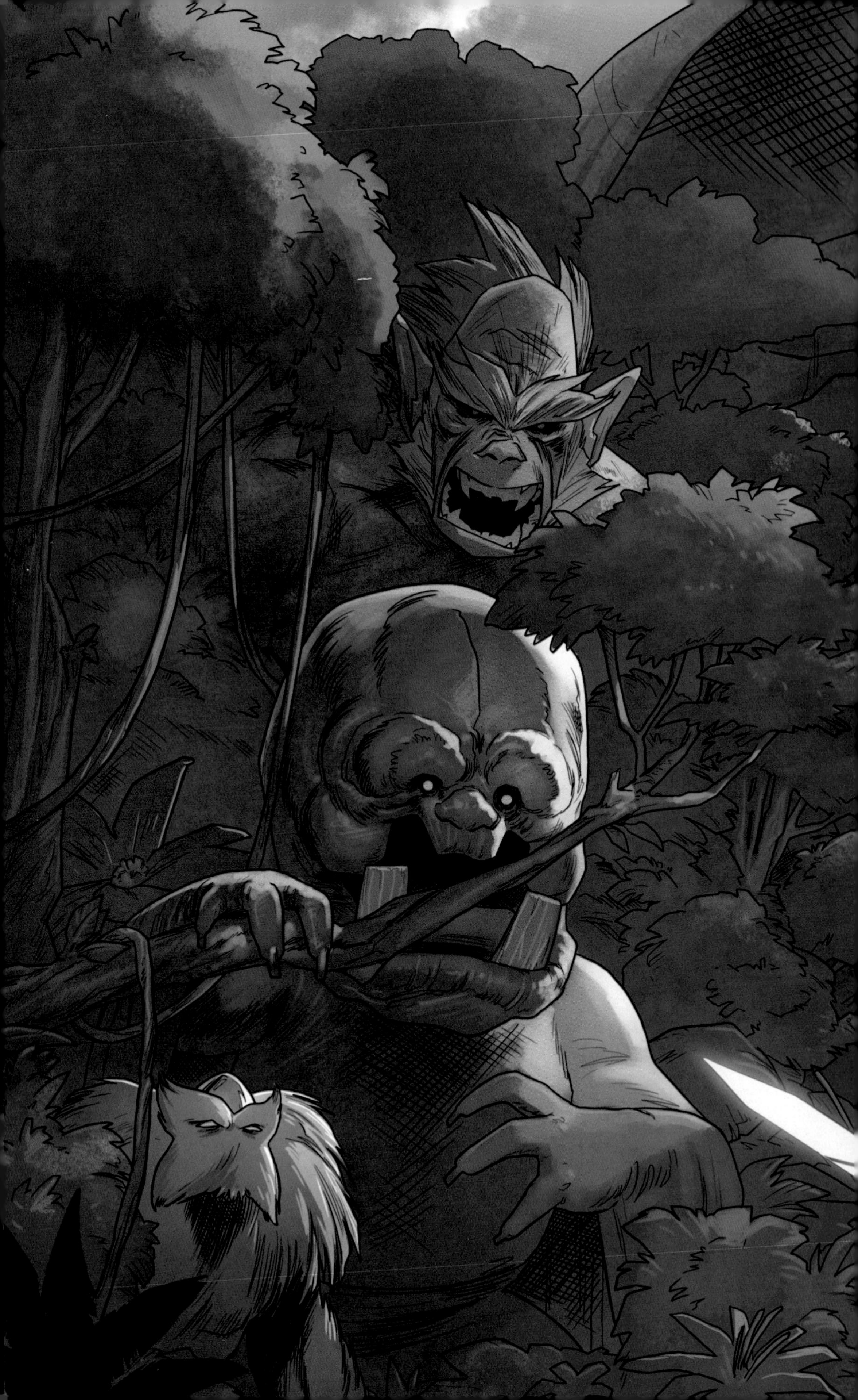

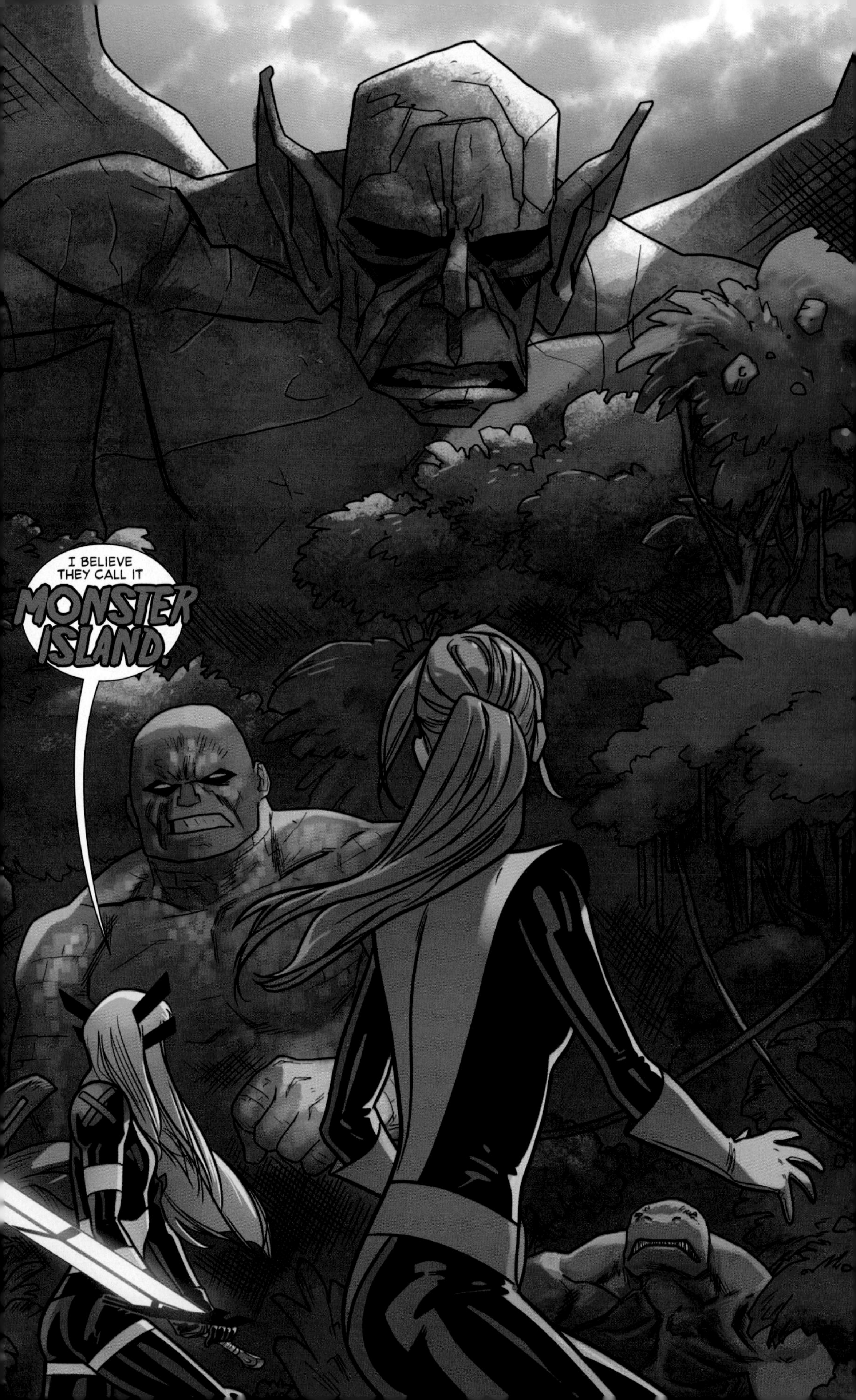
I BELIEVE THEY CALL IT MONSTER ISLAND.

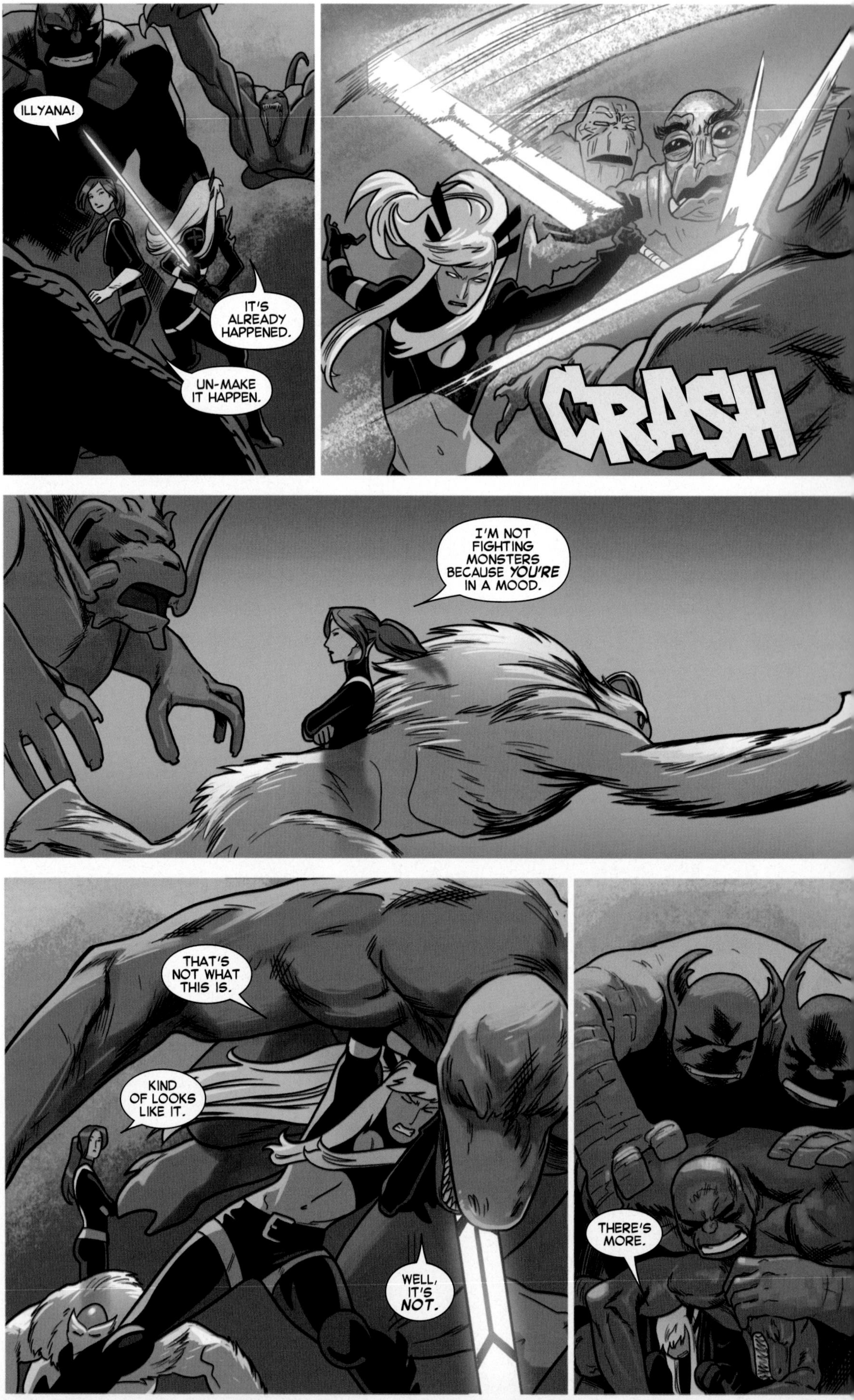
ILLYANA!
IT'S ALREADY HAPPENED.
UN-MAKE IT HAPPEN.
CRASH
I'M NOT FIGHTING MONSTERS BECAUSE *YOU'RE* IN A MOOD.
THAT'S NOT WHAT THIS IS.
KIND OF LOOKS LIKE IT.
WELL, IT'S *NOT*.
THERE'S MORE.

YEAH? WHY ARE WE HERE?

IS THERE AN IN-N-OUT BURGER NEARBY?

THE LAST RECORD STORE ON EARTH?

WE'RE HERE FOR A REASON.

YEAH?

THERE'S A MUTANT HERE AND WE'RE GOING TO SAVE THEM.

THERE'S A MUTANT HERE?

YES.

SMACCCKK

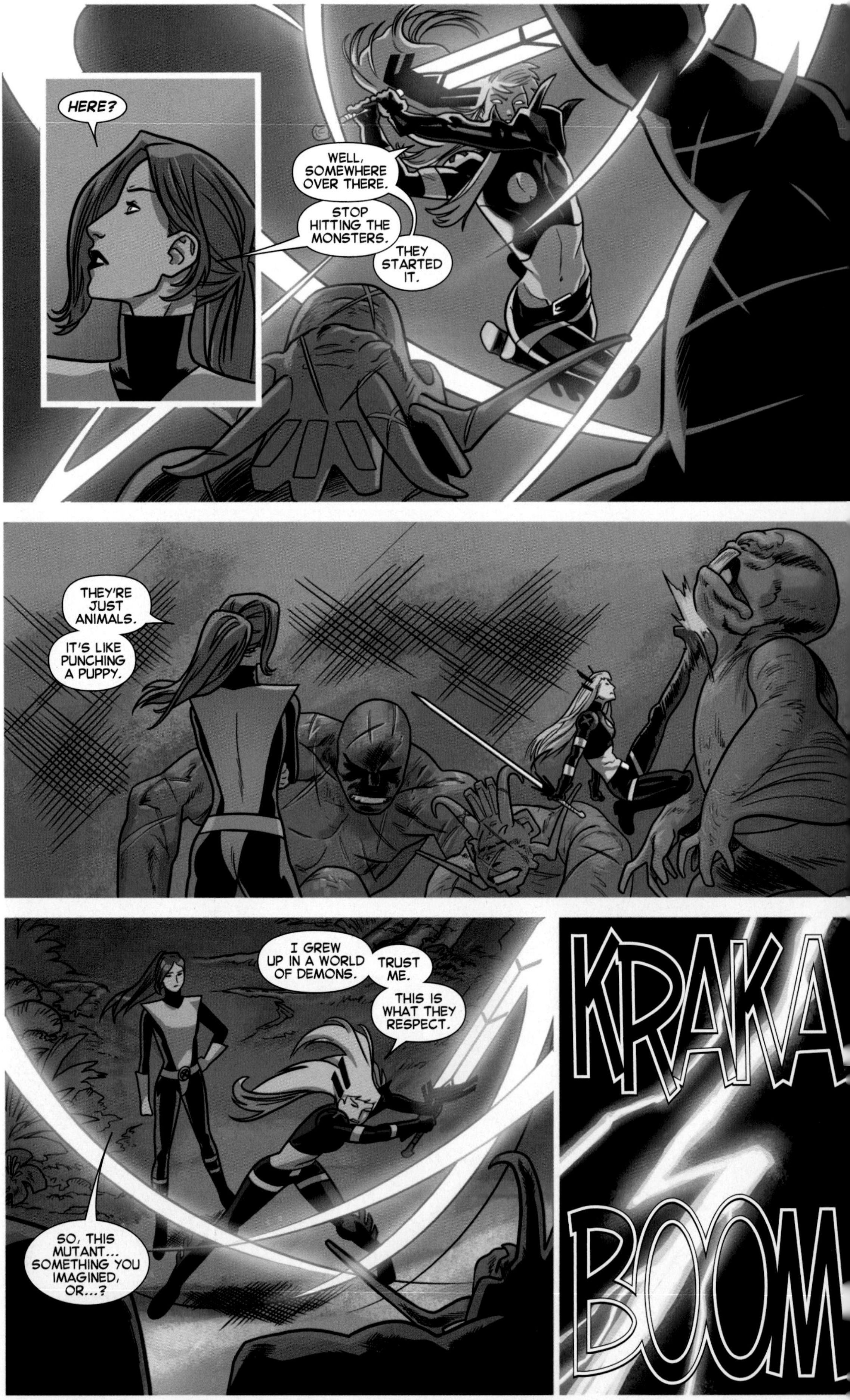
HERE?
WELL, SOMEWHERE OVER THERE.
STOP HITTING THE MONSTERS.
THEY STARTED IT.
THEY'RE JUST ANIMALS.
IT'S LIKE PUNCHING A PUPPY.
I GREW UP IN A WORLD OF DEMONS.
TRUST ME.
THIS IS WHAT THEY RESPECT.
SO, THIS MUTANT... SOMETHING YOU IMAGINED, OR...?
KRAKA
BOOM

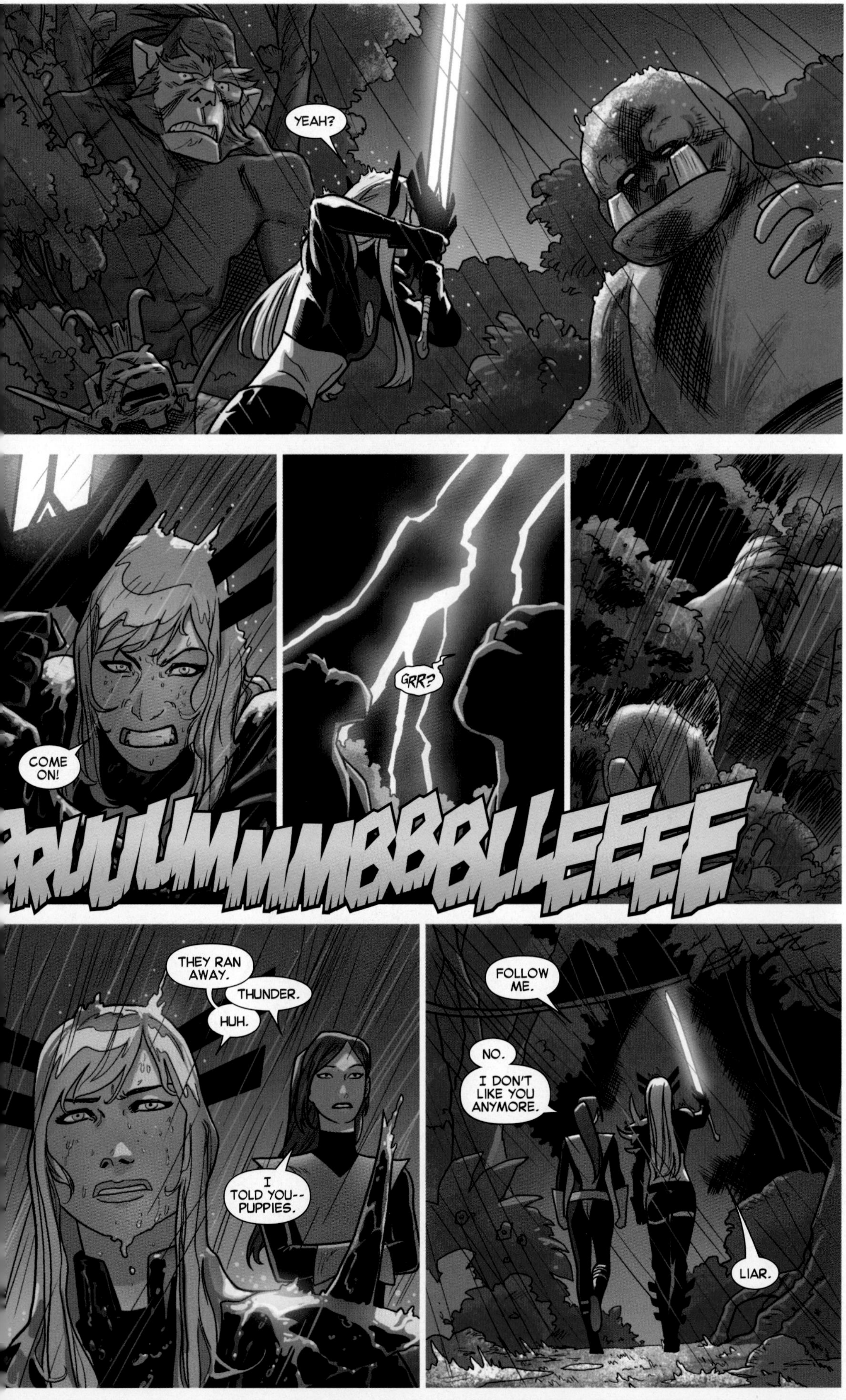
YEAH?
COME ON!
GRR?
RRUUMMMMBBBLLEEEE
THEY RAN AWAY.
THUNDER.
HUH.
I TOLD YOU-- PUPPIES.
FOLLOW ME.
NO.
I DON'T LIKE YOU ANYMORE.
LIAR.

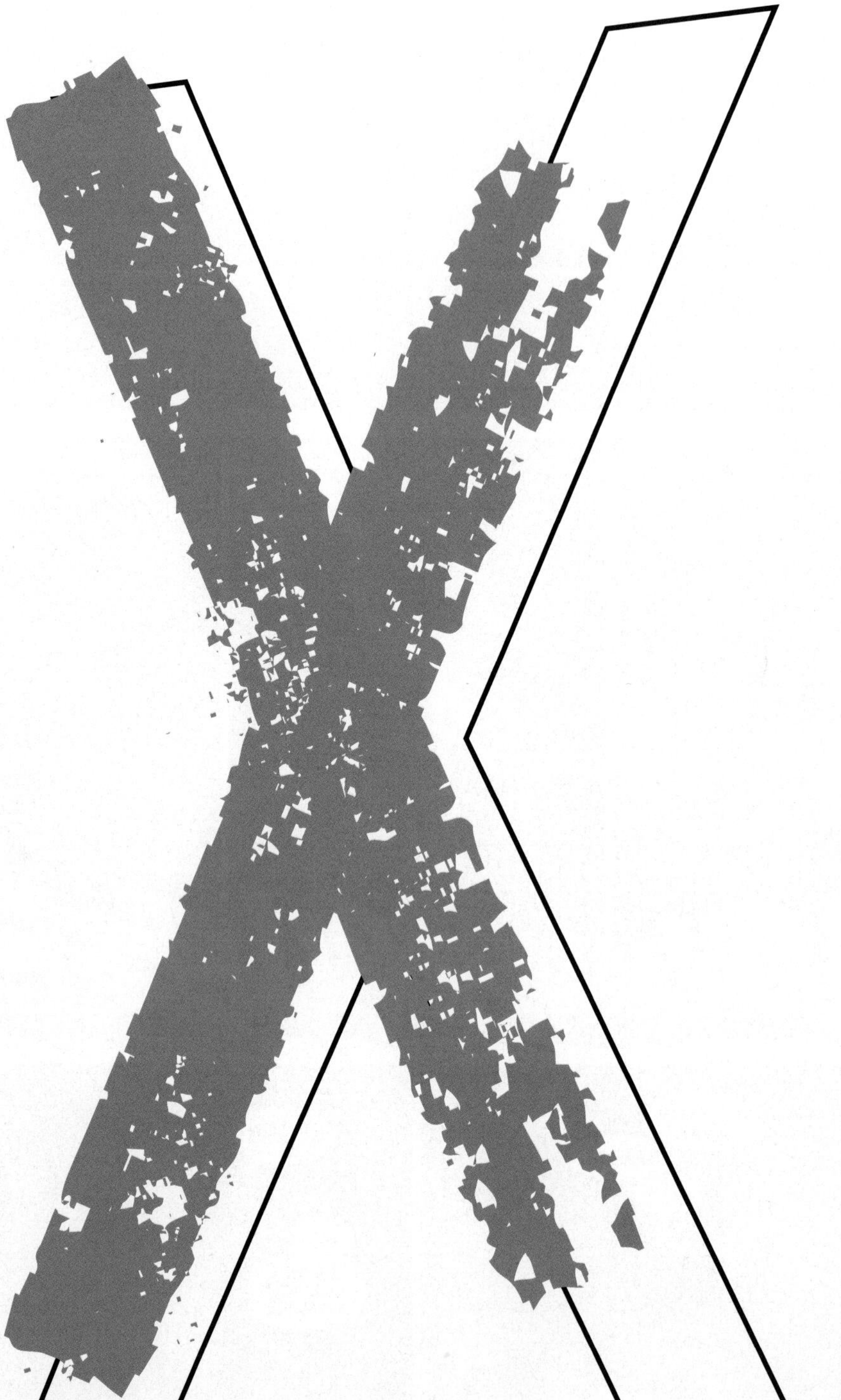

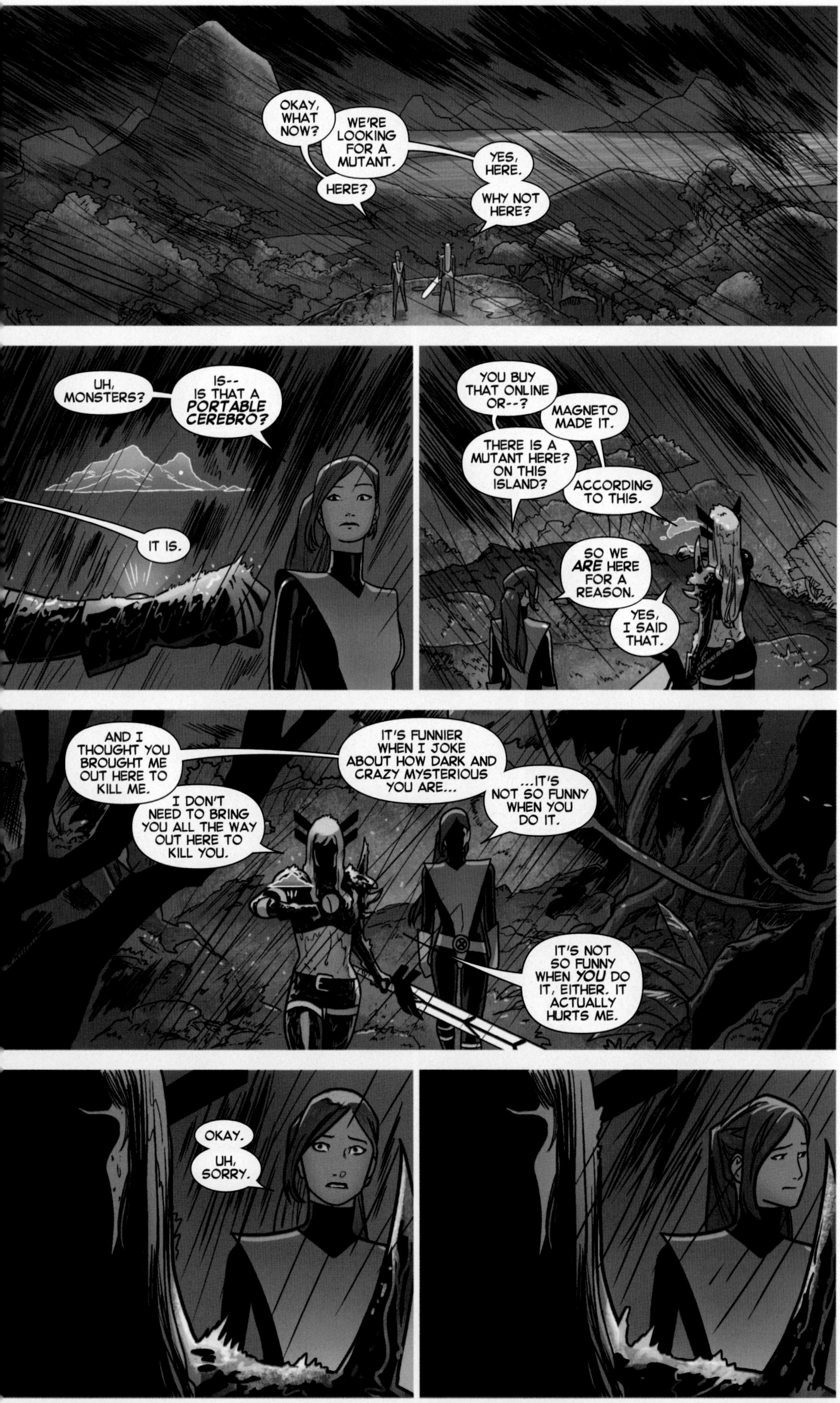
OKAY, WHAT NOW?
WE'RE LOOKING FOR A MUTANT.
HERE?
YES, HERE.
WHY NOT HERE?
UH, MONSTERS?
IS-- IS THAT A PORTABLE CEREBRO?
IT IS.
YOU BUY THAT ONLINE OR--?
MAGNETO MADE IT.
THERE IS A MUTANT HERE? ON THIS ISLAND?
ACCORDING TO THIS.
SO WE ARE HERE FOR A REASON.
YES, I SAID THAT.
AND I THOUGHT YOU BROUGHT ME OUT HERE TO KILL ME.
I DON'T NEED TO BRING YOU ALL THE WAY OUT HERE TO KILL YOU.
IT'S FUNNIER WHEN I JOKE ABOUT HOW DARK AND CRAZY MYSTERIOUS YOU ARE...
...IT'S NOT SO FUNNY WHEN YOU DO IT.
IT'S NOT SO FUNNY WHEN YOU DO IT, EITHER. IT ACTUALLY HURTS ME.
OKAY.
UH, SORRY.

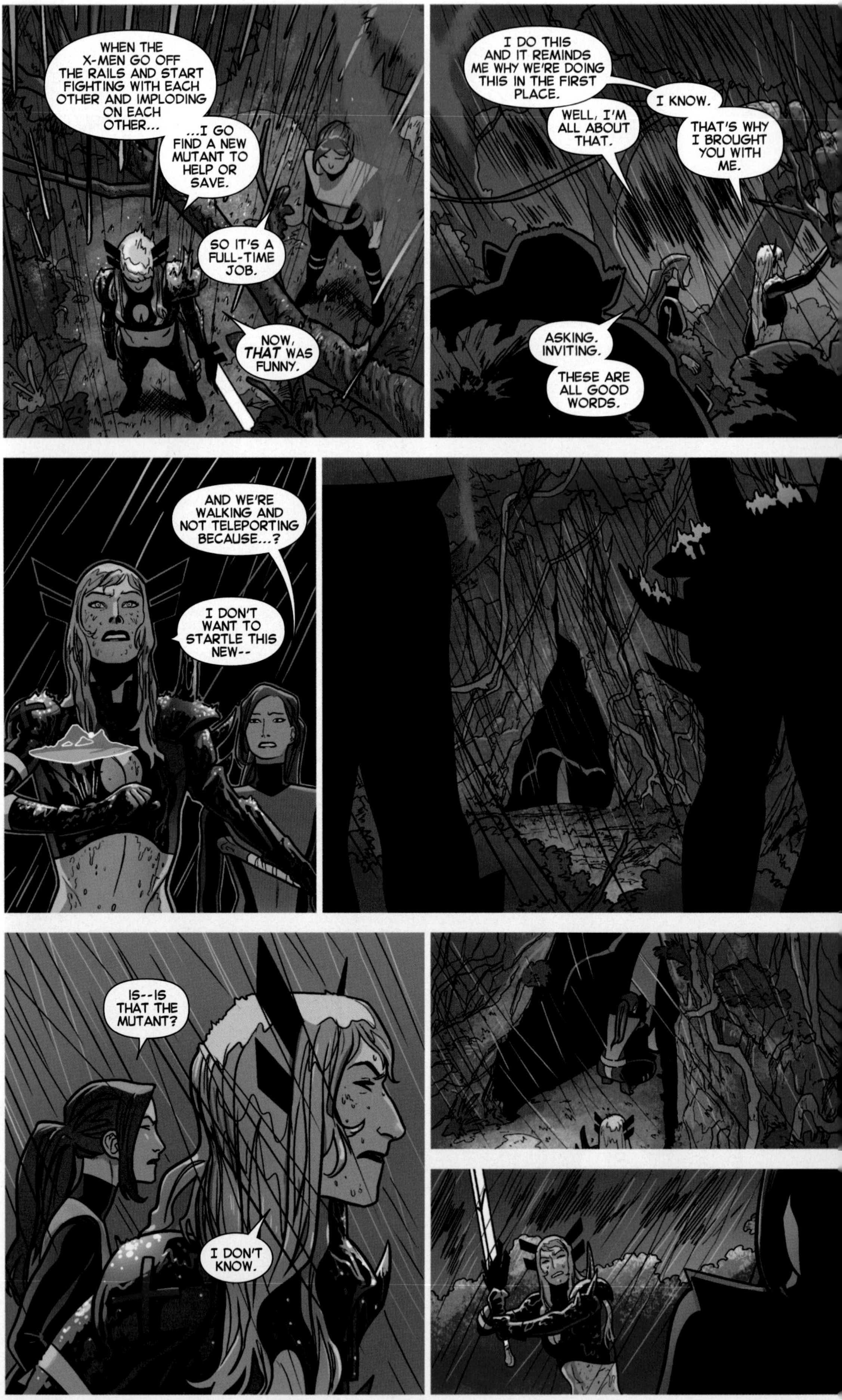
WHEN THE X-MEN GO OFF THE RAILS AND START FIGHTING WITH EACH OTHER AND IMPLODING ON EACH OTHER...
...I GO FIND A NEW MUTANT TO HELP OR SAVE.
SO IT'S A FULL-TIME JOB.
NOW, *THAT* WAS FUNNY.
I DO THIS AND IT REMINDS ME WHY WE'RE DOING THIS IN THE FIRST PLACE.
I KNOW.
WELL, I'M ALL ABOUT THAT.
THAT'S WHY I BROUGHT YOU WITH ME.
ASKING. INVITING.
THESE ARE ALL GOOD WORDS.
AND WE'RE WALKING AND NOT TELEPORTING BECAUSE...?
I DON'T WANT TO STARTLE THIS NEW--
IS--IS THAT THE MUTANT?
I DON'T KNOW.

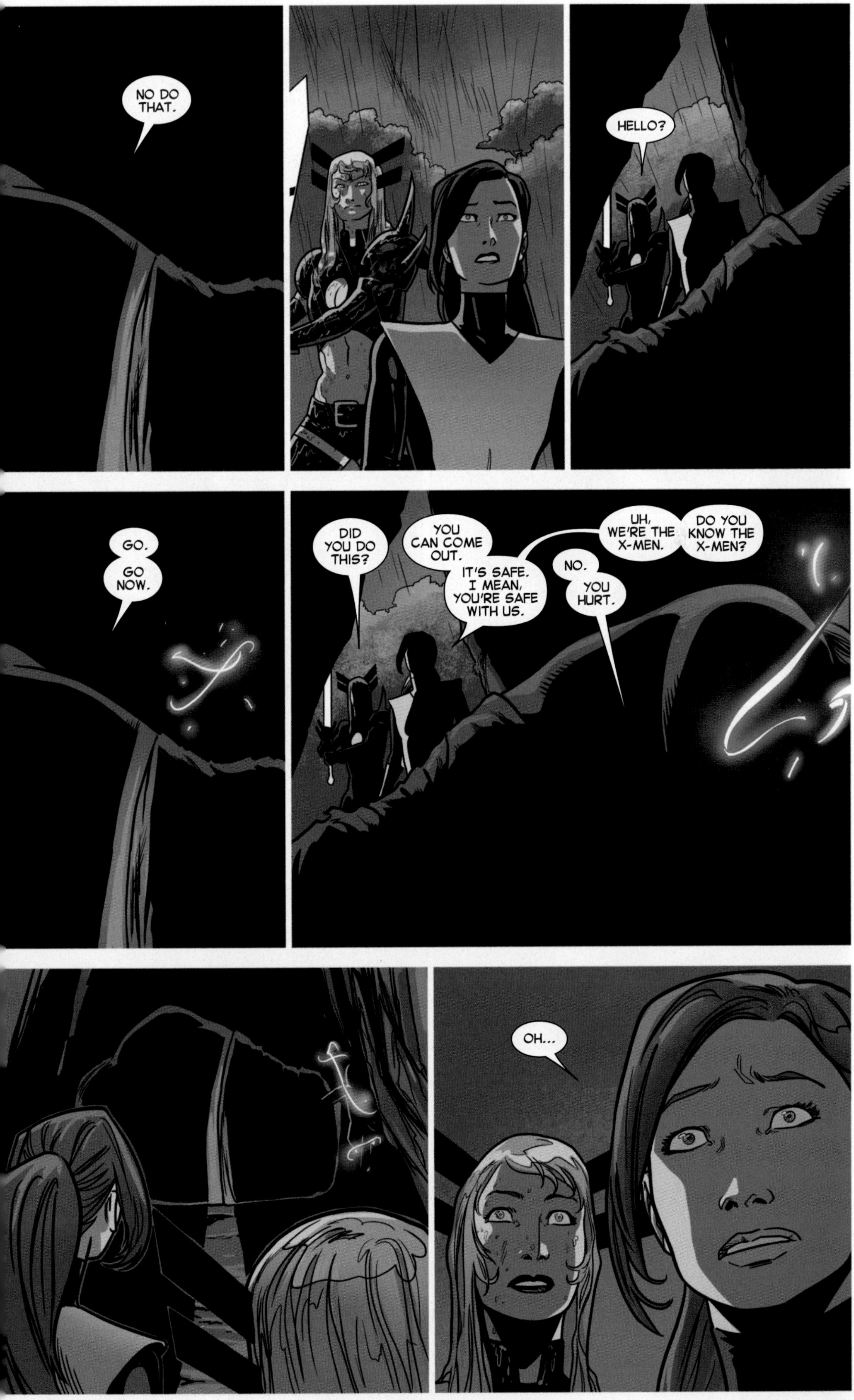
NO DO THAT.
HELLO?
GO.
GO NOW.
DID YOU DO THIS?
YOU CAN COME OUT.
IT'S SAFE. I MEAN, YOU'RE SAFE WITH US.
UH, WE'RE THE X-MEN.
DO YOU KNOW THE X-MEN?
NO.
YOU HURT.
OH...

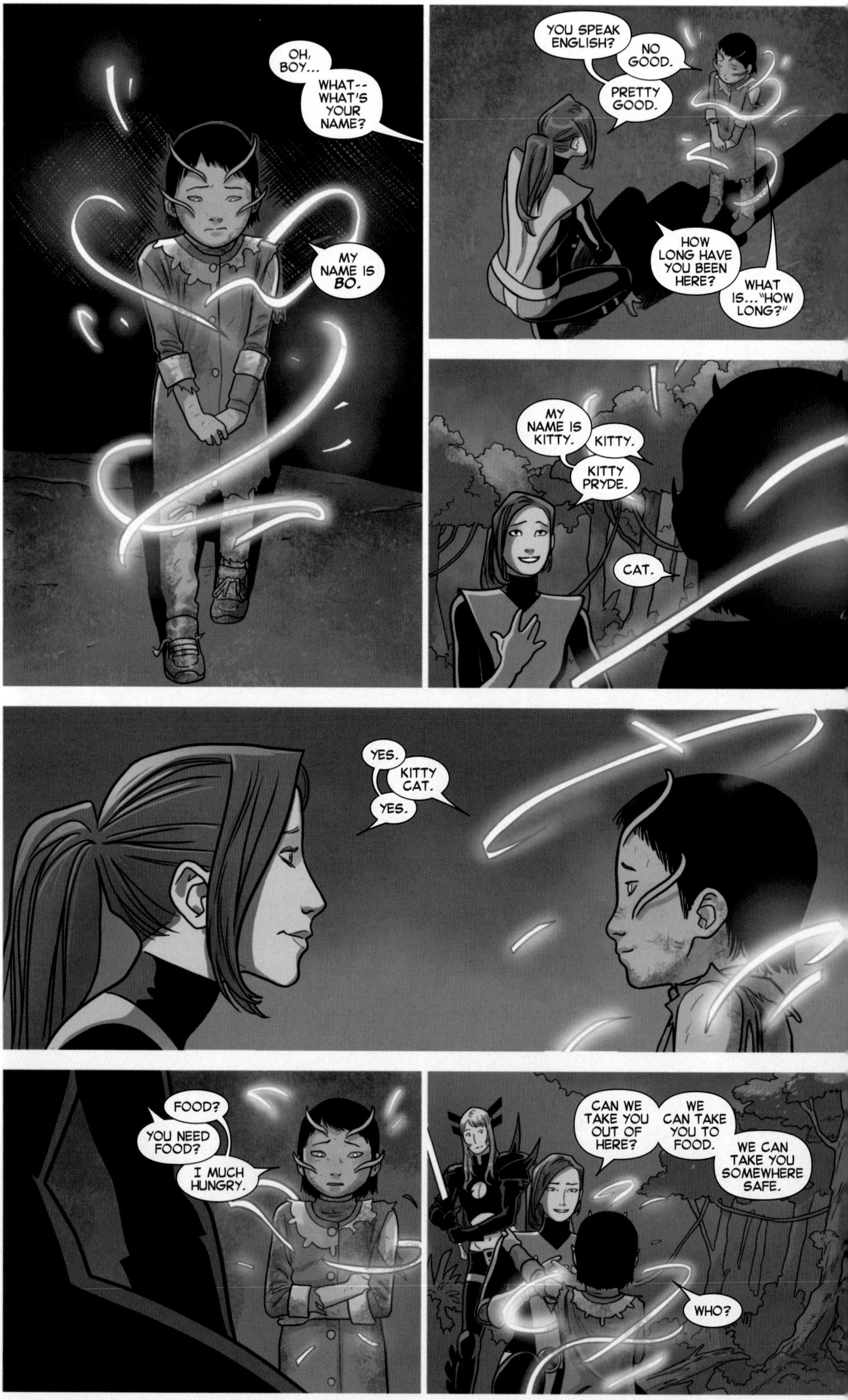
OH, BOY...
WHAT--WHAT'S YOUR NAME?
MY NAME IS BO.
YOU SPEAK ENGLISH?
NO GOOD.
PRETTY GOOD.
HOW LONG HAVE YOU BEEN HERE?
WHAT IS..."HOW LONG?"
MY NAME IS KITTY.
KITTY.
KITTY PRYDE.
CAT.
YES.
KITTY CAT.
YES.
FOOD?
YOU NEED FOOD?
I MUCH HUNGRY.
CAN WE TAKE YOU OUT OF HERE?
WE CAN TAKE YOU TO FOOD.
WE CAN TAKE YOU SOMEWHERE SAFE.
WHO?

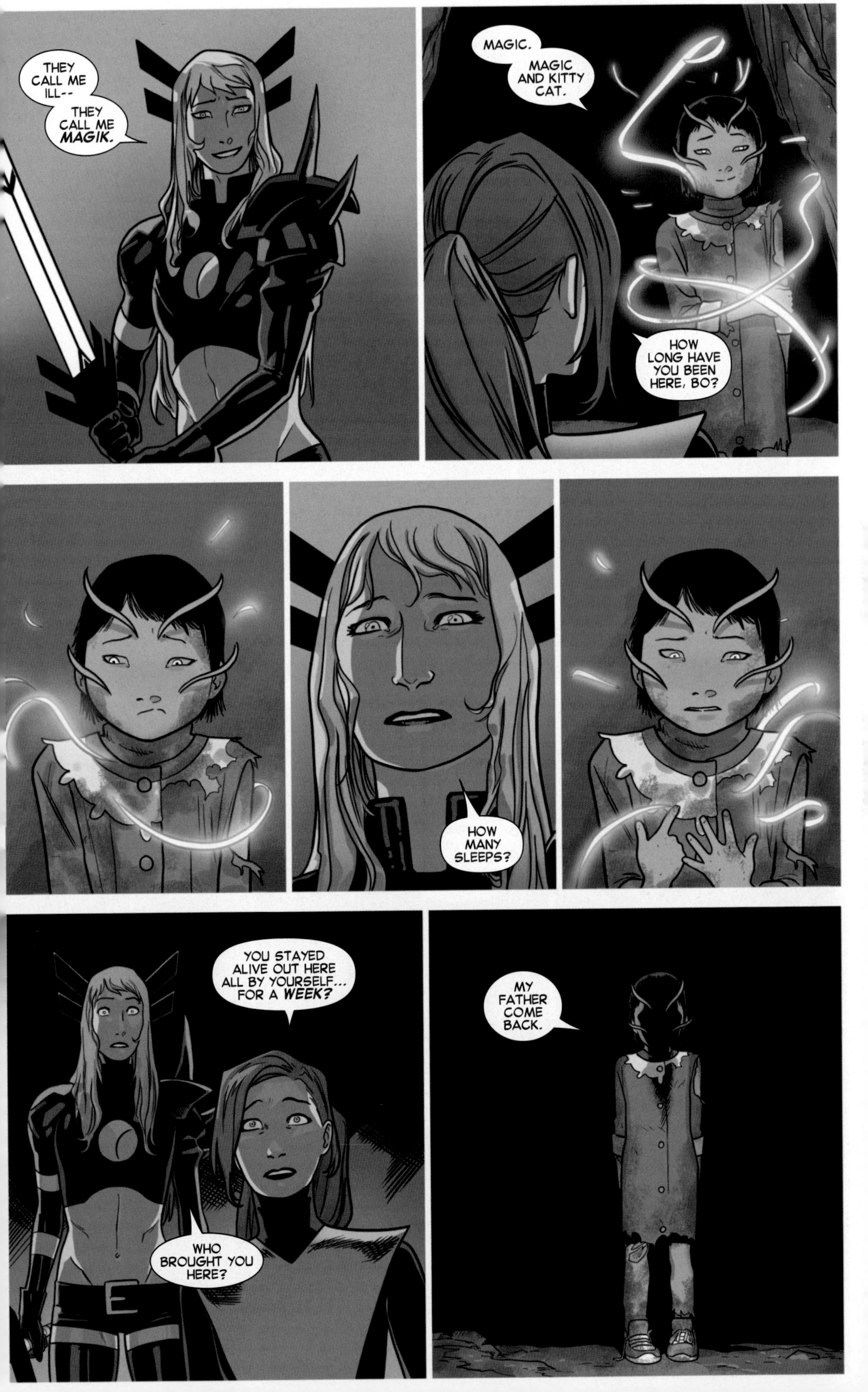
THEY CALL ME ILL--
THEY CALL ME MAGIK.
MAGIC.
MAGIC AND KITTY CAT.
HOW LONG HAVE YOU BEEN HERE, BO?
HOW MANY SLEEPS?
YOU STAYED ALIVE OUT HERE ALL BY YOURSELF... FOR A WEEK?
WHO BROUGHT YOU HERE?
MY FATHER COME BACK.

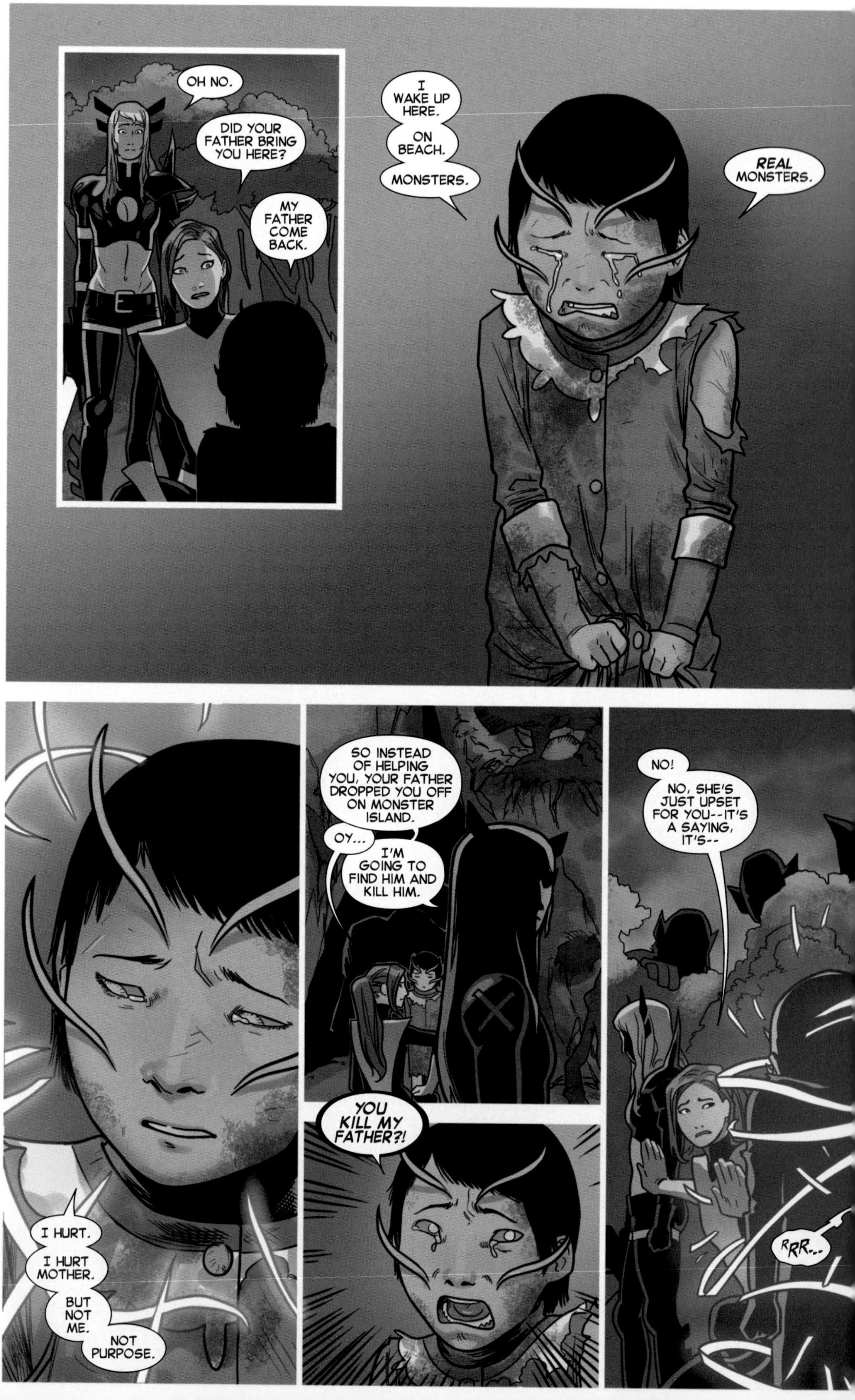
OH NO.
DID YOUR FATHER BRING YOU HERE?
MY FATHER COME BACK.
I WAKE UP HERE.
ON BEACH.
MONSTERS.
REAL MONSTERS.
I HURT.
I HURT MOTHER.
BUT NOT ME.
NOT PURPOSE.
SO INSTEAD OF HELPING YOU, YOUR FATHER DROPPED YOU OFF ON MONSTER ISLAND.
OY...
I'M GOING TO FIND HIM AND KILL HIM.
YOU KILL MY FATHER?!
NO!
NO, SHE'S JUST UPSET FOR YOU--IT'S A SAYING, IT'S--
RRR...

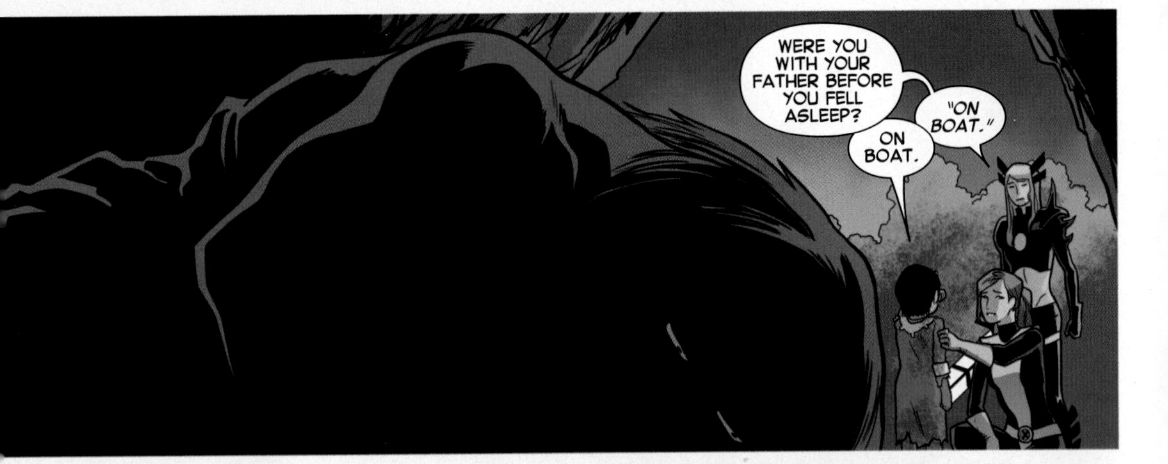
WERE YOU WITH YOUR FATHER BEFORE YOU FELL ASLEEP?
ON BOAT.
"ON BOAT."
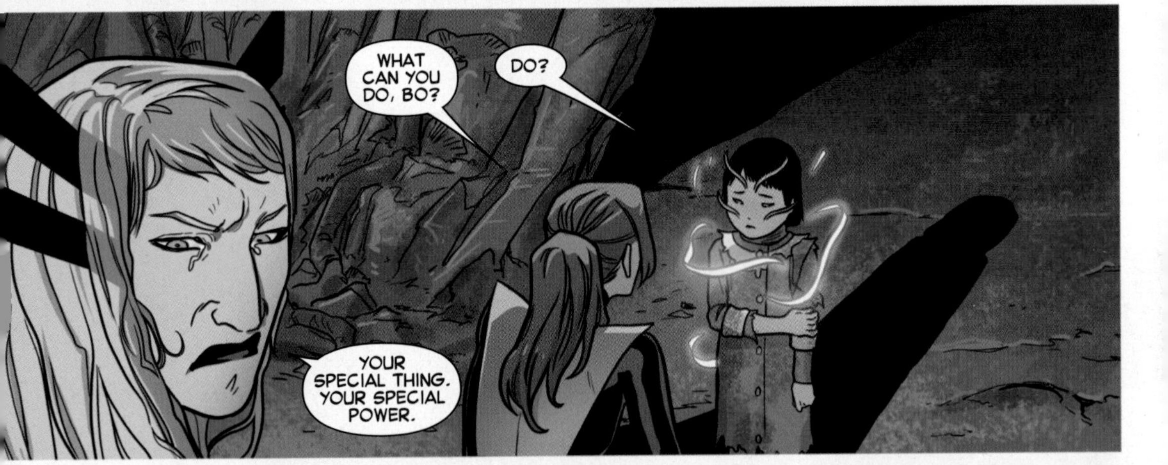
WHAT CAN YOU DO, BO?
DO?
YOUR SPECIAL THING. YOUR SPECIAL POWER.
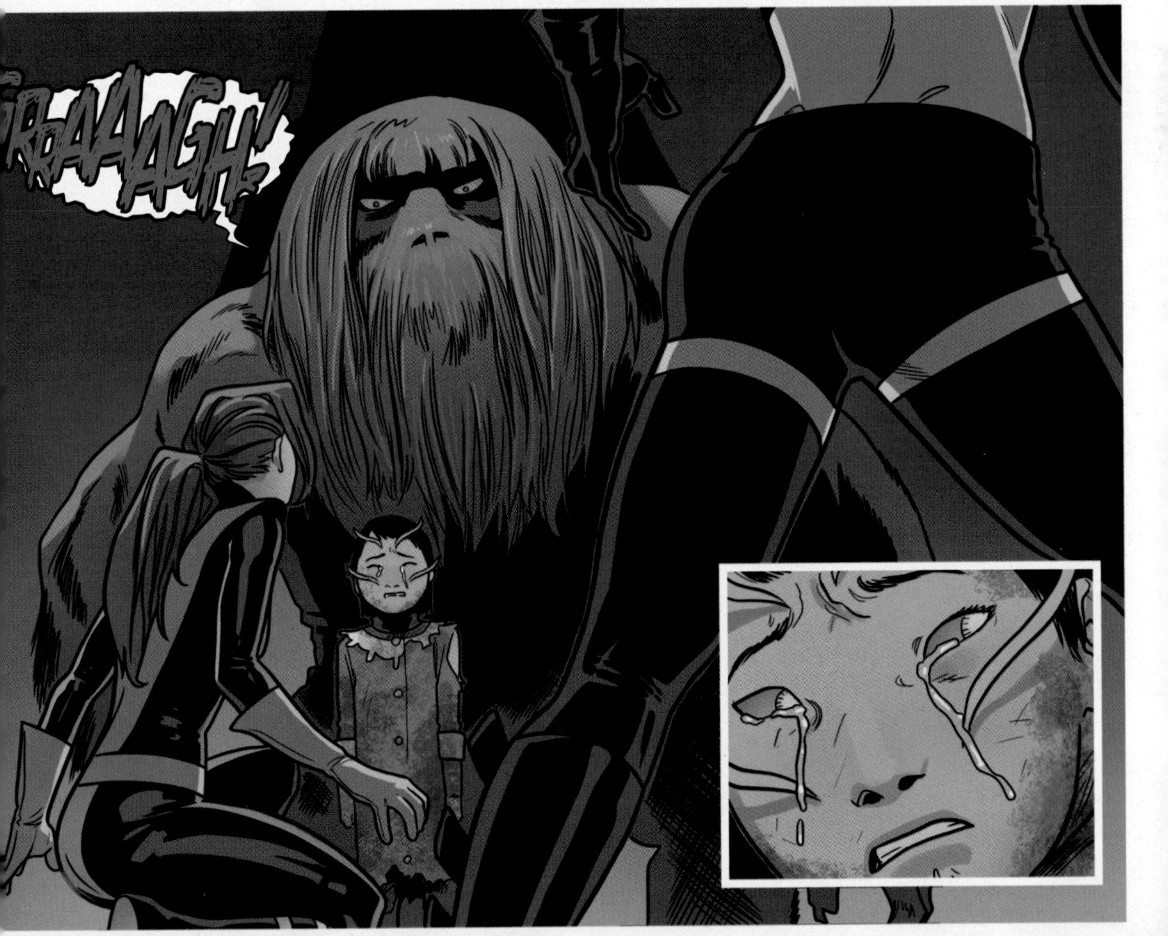
RRAAAAGH!

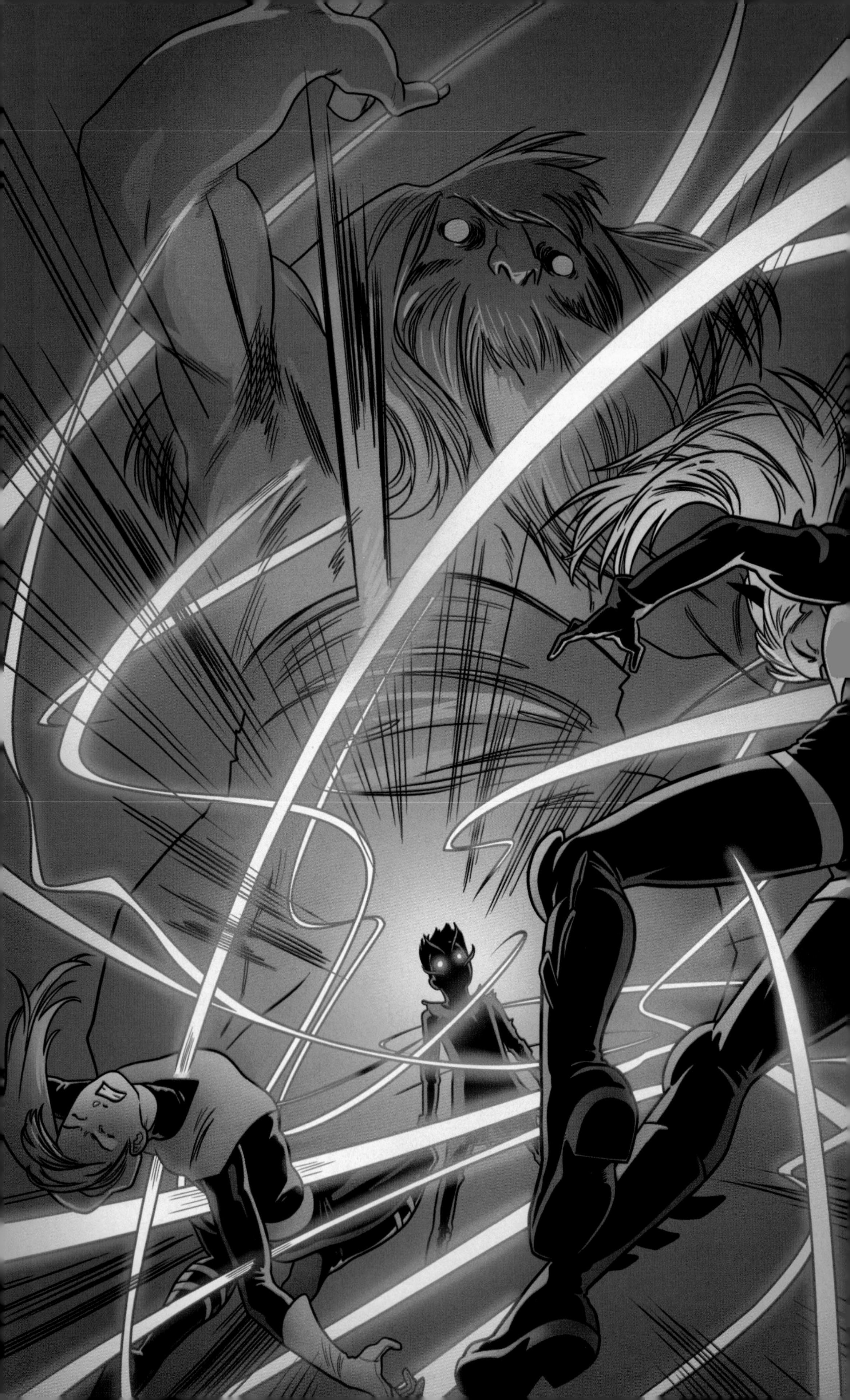

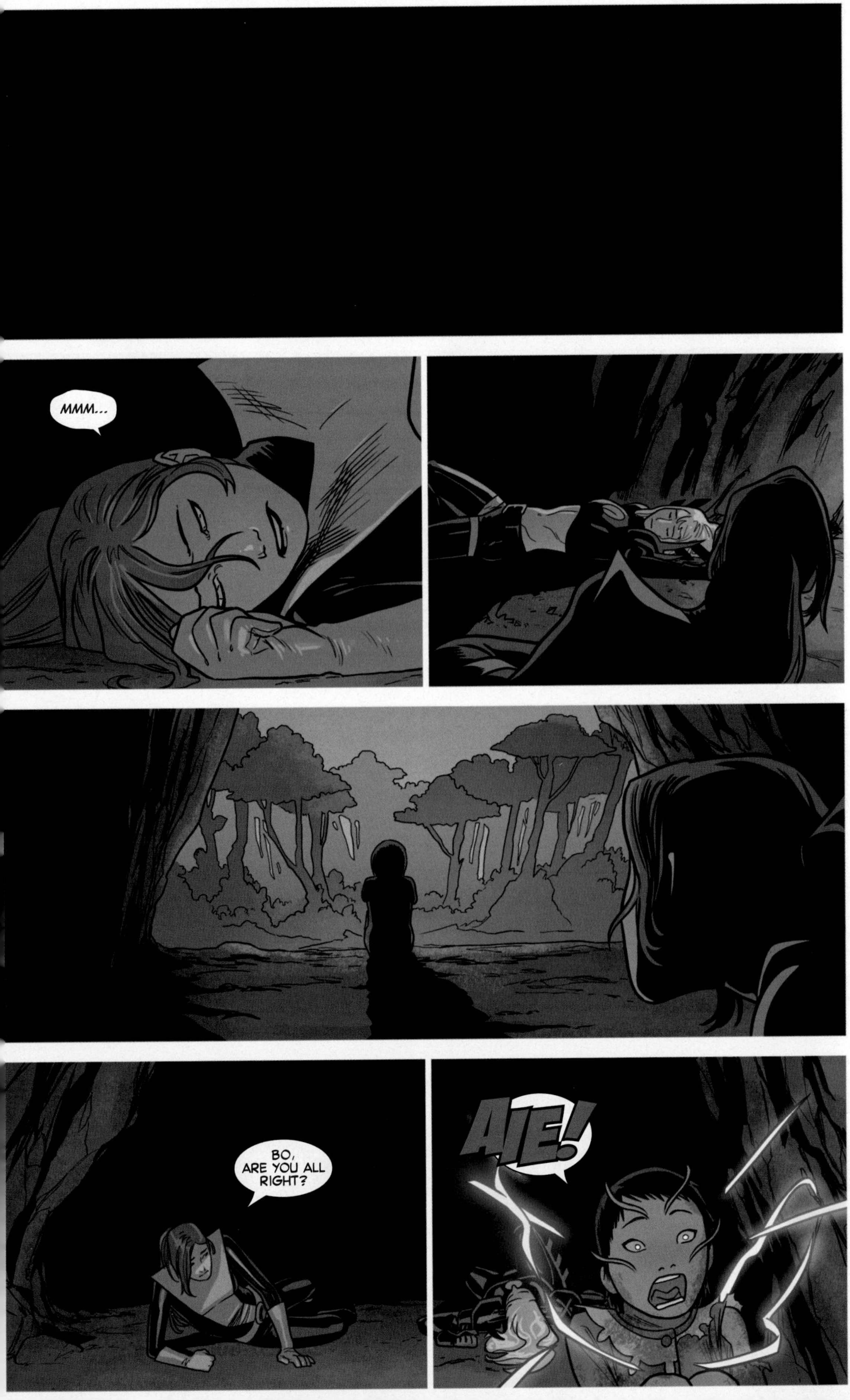
MMM...
BO, ARE YOU ALL RIGHT?
AIE!

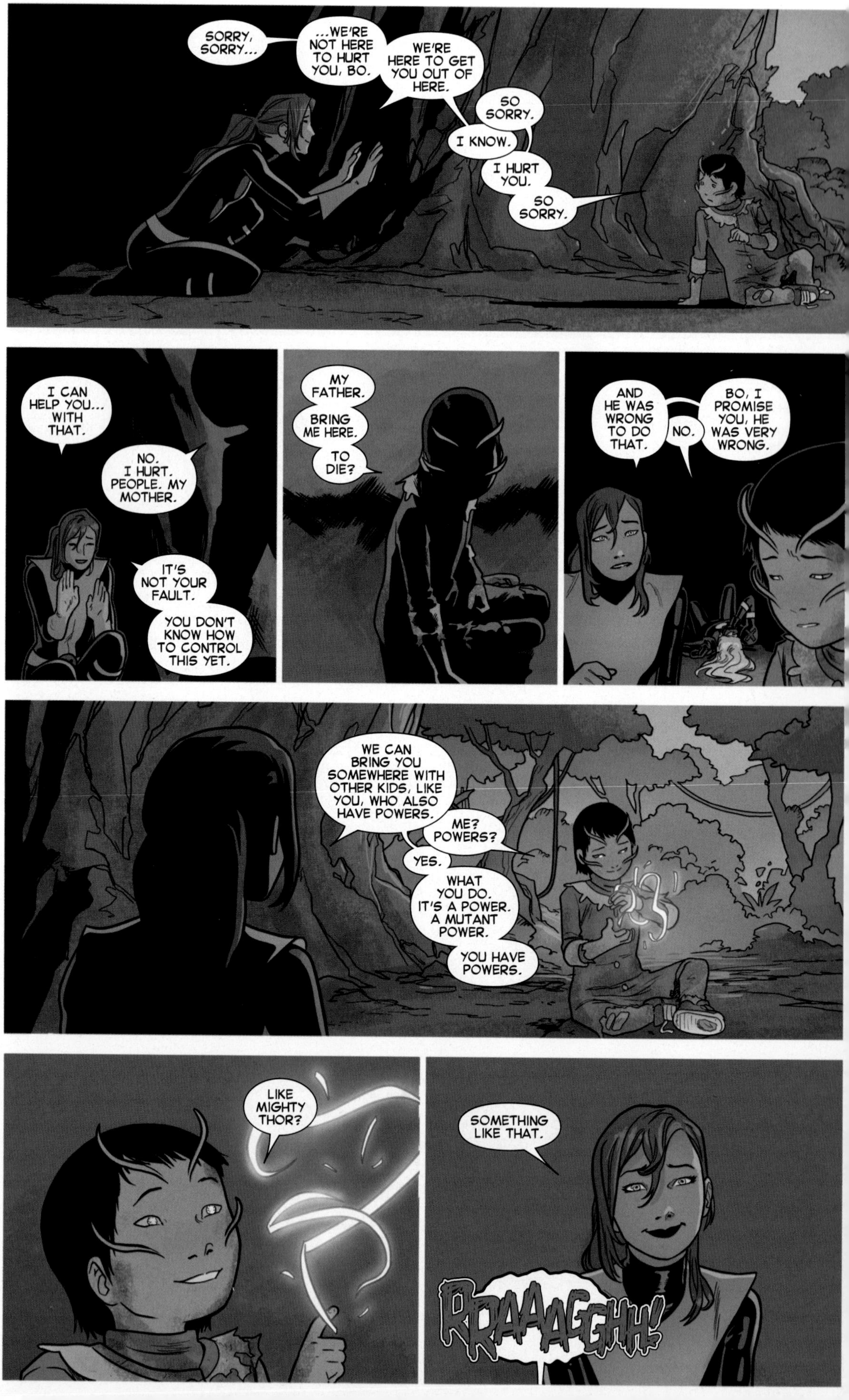
SORRY, SORRY...
...WE'RE NOT HERE TO HURT YOU, BO.
WE'RE HERE TO GET YOU OUT OF HERE.
SO SORRY.
I KNOW.
I HURT YOU.
SO SORRY.
I CAN HELP YOU... WITH THAT.
NO. I HURT. PEOPLE. MY MOTHER.
IT'S NOT YOUR FAULT.
YOU DON'T KNOW HOW TO CONTROL THIS YET.
MY FATHER.
BRING ME HERE.
TO DIE?
AND HE WAS WRONG TO DO THAT.
NO.
BO, I PROMISE YOU, HE WAS VERY WRONG.
WE CAN BRING YOU SOMEWHERE WITH OTHER KIDS, LIKE YOU, WHO ALSO HAVE POWERS.
ME? POWERS?
YES.
WHAT YOU DO. IT'S A POWER. A MUTANT POWER.
YOU HAVE POWERS.
LIKE MIGHTY THOR?
SOMETHING LIKE THAT.
RRAAAGGHH!

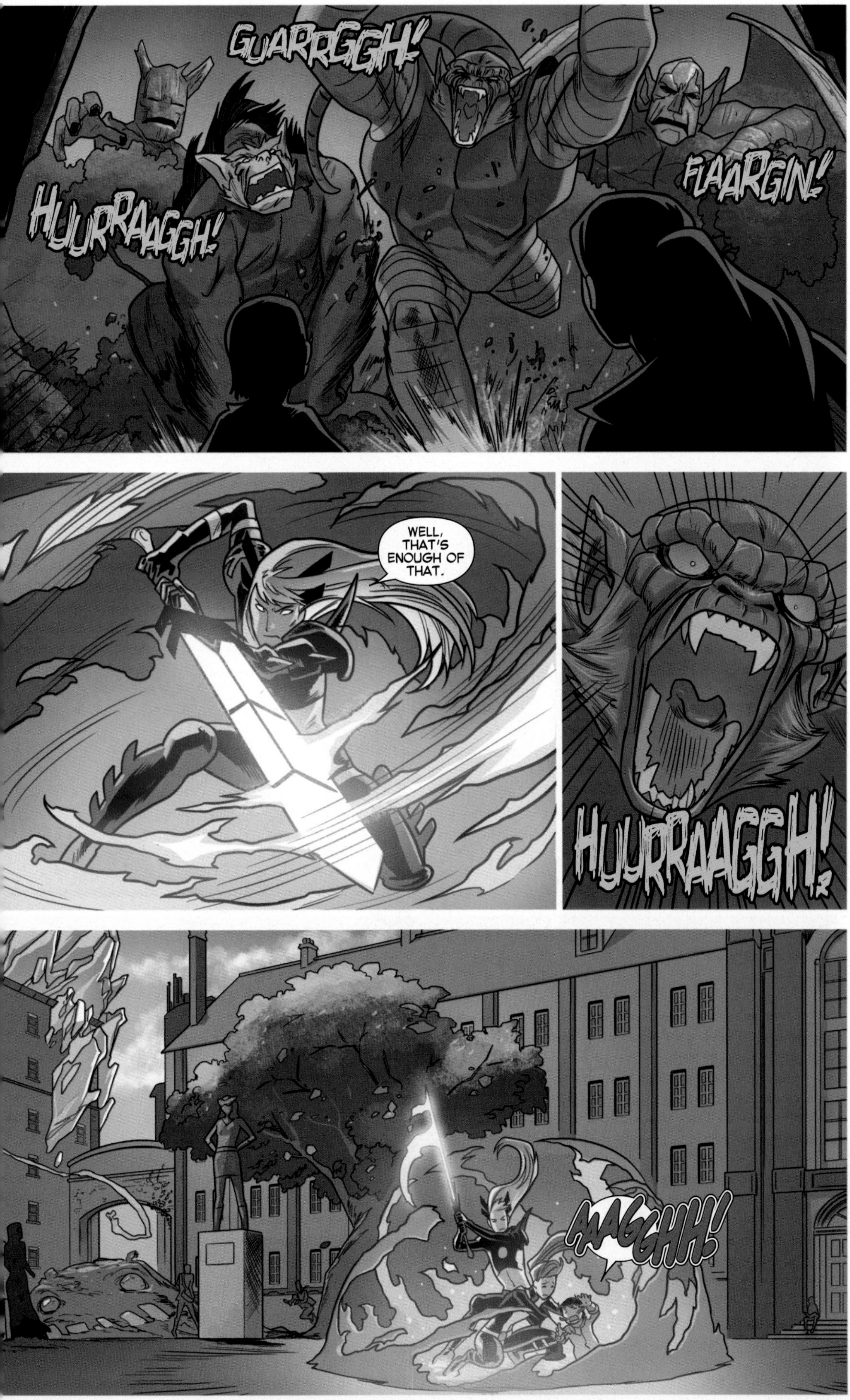
GUARRGGH!
FLAARGIN!
HUURRAAGGH!
WELL, THAT'S ENOUGH OF THAT.
HUURRAAGGH!
AAAGGHH!

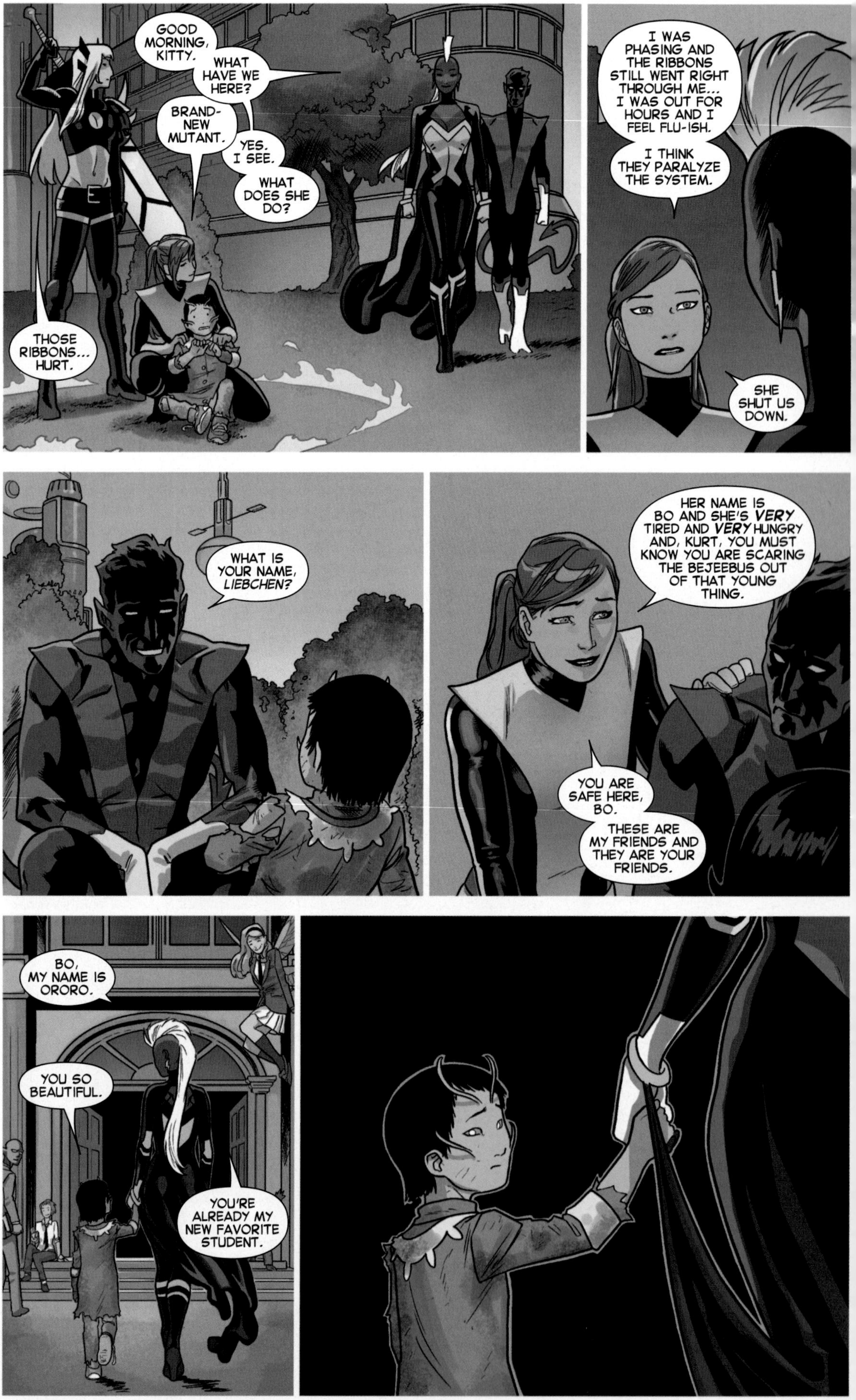
GOOD MORNING, KITTY.
WHAT HAVE WE HERE?
BRAND-NEW MUTANT.
YES. I SEE.
WHAT DOES SHE DO?
THOSE RIBBONS... HURT.
I WAS PHASING AND THE RIBBONS STILL WENT RIGHT THROUGH ME... I WAS OUT FOR HOURS AND I FEEL FLU-ISH.
I THINK THEY PARALYZE THE SYSTEM.
SHE SHUT US DOWN.
WHAT IS YOUR NAME, *LIEBCHEN?*
HER NAME IS BO AND SHE'S ***VERY*** TIRED AND ***VERY*** HUNGRY AND, KURT, YOU MUST KNOW YOU ARE SCARING THE BEJEEBUS OUT OF THAT YOUNG THING.
YOU ARE SAFE HERE, BO.
THESE ARE MY FRIENDS AND THEY ARE YOUR FRIENDS.
BO, MY NAME IS ORORO.
YOU SO BEAUTIFUL.
YOU'RE ALREADY MY NEW FAVORITE STUDENT.

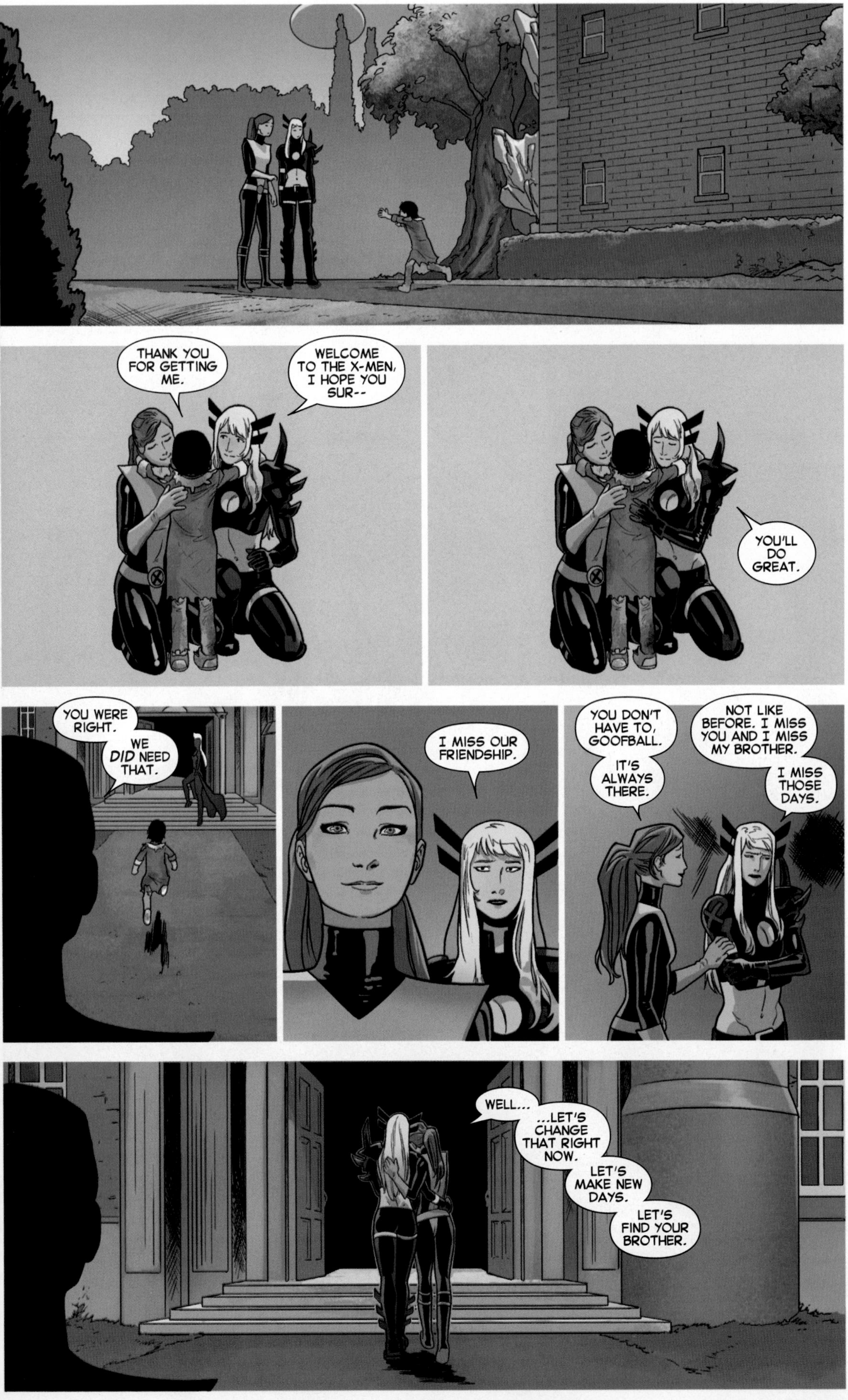
THANK YOU FOR GETTING ME.
WELCOME TO THE X-MEN, I HOPE YOU SUR--
YOU'LL DO GREAT.
YOU WERE RIGHT.
WE *DID* NEED THAT.
I MISS OUR FRIENDSHIP.
YOU DON'T HAVE TO, GOOFBALL.
IT'S ALWAYS THERE.
NOT LIKE BEFORE. I MISS YOU AND I MISS MY BROTHER.
I MISS THOSE DAYS.
WELL...
...LET'S CHANGE THAT RIGHT NOW.
LET'S MAKE NEW DAYS.
LET'S FIND YOUR BROTHER.

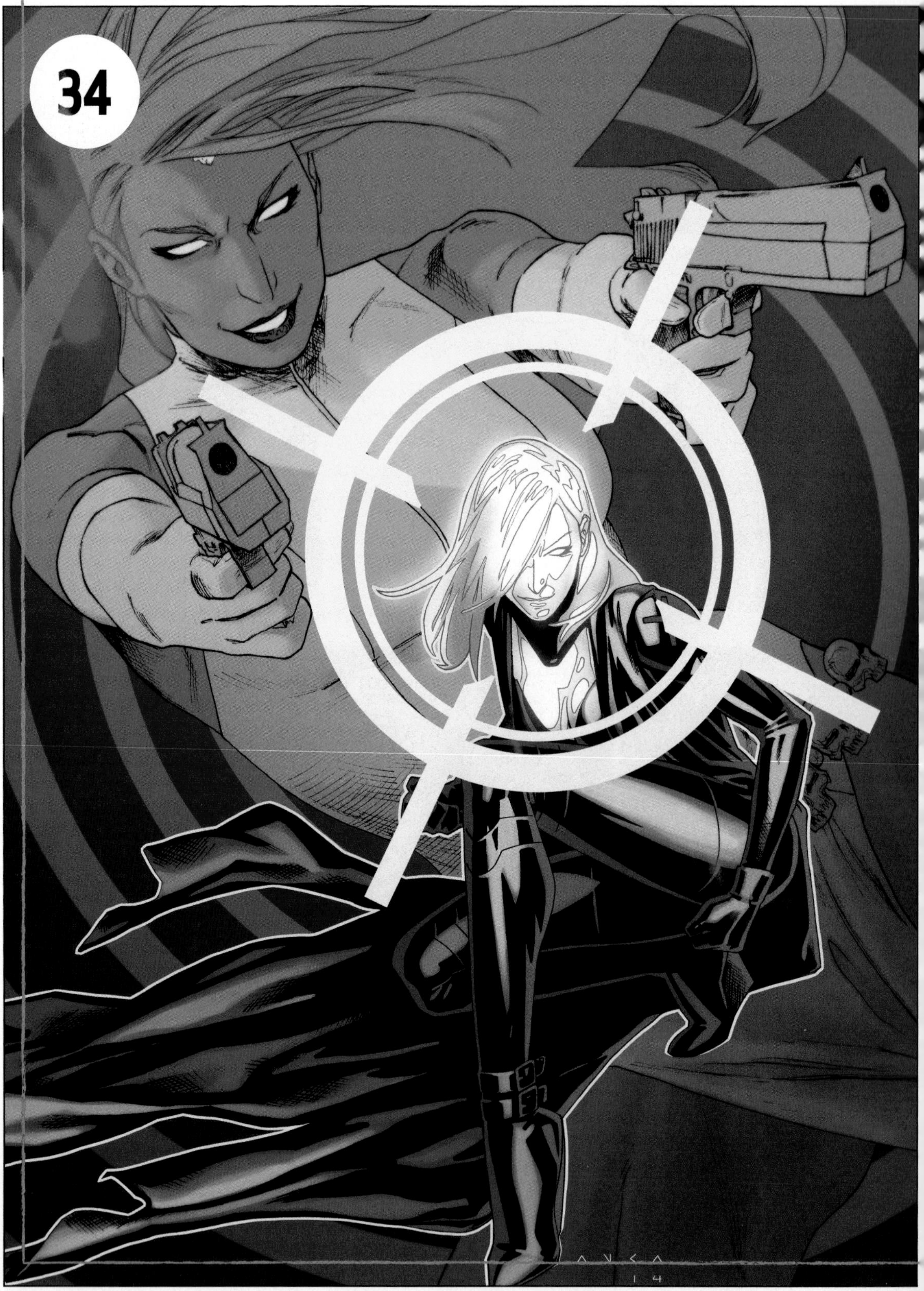
34

DELHI, INDIA.

HELLO, RAVEN.

SCOTT SUMMERS.

HOW DID YOU FIND ME?

YOUR BREAD CRUMBS.

I'M GOING TO HAVE TO WORK ON THAT.

YOU'RE A BOLLYWOOD STAR NOW?

ONLY FOR A WEEK OR TWO.

JUST TAKING A VACATION FROM MYSELF.

AGAIN.

AGAIN.

SO, HOW GOES THE MUTANT REVOLUTION?

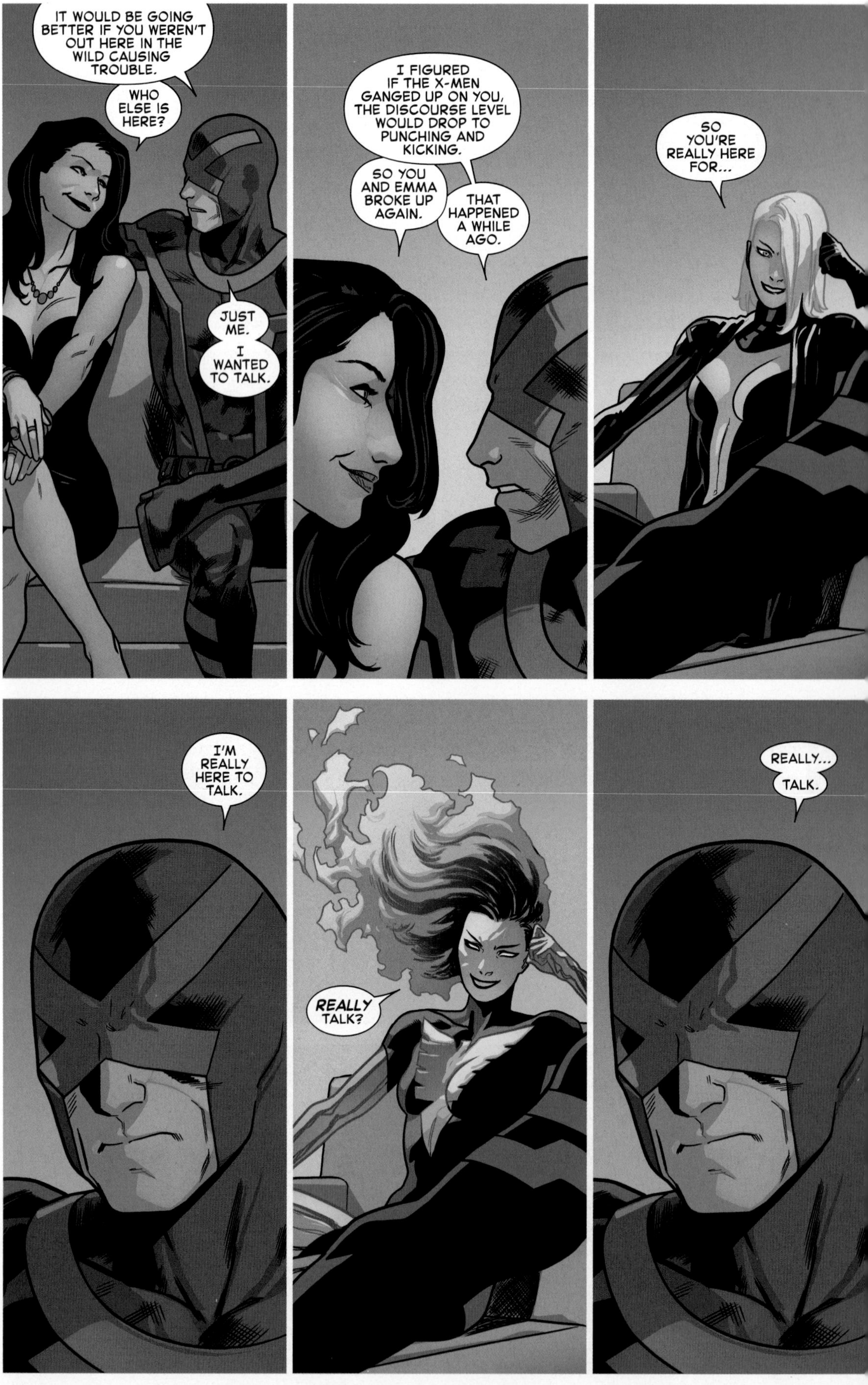
IT WOULD BE GOING BETTER IF YOU WEREN'T OUT HERE IN THE WILD CAUSING TROUBLE.
WHO ELSE IS HERE?
JUST ME.
I WANTED TO TALK.
I FIGURED IF THE X-MEN GANGED UP ON YOU, THE DISCOURSE LEVEL WOULD DROP TO PUNCHING AND KICKING.
SO YOU AND EMMA BROKE UP AGAIN.
THAT HAPPENED A WHILE AGO.
SO YOU'RE REALLY HERE FOR...
I'M REALLY HERE TO TALK.
REALLY TALK?
REALLY...
TALK.

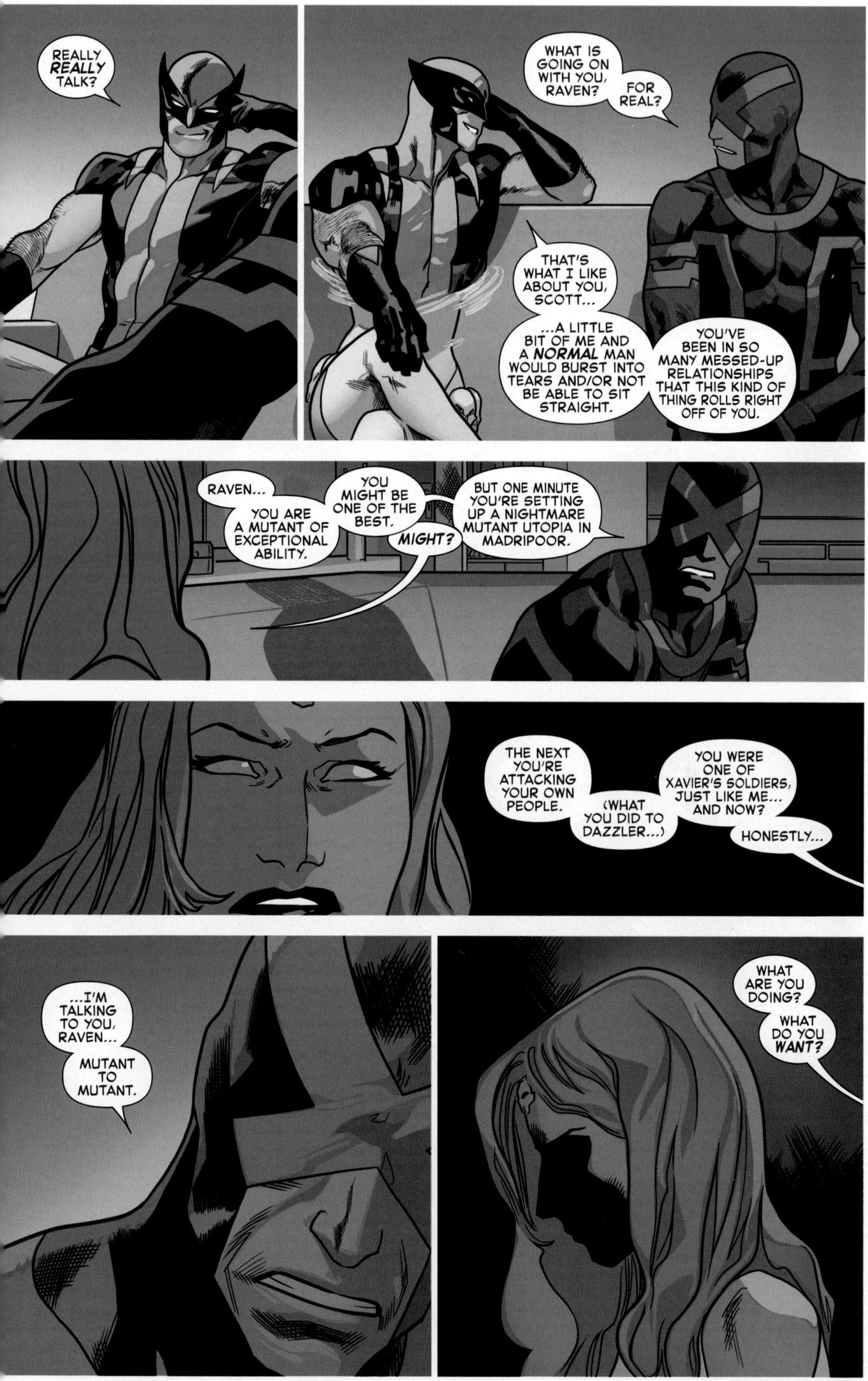

REALLY *REALLY* TALK?
WHAT IS GOING ON WITH YOU, RAVEN?
FOR REAL?
THAT'S WHAT I LIKE ABOUT YOU, SCOTT...
...A LITTLE BIT OF ME AND A *NORMAL* MAN WOULD BURST INTO TEARS AND/OR NOT BE ABLE TO SIT STRAIGHT.
YOU'VE BEEN IN SO MANY MESSED-UP RELATIONSHIPS THAT THIS KIND OF THING ROLLS RIGHT OFF OF YOU.
RAVEN...
YOU ARE A MUTANT OF EXCEPTIONAL ABILITY.
YOU MIGHT BE ONE OF THE BEST.
MIGHT?
BUT ONE MINUTE YOU'RE SETTING UP A NIGHTMARE MUTANT UTOPIA IN MADRIPOOR.
THE NEXT YOU'RE ATTACKING YOUR OWN PEOPLE.
(WHAT YOU DID TO DAZZLER...)
YOU WERE ONE OF XAVIER'S SOLDIERS, JUST LIKE ME... AND NOW?
HONESTLY...
...I'M TALKING TO YOU, RAVEN...
MUTANT TO MUTANT.
WHAT ARE YOU DOING?
WHAT DO YOU *WANT?*

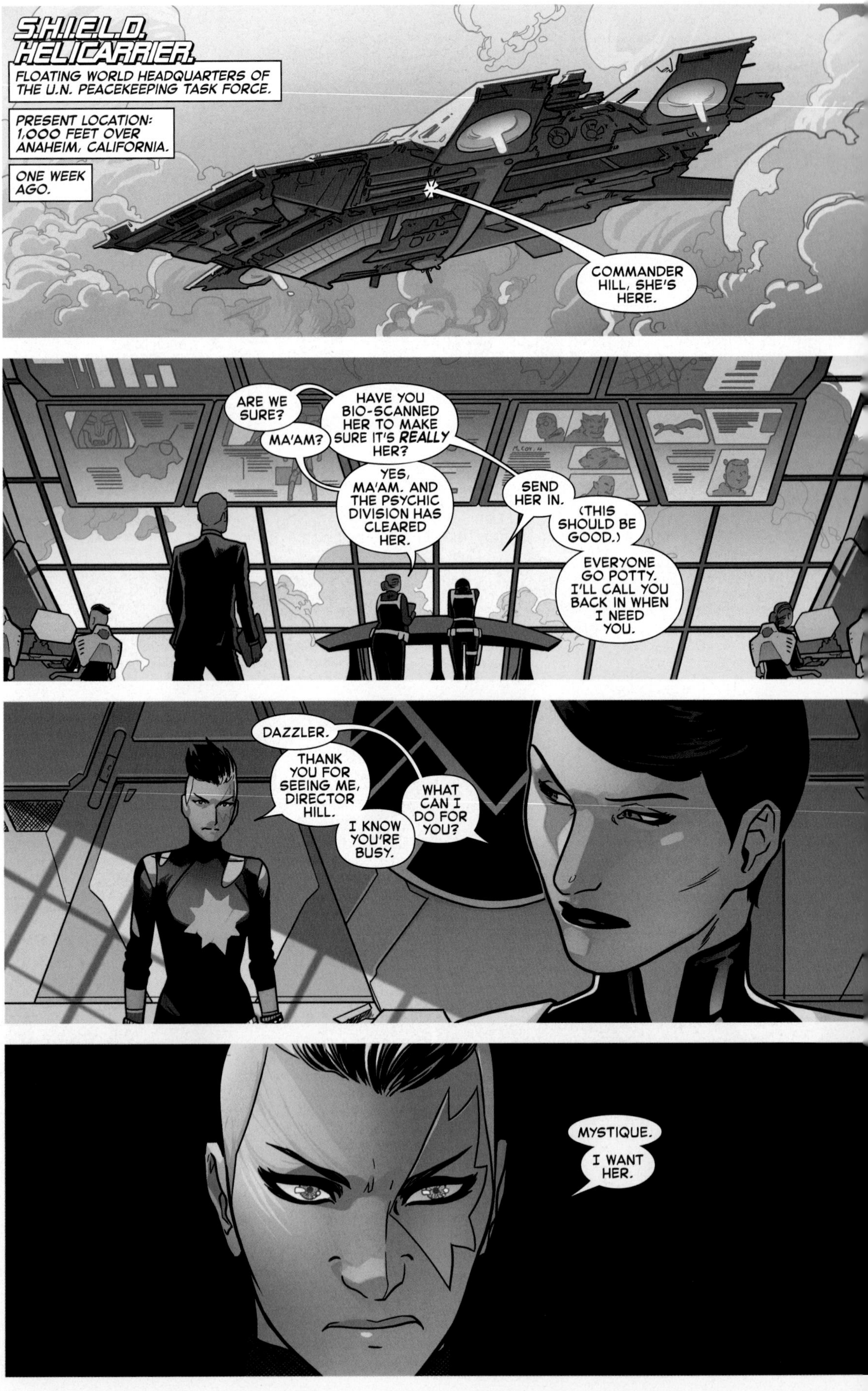
S.H.I.E.L.D. HELICARRIER.
FLOATING WORLD HEADQUARTERS OF THE U.N. PEACEKEEPING TASK FORCE.
PRESENT LOCATION: 1,000 FEET OVER ANAHEIM, CALIFORNIA.
ONE WEEK AGO.
COMMANDER HILL, SHE'S HERE.
ARE WE SURE?
HAVE YOU BIO-SCANNED HER TO MAKE SURE IT'S REALLY HER?
MA'AM?
YES, MA'AM. AND THE PSYCHIC DIVISION HAS CLEARED HER.
SEND HER IN.
(THIS SHOULD BE GOOD.)
EVERYONE GO POTTY. I'LL CALL YOU BACK IN WHEN I NEED YOU.
DAZZLER.
THANK YOU FOR SEEING ME, DIRECTOR HILL.
I KNOW YOU'RE BUSY.
WHAT CAN I DO FOR YOU?
MYSTIQUE.
I WANT HER.

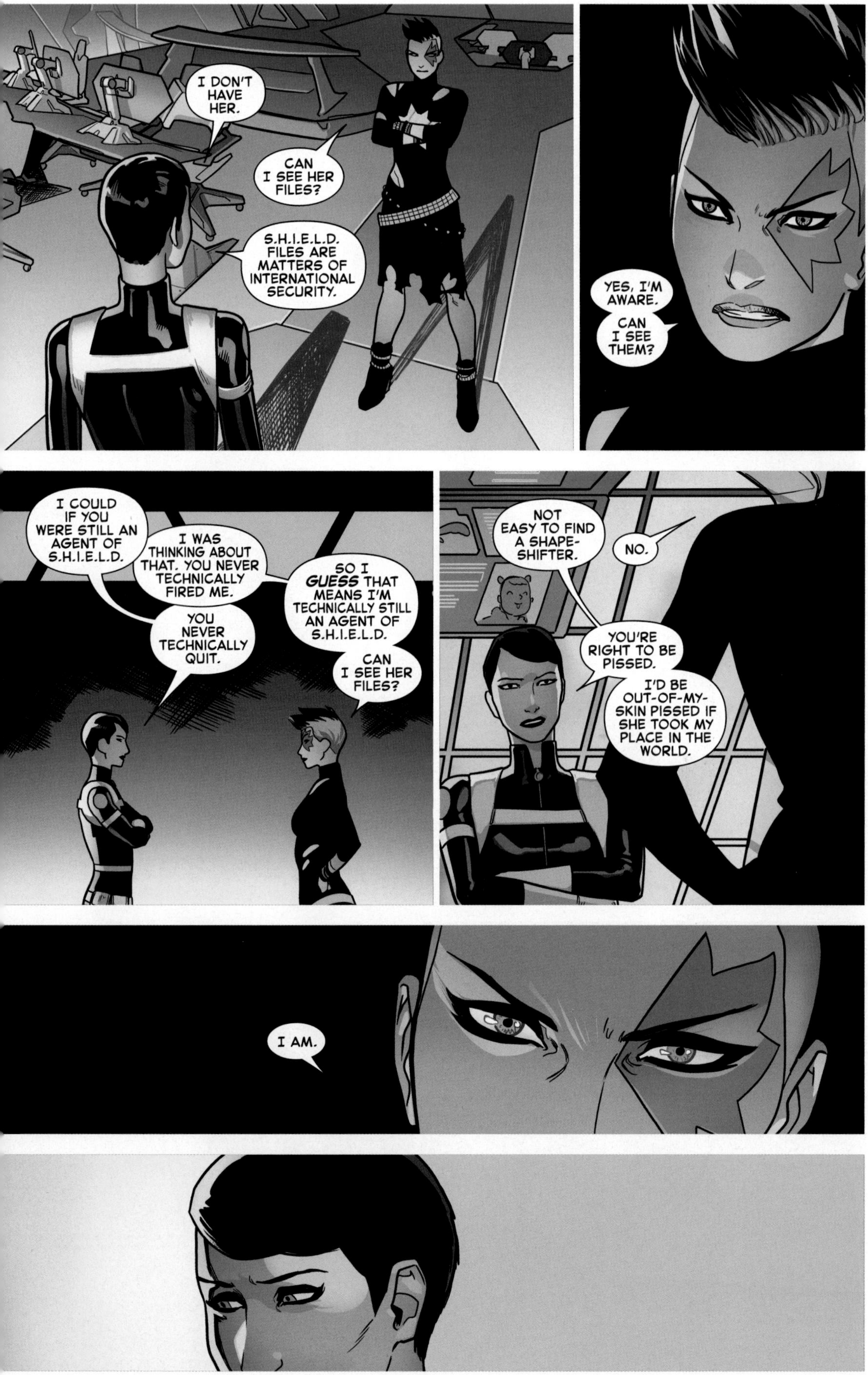
I DON'T HAVE HER.
CAN I SEE HER FILES?
S.H.I.E.L.D. FILES ARE MATTERS OF INTERNATIONAL SECURITY.
YES, I'M AWARE.
CAN I SEE THEM?
I COULD IF YOU WERE STILL AN AGENT OF S.H.I.E.L.D.
I WAS THINKING ABOUT THAT. YOU NEVER TECHNICALLY FIRED ME.
YOU NEVER TECHNICALLY QUIT.
SO I GUESS THAT MEANS I'M TECHNICALLY STILL AN AGENT OF S.H.I.E.L.D.
CAN I SEE HER FILES?
NO.
NOT EASY TO FIND A SHAPE-SHIFTER.
YOU'RE RIGHT TO BE PISSED.
I'D BE OUT-OF-MY-SKIN PISSED IF SHE TOOK MY PLACE IN THE WORLD.
I AM.

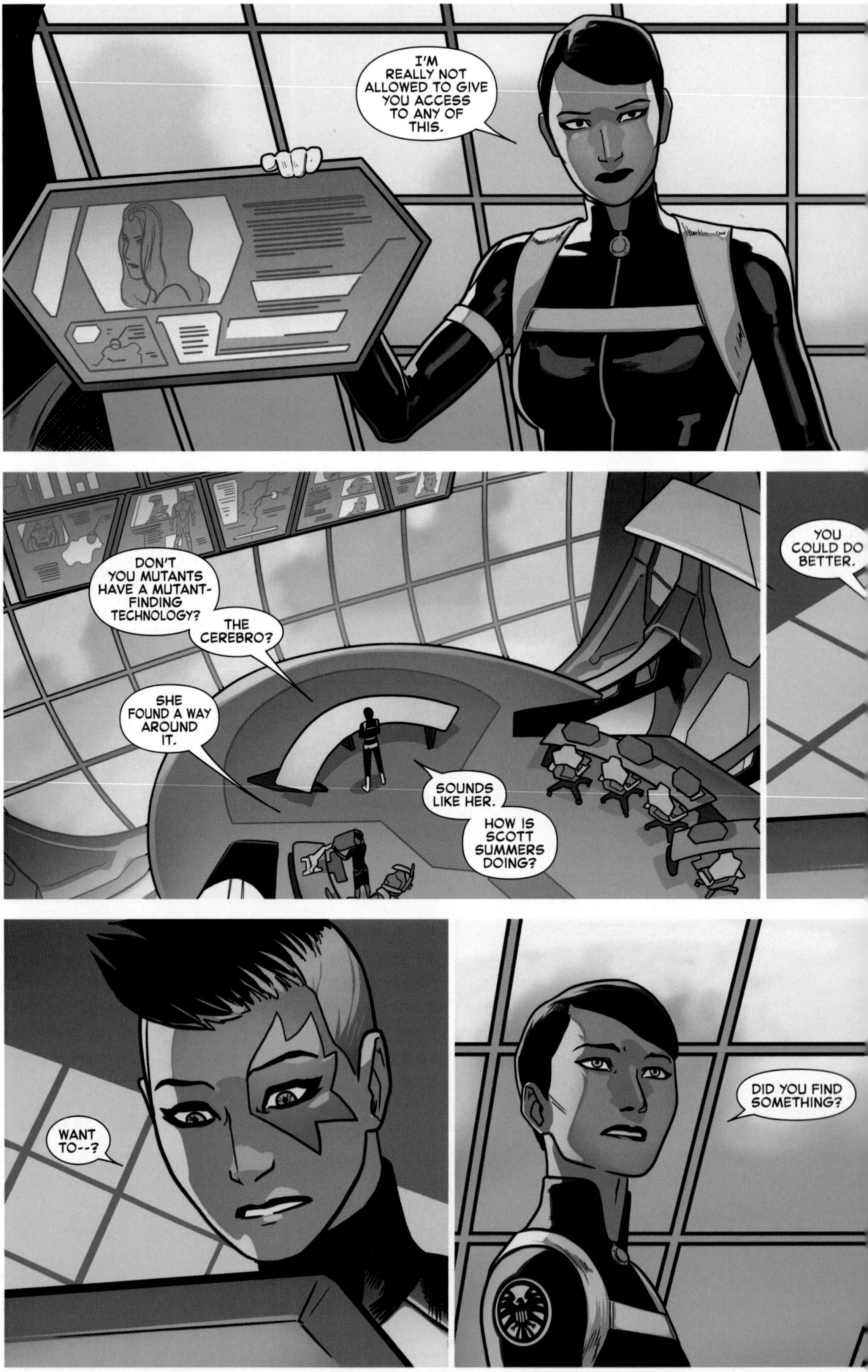
I'M REALLY NOT ALLOWED TO GIVE YOU ACCESS TO ANY OF THIS.
DON'T YOU MUTANTS HAVE A MUTANT-FINDING TECHNOLOGY?
THE CEREBRO?
SHE FOUND A WAY AROUND IT.
SOUNDS LIKE HER.
HOW IS SCOTT SUMMERS DOING?
YOU COULD DO BETTER.
WANT TO--?
DID YOU FIND SOMETHING?

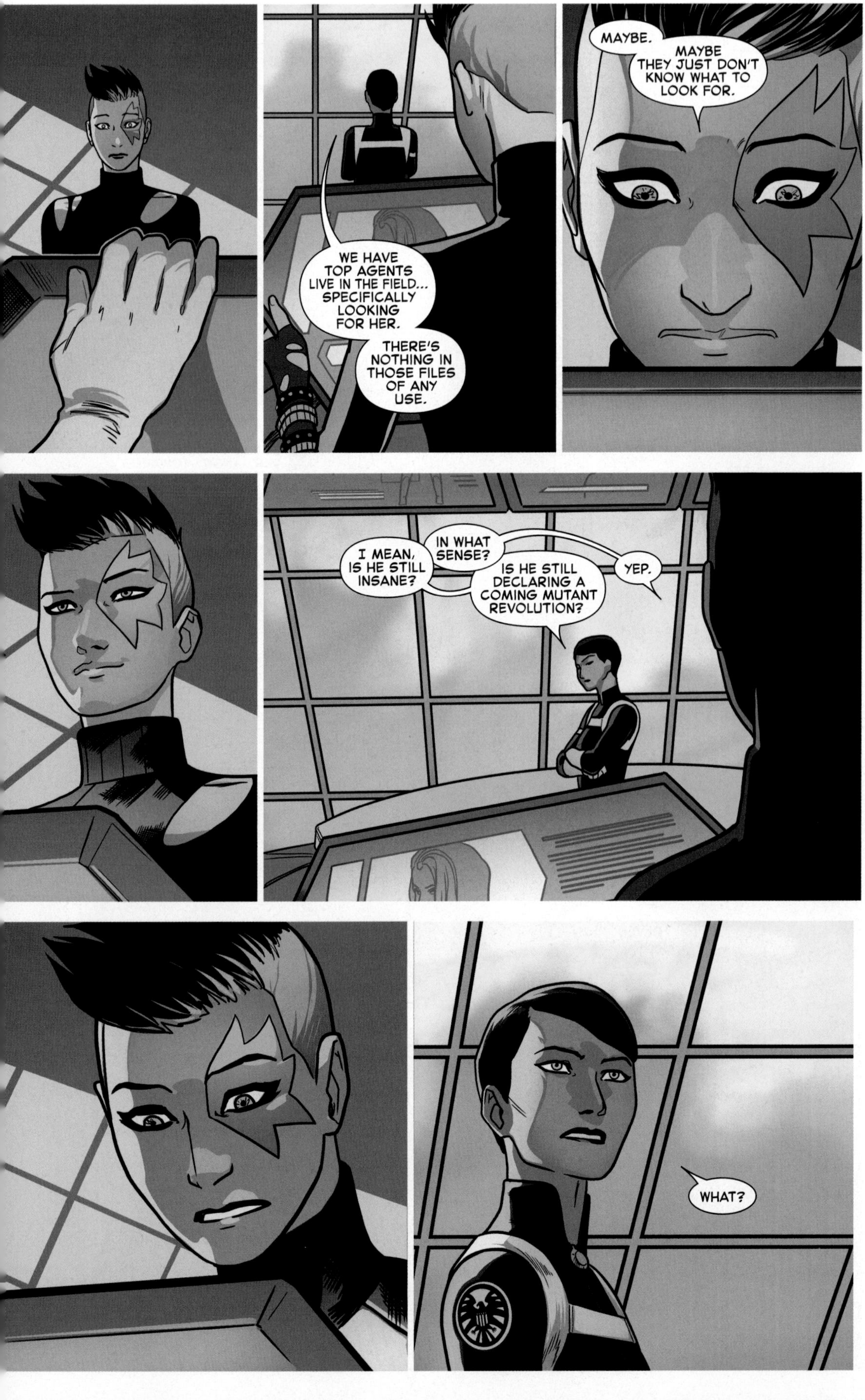
WE HAVE TOP AGENTS LIVE IN THE FIELD... SPECIFICALLY LOOKING FOR HER.
THERE'S NOTHING IN THOSE FILES OF ANY USE.
MAYBE.
MAYBE THEY JUST DON'T KNOW WHAT TO LOOK FOR.
I MEAN, IS HE STILL INSANE?
IN WHAT SENSE?
IS HE STILL DECLARING A COMING MUTANT REVOLUTION?
YEP.
WHAT?

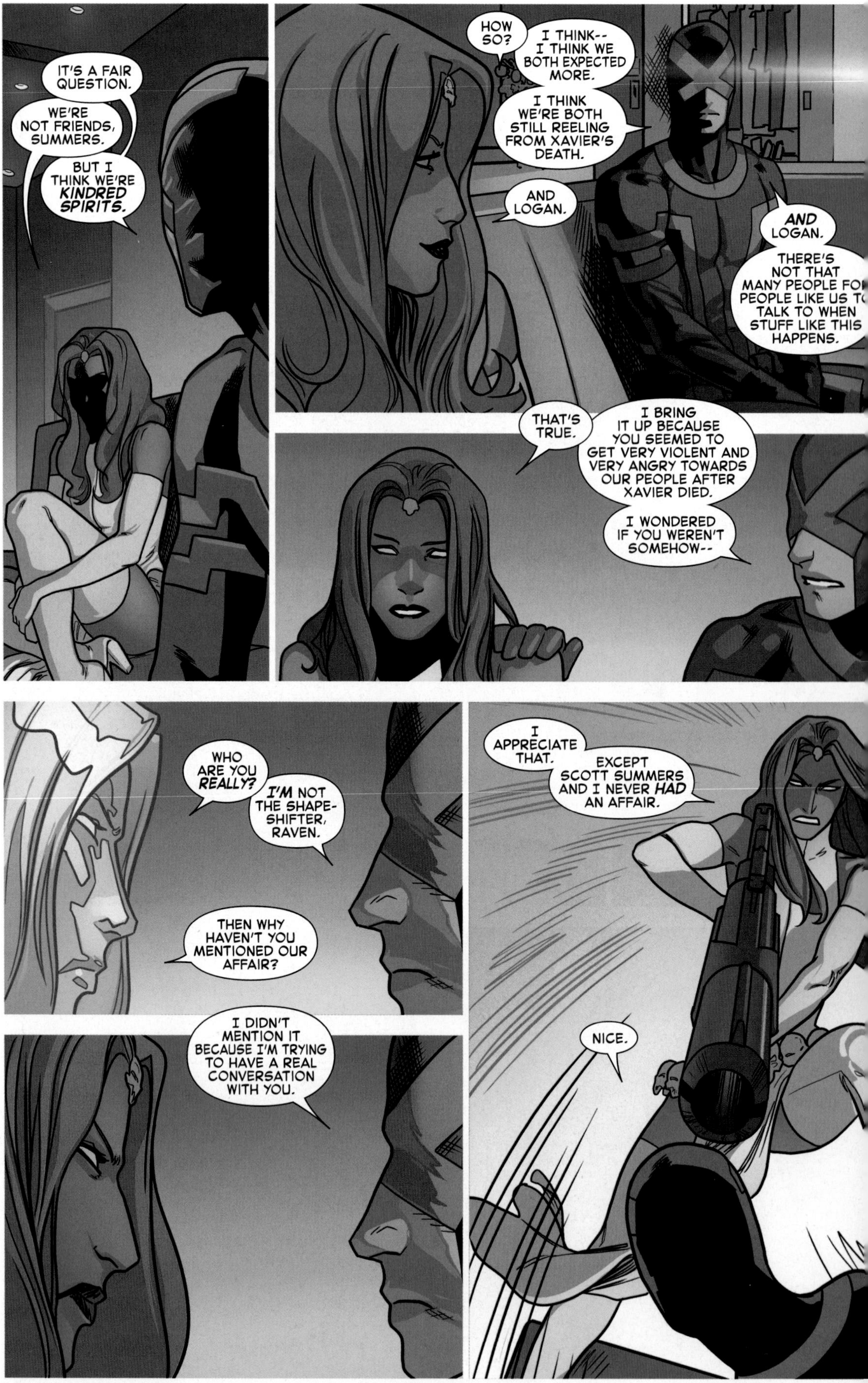
IT'S A FAIR QUESTION.
WE'RE NOT FRIENDS, SUMMERS.
BUT I THINK WE'RE *KINDRED SPIRITS.*
HOW SO?
I THINK-- I THINK WE BOTH EXPECTED MORE.
I THINK WE'RE BOTH STILL REELING FROM XAVIER'S DEATH.
AND LOGAN.
AND LOGAN.
THERE'S NOT THAT MANY PEOPLE FO PEOPLE LIKE US T TALK TO WHEN STUFF LIKE THIS HAPPENS.
THAT'S TRUE.
I BRING IT UP BECAUSE YOU SEEMED TO GET VERY VIOLENT AND VERY ANGRY TOWARDS OUR PEOPLE AFTER XAVIER DIED.
I WONDERED IF YOU WEREN'T SOMEHOW--
WHO ARE YOU *REALLY?*
I'M NOT THE SHAPE-SHIFTER, RAVEN.
THEN WHY HAVEN'T YOU MENTIONED OUR AFFAIR?
I DIDN'T MENTION IT BECAUSE I'M TRYING TO HAVE A REAL CONVERSATION WITH YOU.
I APPRECIATE THAT.
EXCEPT SCOTT SUMMERS AND I NEVER *HAD* AN AFFAIR.
NICE.

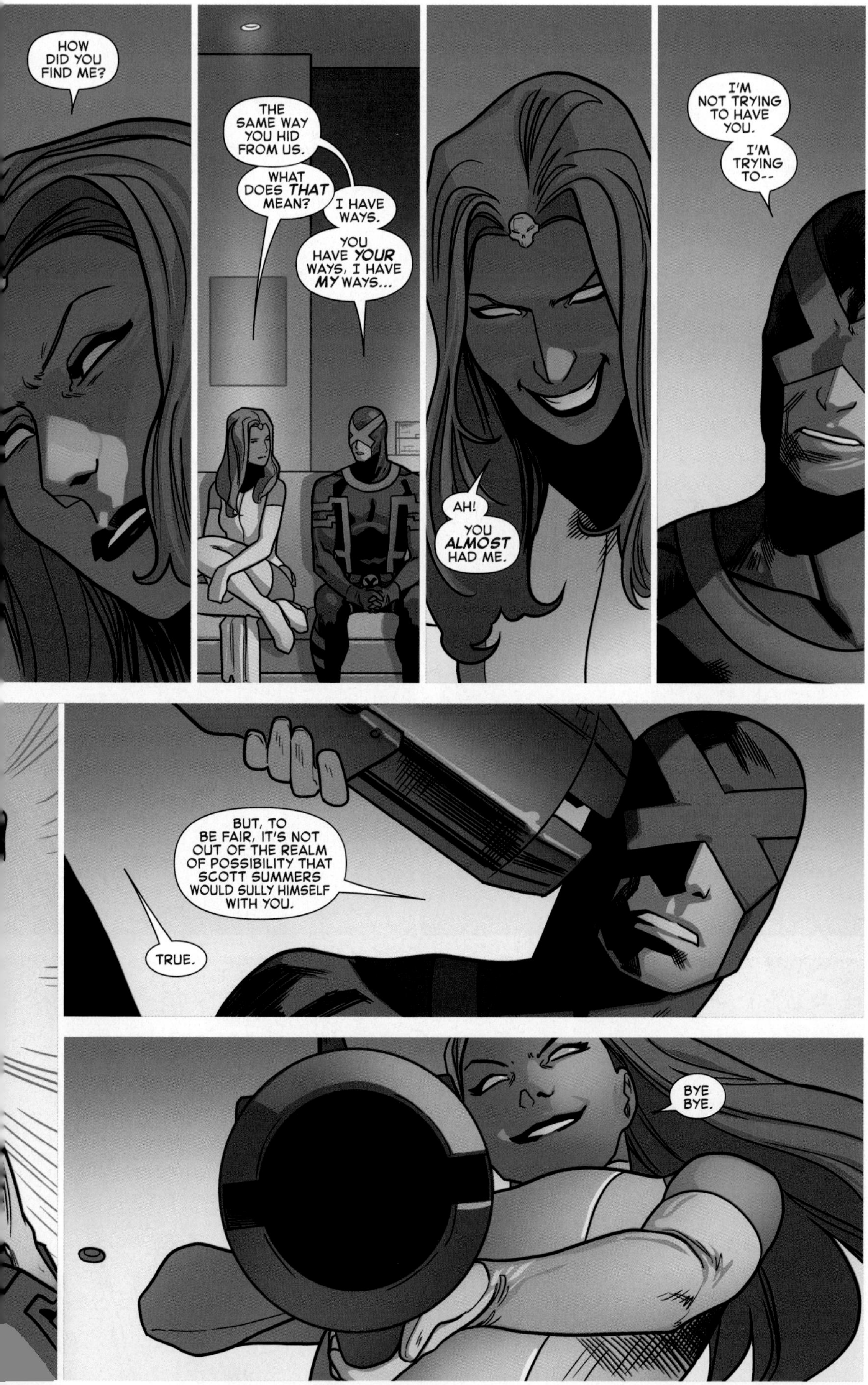
HOW DID YOU FIND ME?
THE SAME WAY YOU HID FROM US.
WHAT DOES THAT MEAN?
I HAVE WAYS.
YOU HAVE YOUR WAYS, I HAVE MY WAYS...
AH! YOU ALMOST HAD ME.
I'M NOT TRYING TO HAVE YOU.
I'M TRYING TO--
BUT, TO BE FAIR, IT'S NOT OUT OF THE REALM OF POSSIBILITY THAT SCOTT SUMMERS WOULD SULLY HIMSELF WITH YOU.
TRUE.
BYE BYE.

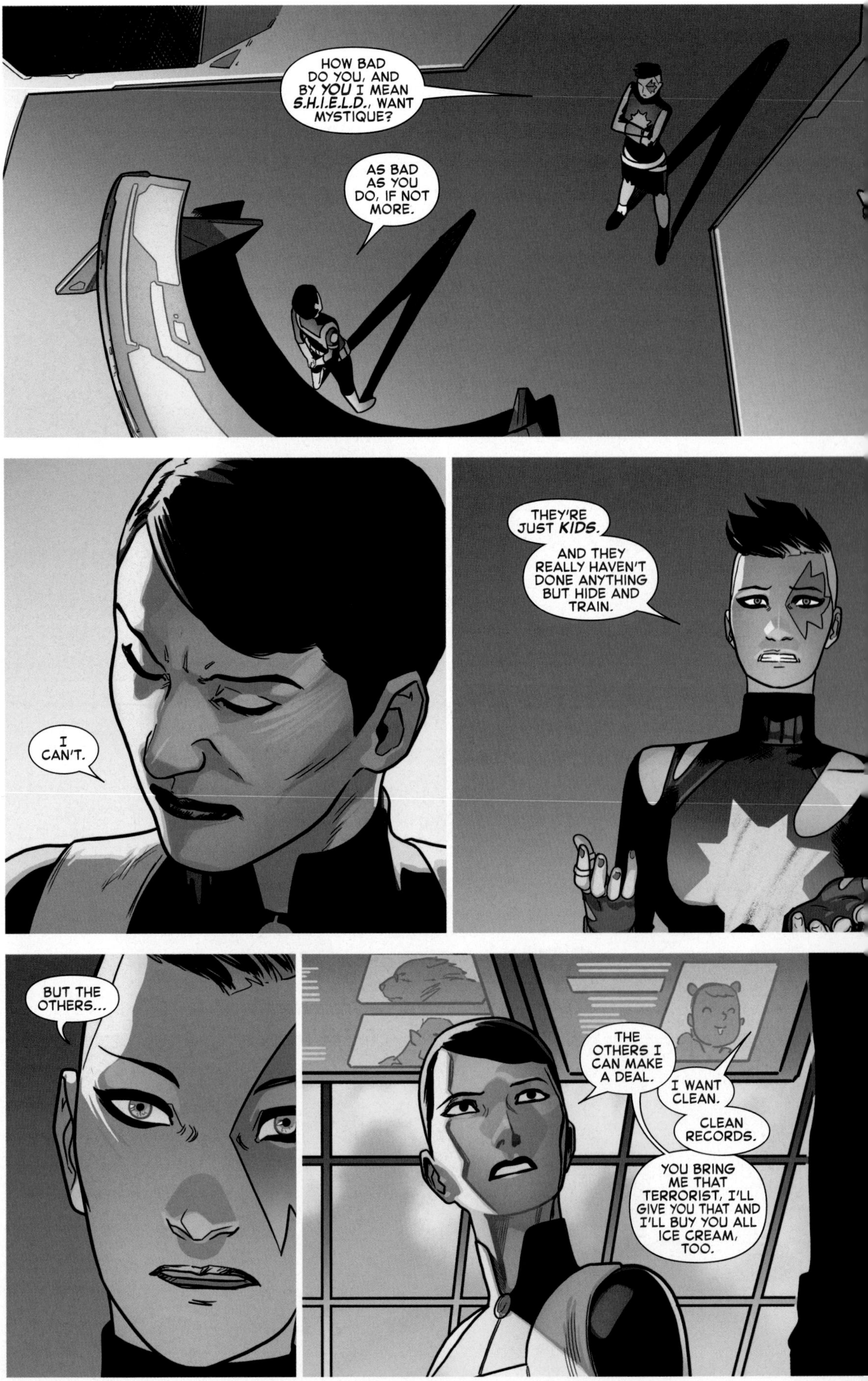
HOW BAD DO YOU, AND BY *YOU* I MEAN *S.H.I.E.L.D.*, WANT MYSTIQUE?
AS BAD AS YOU DO, IF NOT MORE.
I CAN'T.
THEY'RE JUST *KIDS.*
AND THEY REALLY HAVEN'T DONE ANYTHING BUT HIDE AND TRAIN.
BUT THE OTHERS...
THE OTHERS I CAN MAKE A DEAL.
I WANT CLEAN.
CLEAN RECORDS.
YOU BRING ME THAT TERRORIST, I'LL GIVE YOU THAT AND I'LL BUY YOU ALL ICE CREAM, TOO.

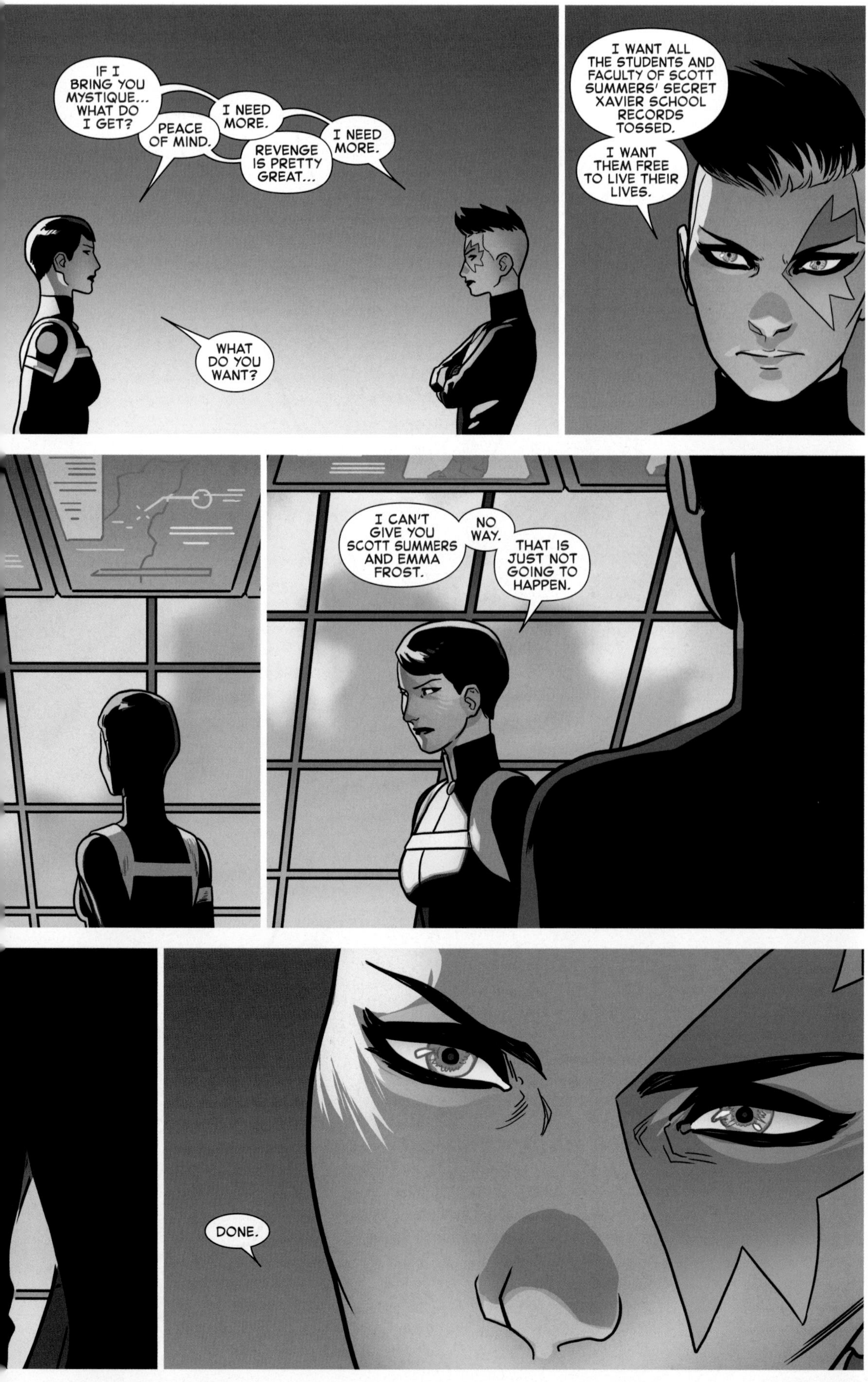
IF I BRING YOU MYSTIQUE... WHAT DO I GET?
PEACE OF MIND.
I NEED MORE.
REVENGE IS PRETTY GREAT...
I NEED MORE.
WHAT DO YOU WANT?
I WANT ALL THE STUDENTS AND FACULTY OF SCOTT SUMMERS' SECRET XAVIER SCHOOL RECORDS TOSSED.
I WANT THEM FREE TO LIVE THEIR LIVES.
I CAN'T GIVE YOU SCOTT SUMMERS AND EMMA FROST.
NO WAY.
THAT IS JUST NOT GOING TO HAPPEN.
DONE.

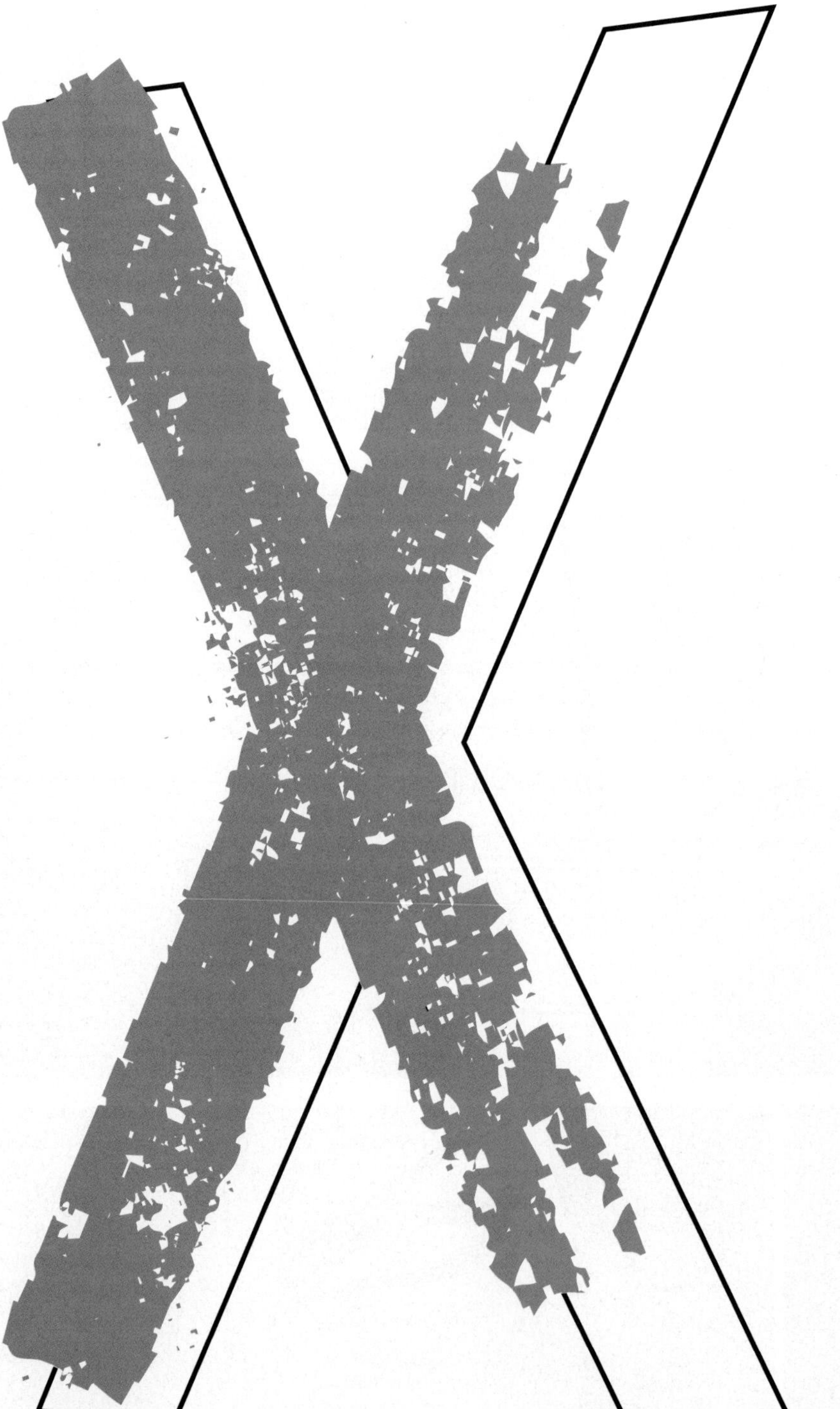

BYE BYE.

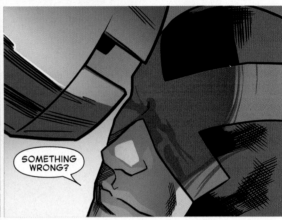

SOMETHING WRONG?

I CAN'T PULL THE TRIGGER.

I NOTICED.

HOW ARE YOU DOING THIS?

WHO ARE YOU?

THERE SHE IS.

THERE IS THAT SAD, SCARED LITTLE GIRL HIDING BEHIND ALL HER MASKS.

GET OUT OF THERE.

SHE'S ON TO YOU AND SHE HAS ALL KINDS OF PSYCHIC SHIELDS UP.

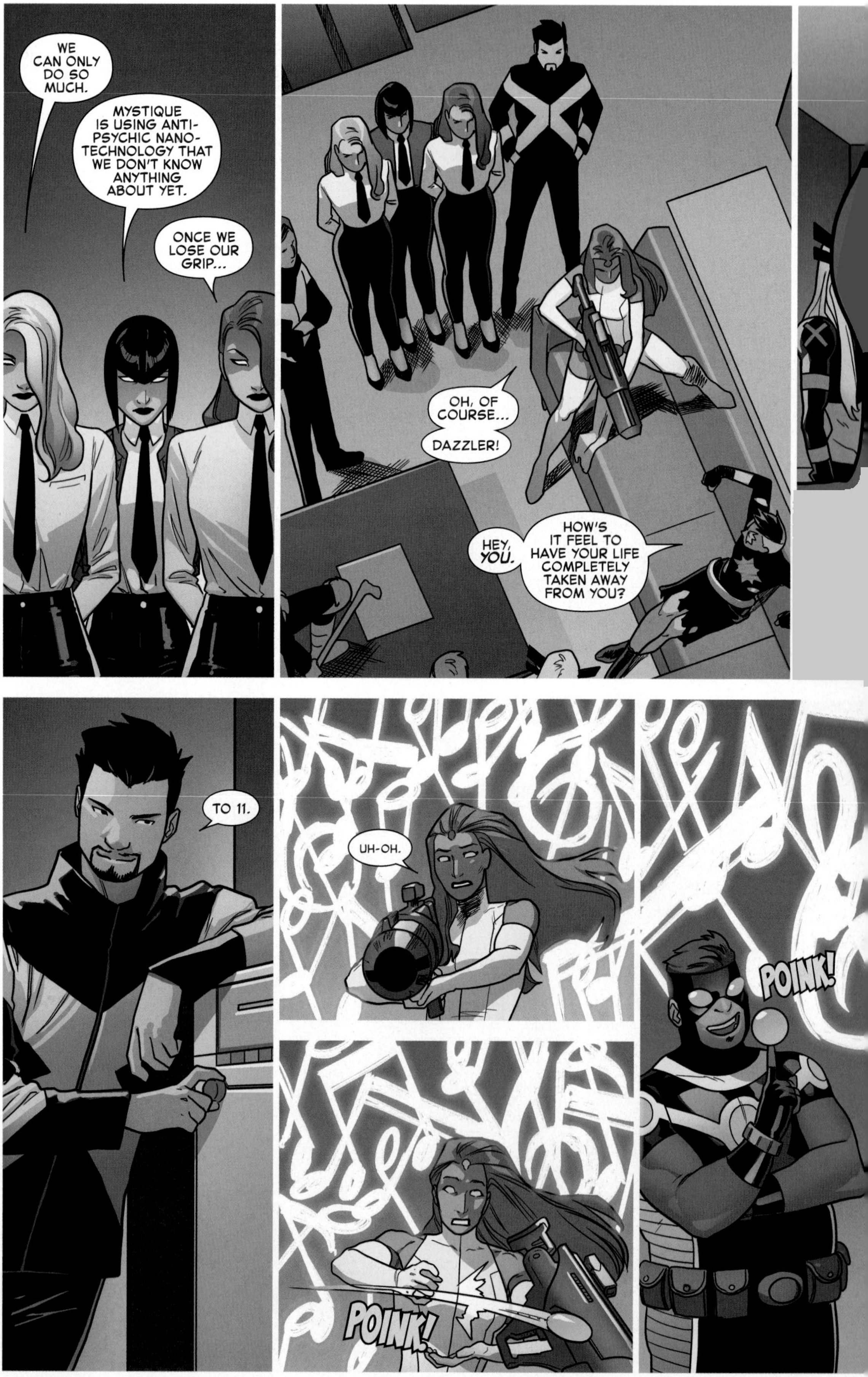
WE CAN ONLY DO SO MUCH.
MYSTIQUE IS USING ANTI-PSYCHIC NANO-TECHNOLOGY THAT WE DON'T KNOW ANYTHING ABOUT YET.
ONCE WE LOSE OUR GRIP...
OH, OF COURSE...
DAZZLER!
HEY, YOU.
HOW'S IT FEEL TO HAVE YOUR LIFE COMPLETELY TAKEN AWAY FROM YOU?
TO 11.
UH-OH.
POINK!
POINK!

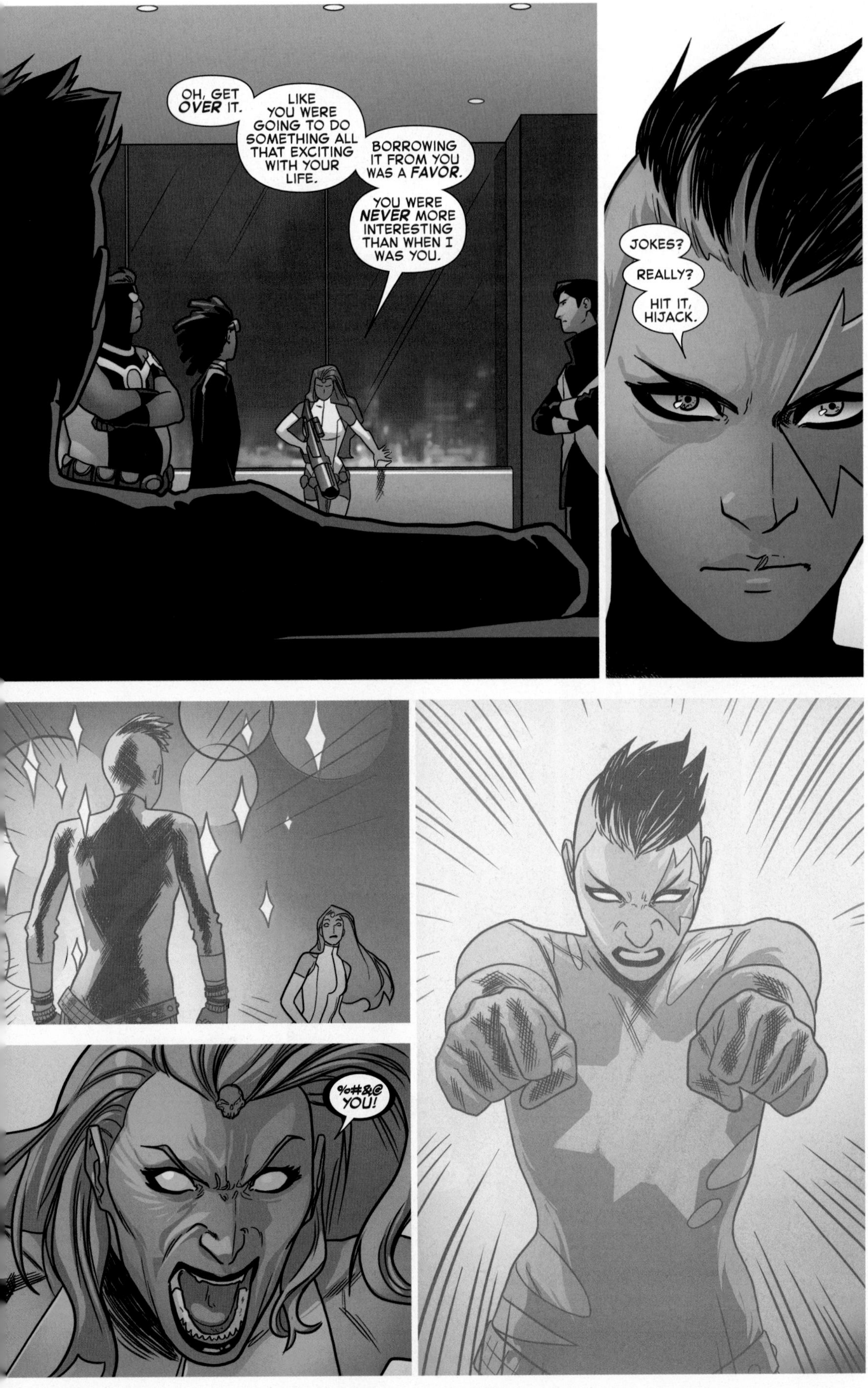
OH, GET OVER IT.
LIKE YOU WERE GOING TO DO SOMETHING ALL THAT EXCITING WITH YOUR LIFE.
BORROWING IT FROM YOU WAS A FAVOR.
YOU WERE NEVER MORE INTERESTING THAN WHEN I WAS YOU.
JOKES?
REALLY?
HIT IT, HIJACK.
%#&@ YOU!

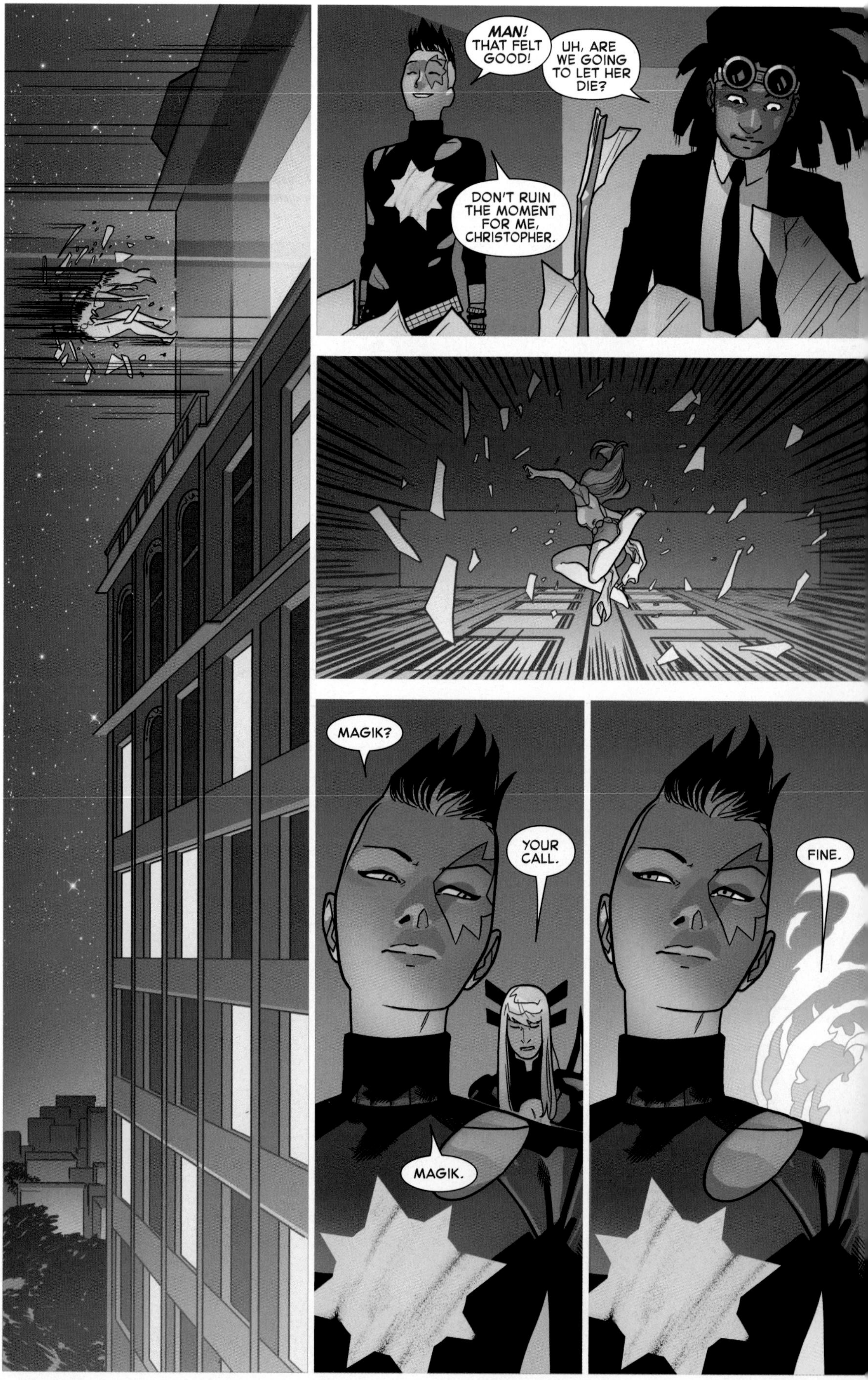

MAN! THAT FELT GOOD!
UH, ARE WE GOING TO LET HER DIE?
DON'T RUIN THE MOMENT FOR ME, CHRISTOPHER.
MAGIK?
YOUR CALL.
MAGIK.
FINE.

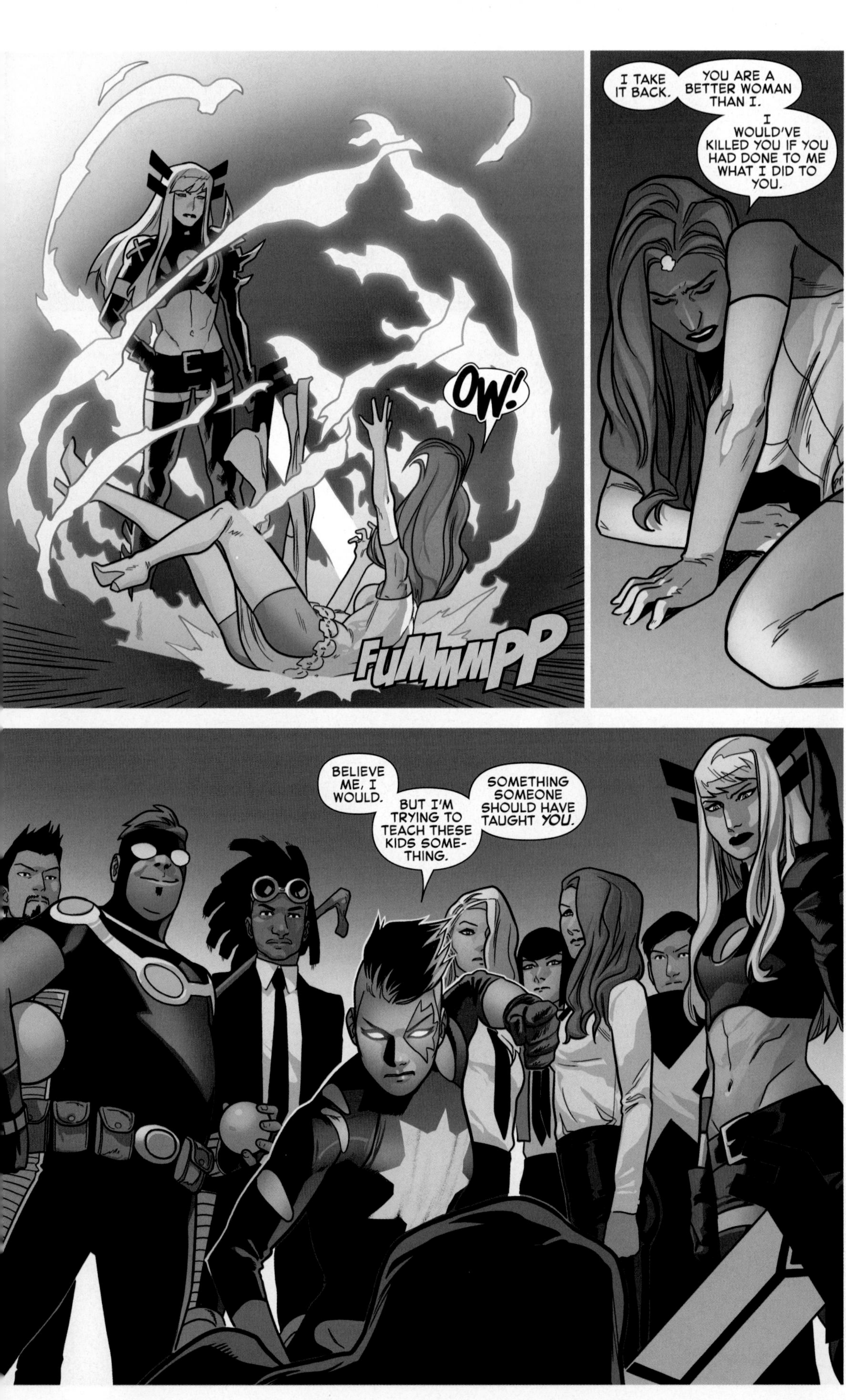
OW!
FUMMMMPP
I TAKE IT BACK.
YOU ARE A BETTER WOMAN THAN I.
I WOULD'VE KILLED YOU IF YOU HAD DONE TO ME WHAT I DID TO YOU.
BELIEVE ME, I WOULD.
BUT I'M TRYING TO TEACH THESE KIDS SOME-THING.
SOMETHING SOMEONE SHOULD HAVE TAUGHT *YOU*.

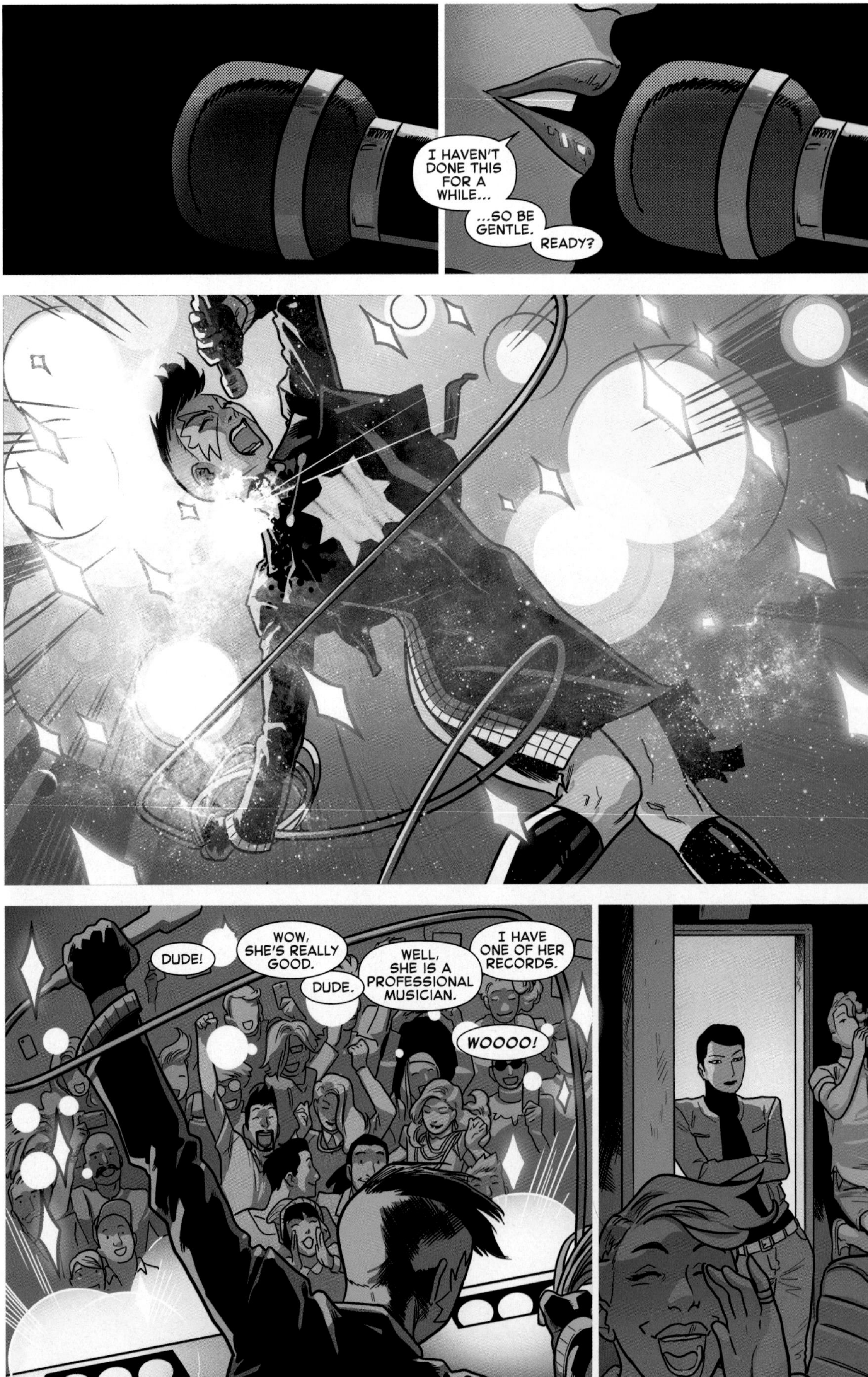
I HAVEN'T DONE THIS FOR A WHILE...
...SO BE GENTLE.
READY?
DUDE!
WOW, SHE'S REALLY GOOD.
DUDE.
WELL, SHE IS A PROFESSIONAL MUSICIAN.
I HAVE ONE OF HER RECORDS.
WOOOO!

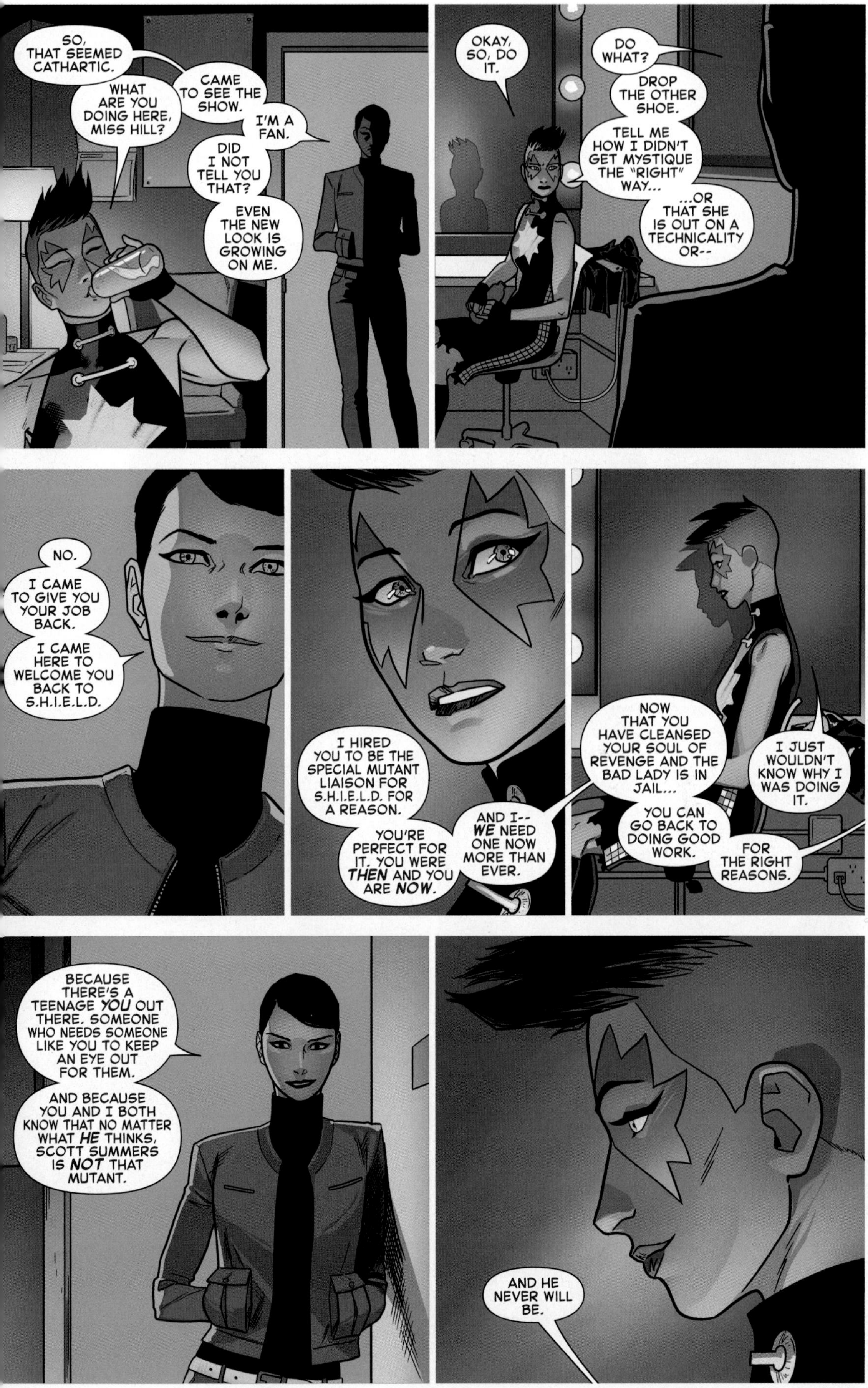
SO, THAT SEEMED CATHARTIC.
WHAT ARE YOU DOING HERE, MISS HILL?
CAME TO SEE THE SHOW.
I'M A FAN.
DID I NOT TELL YOU THAT?
EVEN THE NEW LOOK IS GROWING ON ME.
OKAY, SO, DO IT.
DO WHAT?
DROP THE OTHER SHOE.
TELL ME HOW I DIDN'T GET MYSTIQUE THE "RIGHT" WAY...
...OR THAT SHE IS OUT ON A TECHNICALITY OR--
NO.
I CAME TO GIVE YOU YOUR JOB BACK.
I CAME HERE TO WELCOME YOU BACK TO S.H.I.E.L.D.
I HIRED YOU TO BE THE SPECIAL MUTANT LIAISON FOR S.H.I.E.L.D. FOR A REASON.
YOU'RE PERFECT FOR IT. YOU WERE THEN AND YOU ARE NOW.
AND I-- WE NEED ONE NOW MORE THAN EVER.
NOW THAT YOU HAVE CLEANSED YOUR SOUL OF REVENGE AND THE BAD LADY IS IN JAIL...
YOU CAN GO BACK TO DOING GOOD WORK.
FOR THE RIGHT REASONS.
I JUST WOULDN'T KNOW WHY I WAS DOING IT.
BECAUSE THERE'S A TEENAGE YOU OUT THERE. SOMEONE WHO NEEDS SOMEONE LIKE YOU TO KEEP AN EYE OUT FOR THEM.
AND BECAUSE YOU AND I BOTH KNOW THAT NO MATTER WHAT HE THINKS, SCOTT SUMMERS IS NOT THAT MUTANT.
AND HE NEVER WILL BE.

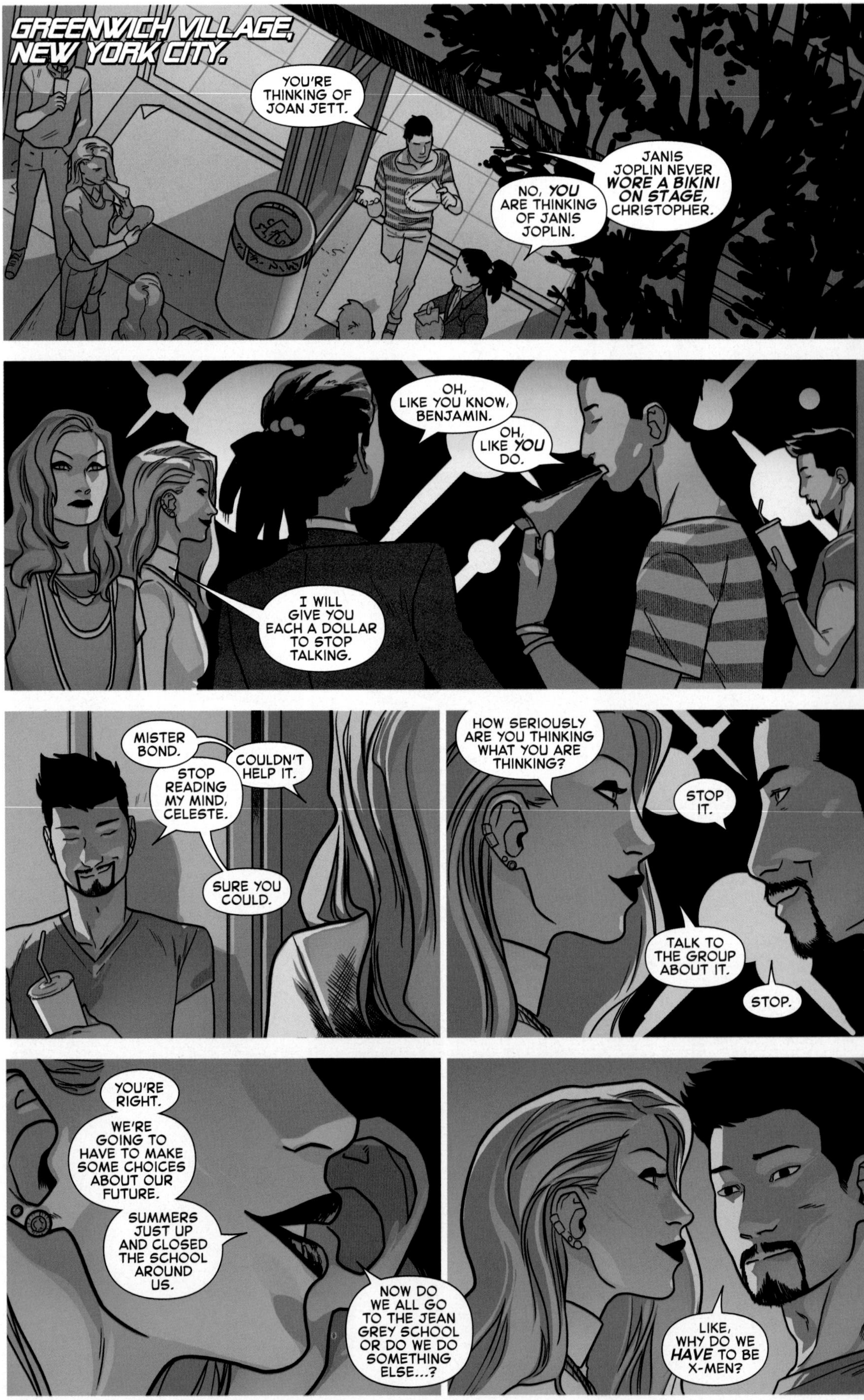
GREENWICH VILLAGE, NEW YORK CITY.
YOU'RE THINKING OF JOAN JETT.
NO, *YOU* ARE THINKING OF JANIS JOPLIN.
JANIS JOPLIN NEVER *WORE A BIKINI ON STAGE,* CHRISTOPHER.
OH, LIKE YOU KNOW, BENJAMIN.
OH, LIKE *YOU* DO.
I WILL GIVE YOU EACH A DOLLAR TO STOP TALKING.
MISTER BOND.
COULDN'T HELP IT.
STOP READING MY MIND, CELESTE.
SURE YOU COULD.
HOW SERIOUSLY ARE YOU THINKING WHAT YOU ARE THINKING?
STOP IT.
TALK TO THE GROUP ABOUT IT.
STOP.
YOU'RE RIGHT.
WE'RE GOING TO HAVE TO MAKE SOME CHOICES ABOUT OUR FUTURE.
SUMMERS JUST UP AND CLOSED THE SCHOOL AROUND US.
NOW DO WE ALL GO TO THE JEAN GREY SCHOOL OR DO WE DO SOMETHING ELSE...?
LIKE, WHY DO WE *HAVE* TO BE X-MEN?

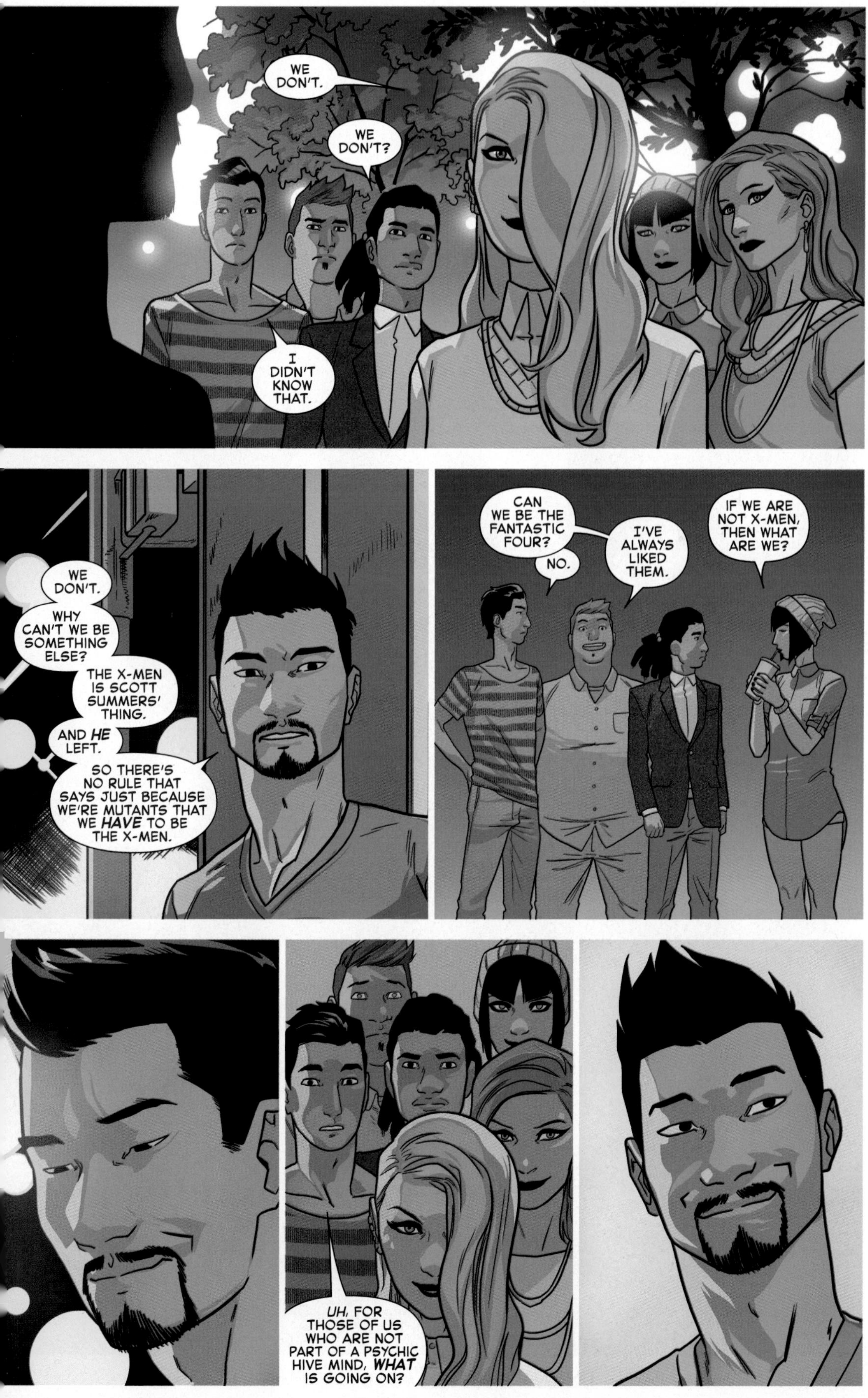

WE DON'T.
WE DON'T?
I DIDN'T KNOW THAT.
WE DON'T.
WHY CAN'T WE BE SOMETHING ELSE?
THE X-MEN IS SCOTT SUMMERS' THING.
AND *HE* LEFT.
SO THERE'S NO RULE THAT SAYS JUST BECAUSE WE'RE MUTANTS THAT WE *HAVE* TO BE THE X-MEN.
CAN WE BE THE FANTASTIC FOUR?
NO.
I'VE ALWAYS LIKED THEM.
IF WE ARE NOT X-MEN, THEN WHAT ARE WE?
UH, FOR THOSE OF US WHO ARE NOT PART OF A PSYCHIC HIVE MIND, ***WHAT*** IS GOING ON?

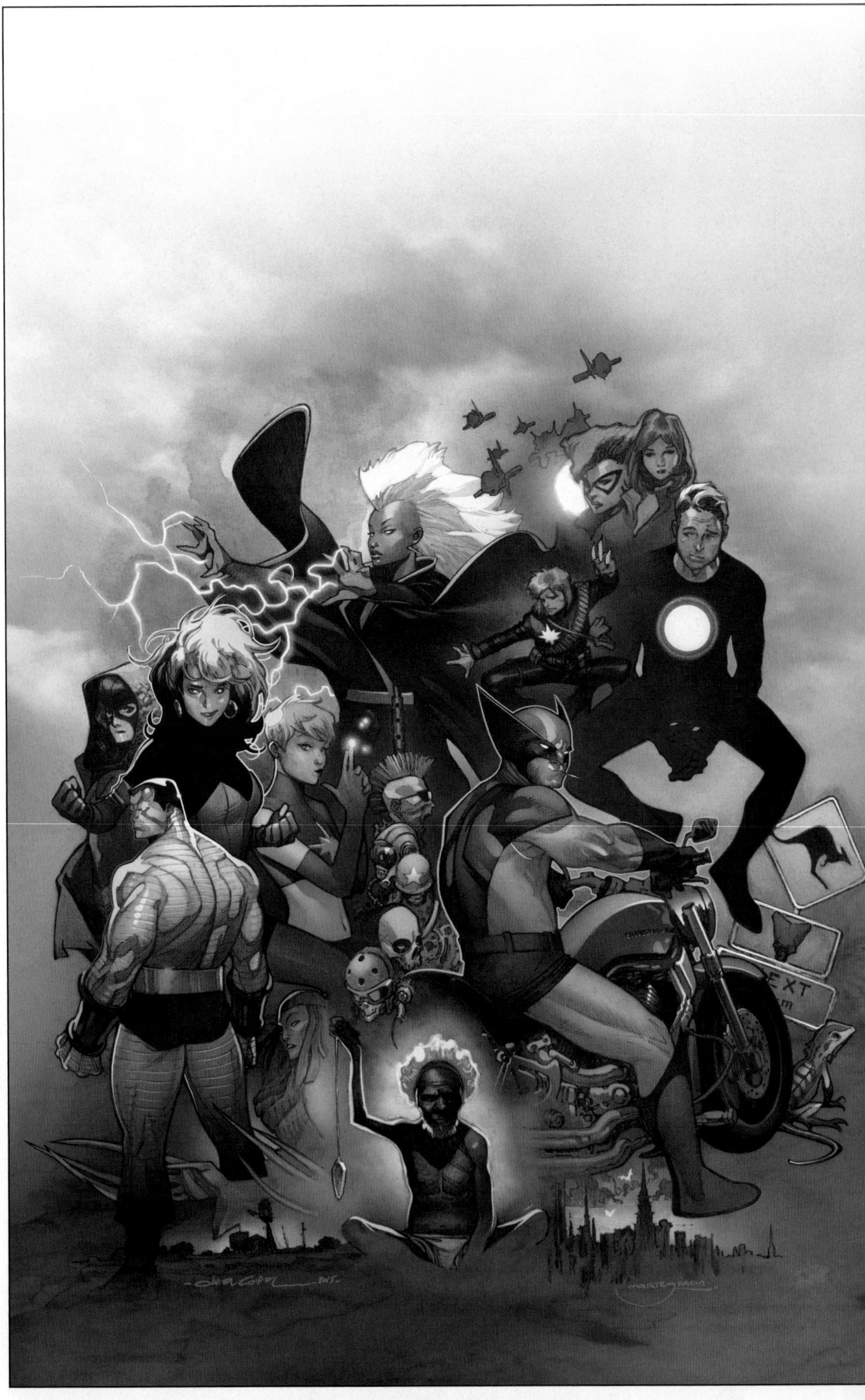

UNCANNY X-MEN #600 VARIANT

BY OLIVIER COIPEL & MARTE GRACIA

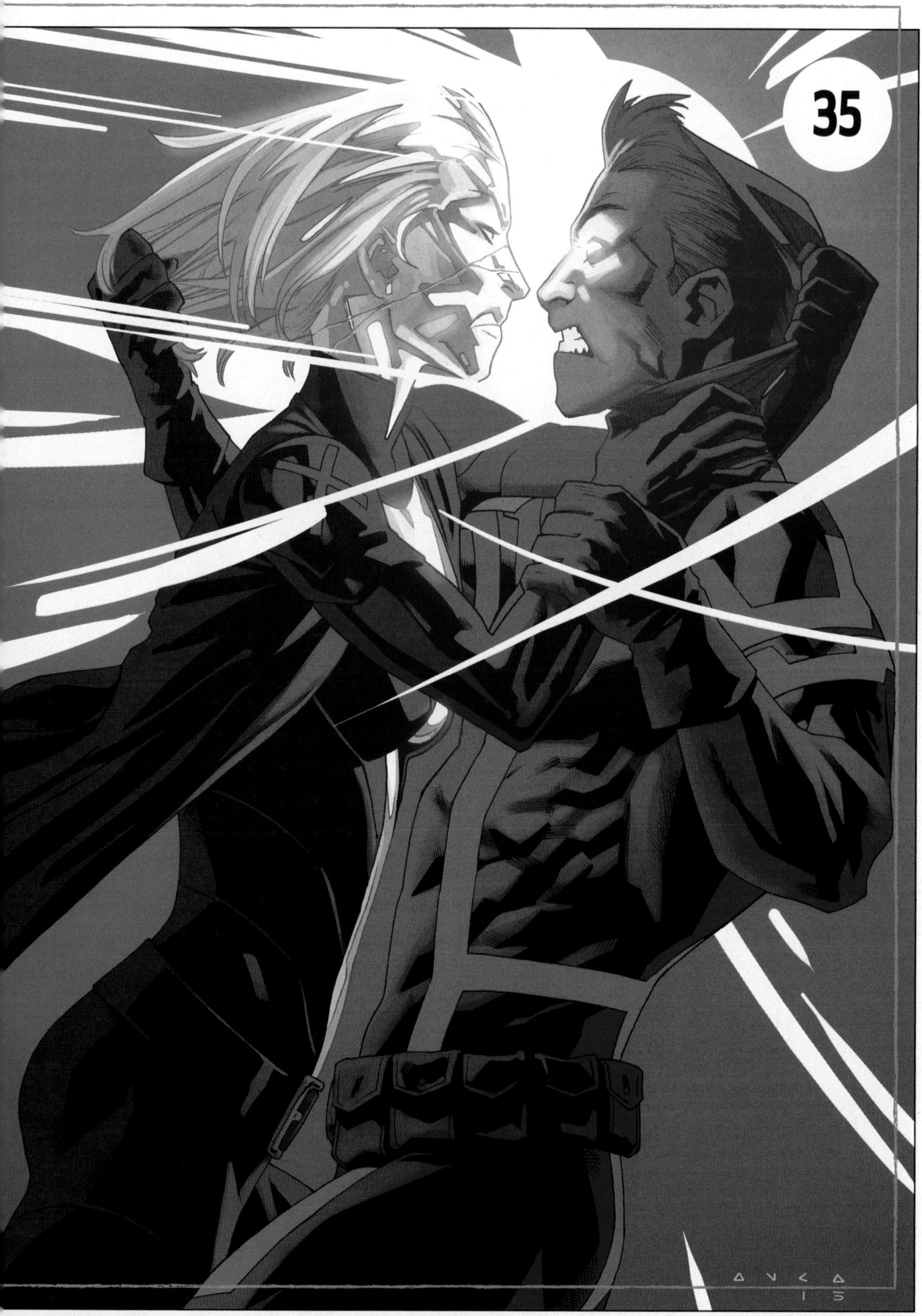
35

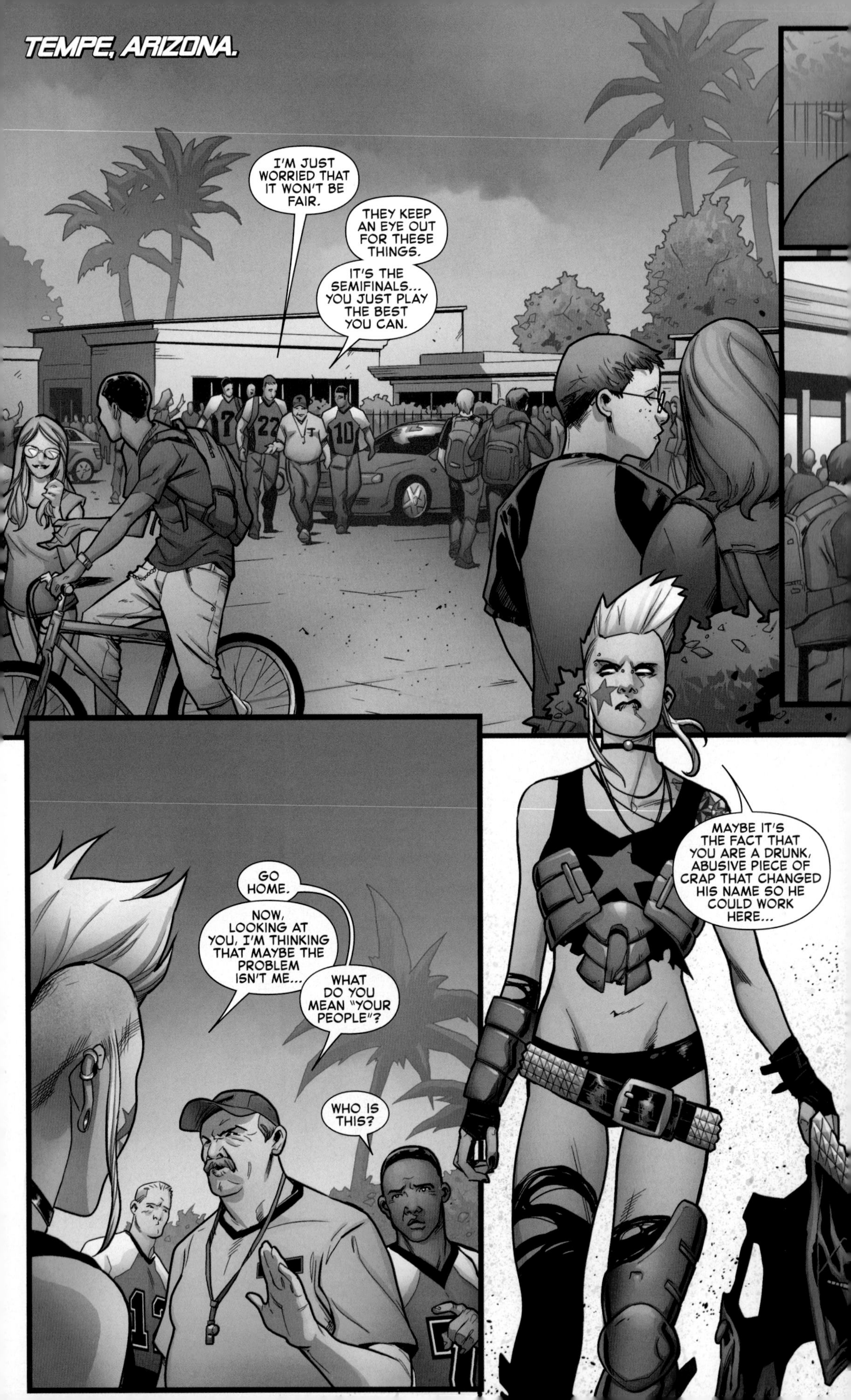
TEMPE, ARIZONA.
I'M JUST WORRIED THAT IT WON'T BE FAIR.
THEY KEEP AN EYE OUT FOR THESE THINGS.
IT'S THE SEMIFINALS... YOU JUST PLAY THE BEST YOU CAN.
GO HOME.
NOW, LOOKING AT YOU, I'M THINKING THAT MAYBE THE PROBLEM ISN'T ME...
WHAT DO YOU MEAN "YOUR PEOPLE"?
WHO IS THIS?
MAYBE IT'S THE FACT THAT YOU ARE A DRUNK, ABUSIVE PIECE OF CRAP THAT CHANGED HIS NAME SO HE COULD WORK HERE...

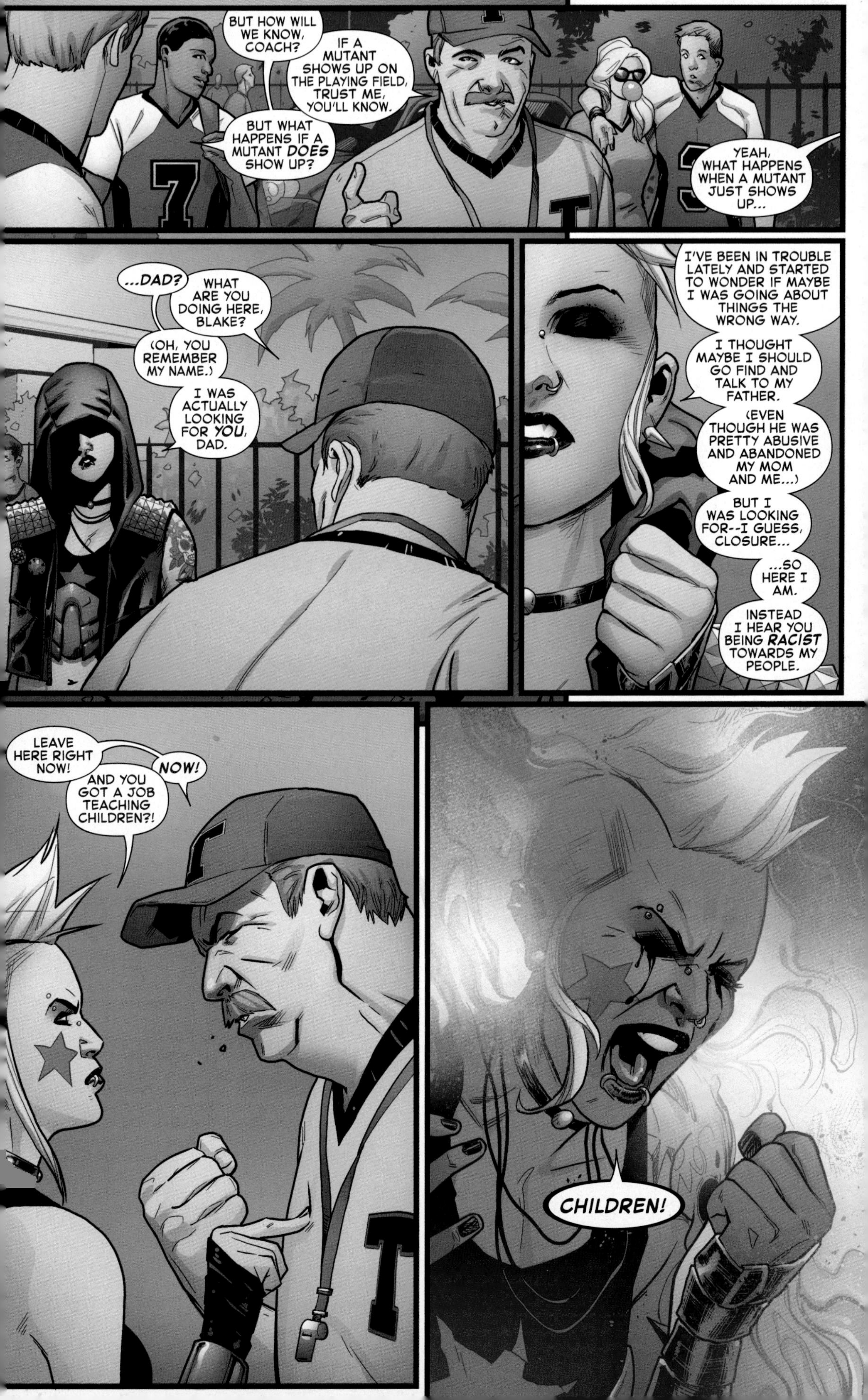
BUT HOW WILL WE KNOW, COACH?
IF A MUTANT SHOWS UP ON THE PLAYING FIELD, TRUST ME, YOU'LL KNOW.
BUT WHAT HAPPENS IF A MUTANT DOES SHOW UP?
YEAH, WHAT HAPPENS WHEN A MUTANT JUST SHOWS UP...
...DAD?
WHAT ARE YOU DOING HERE, BLAKE?
(OH, YOU REMEMBER MY NAME.)
I WAS ACTUALLY LOOKING FOR YOU, DAD.
I'VE BEEN IN TROUBLE LATELY AND STARTED TO WONDER IF MAYBE I WAS GOING ABOUT THINGS THE WRONG WAY.
I THOUGHT MAYBE I SHOULD GO FIND AND TALK TO MY FATHER.
(EVEN THOUGH HE WAS PRETTY ABUSIVE AND ABANDONED MY MOM AND ME...)
BUT I WAS LOOKING FOR--I GUESS, CLOSURE...
...SO HERE I AM.
INSTEAD I HEAR YOU BEING RACIST TOWARDS MY PEOPLE.
LEAVE HERE RIGHT NOW!
NOW!
AND YOU GOT A JOB TEACHING CHILDREN?!
CHILDREN!

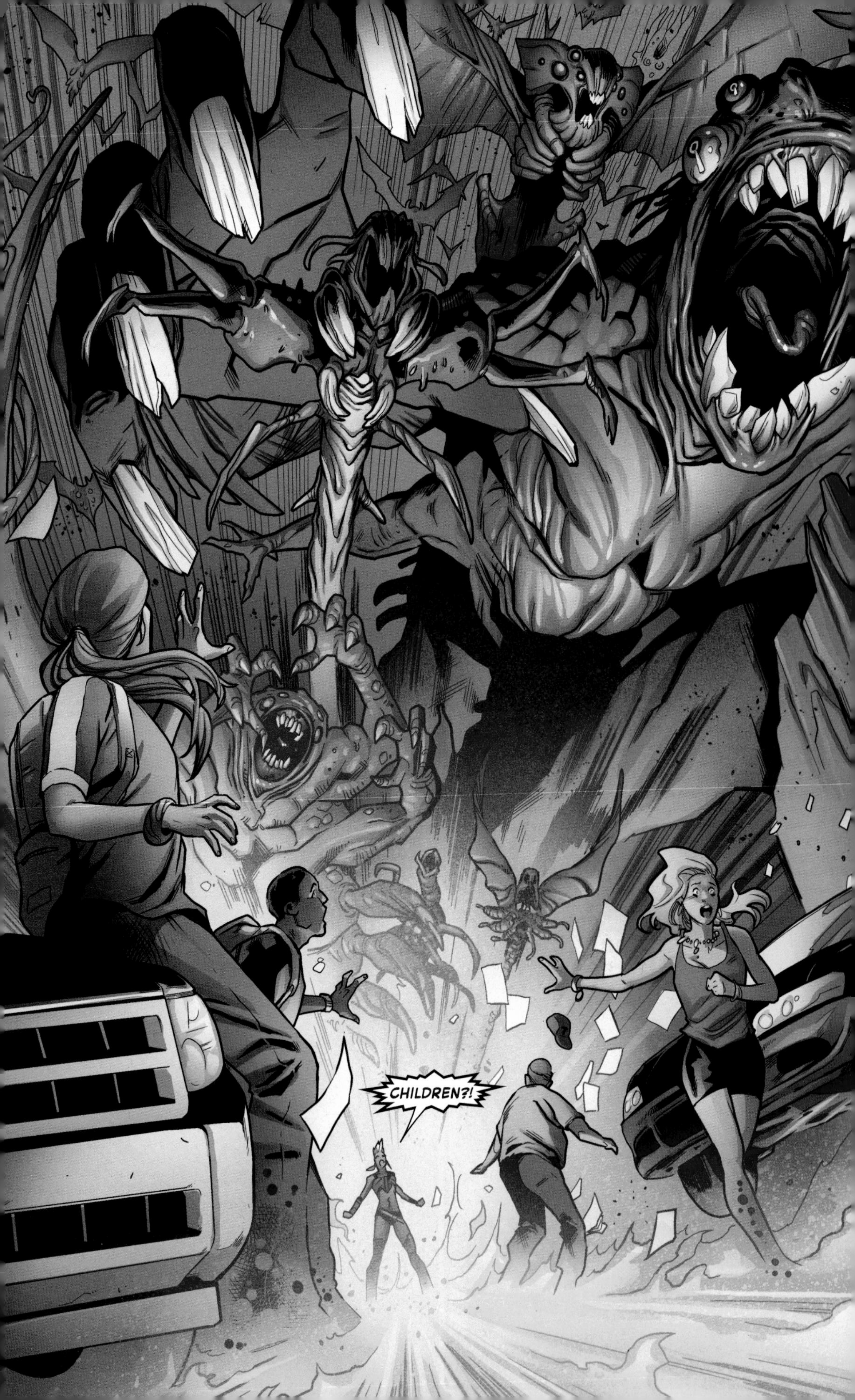
CHILDREN?!

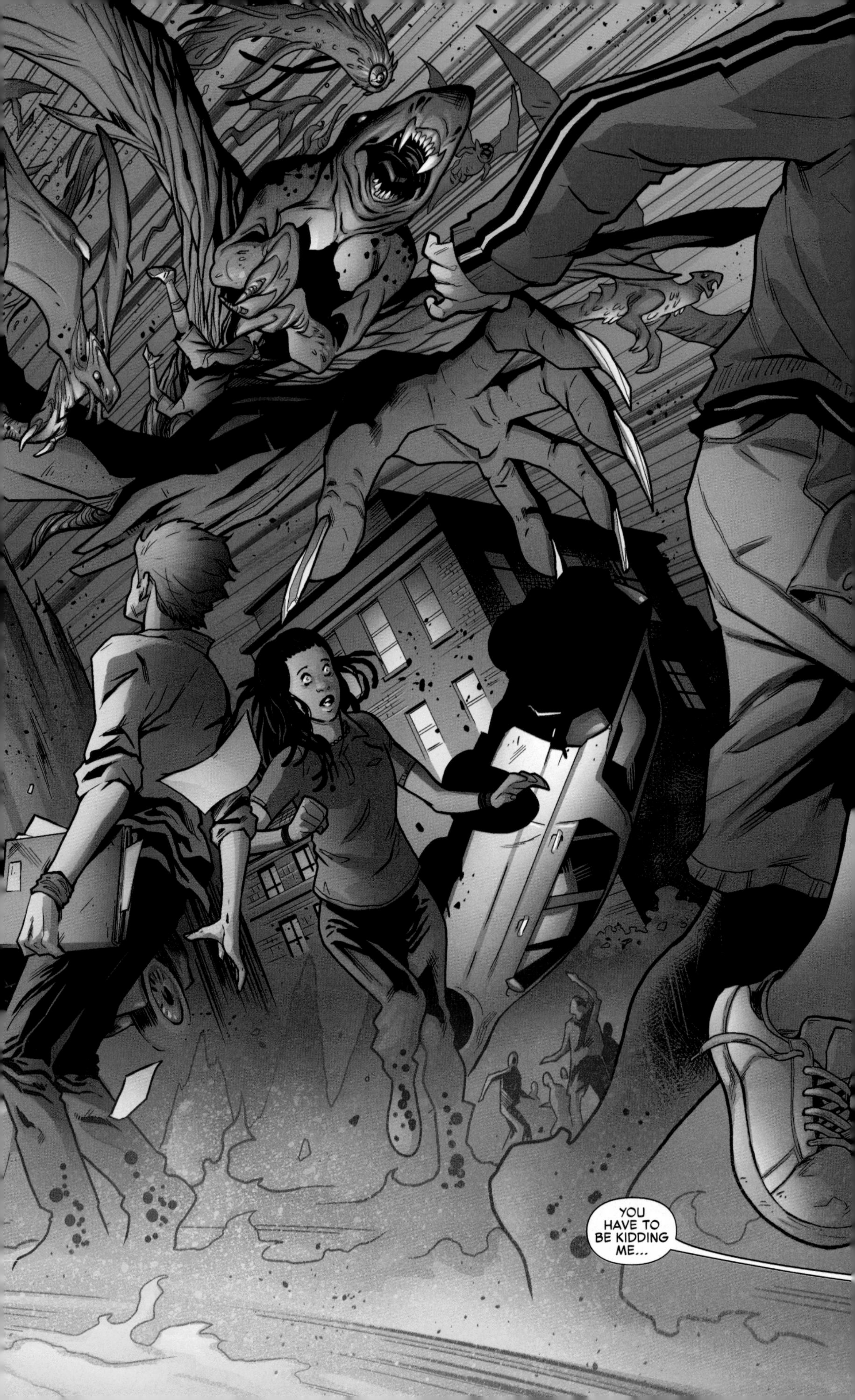
YOU HAVE TO BE KIDDING ME...

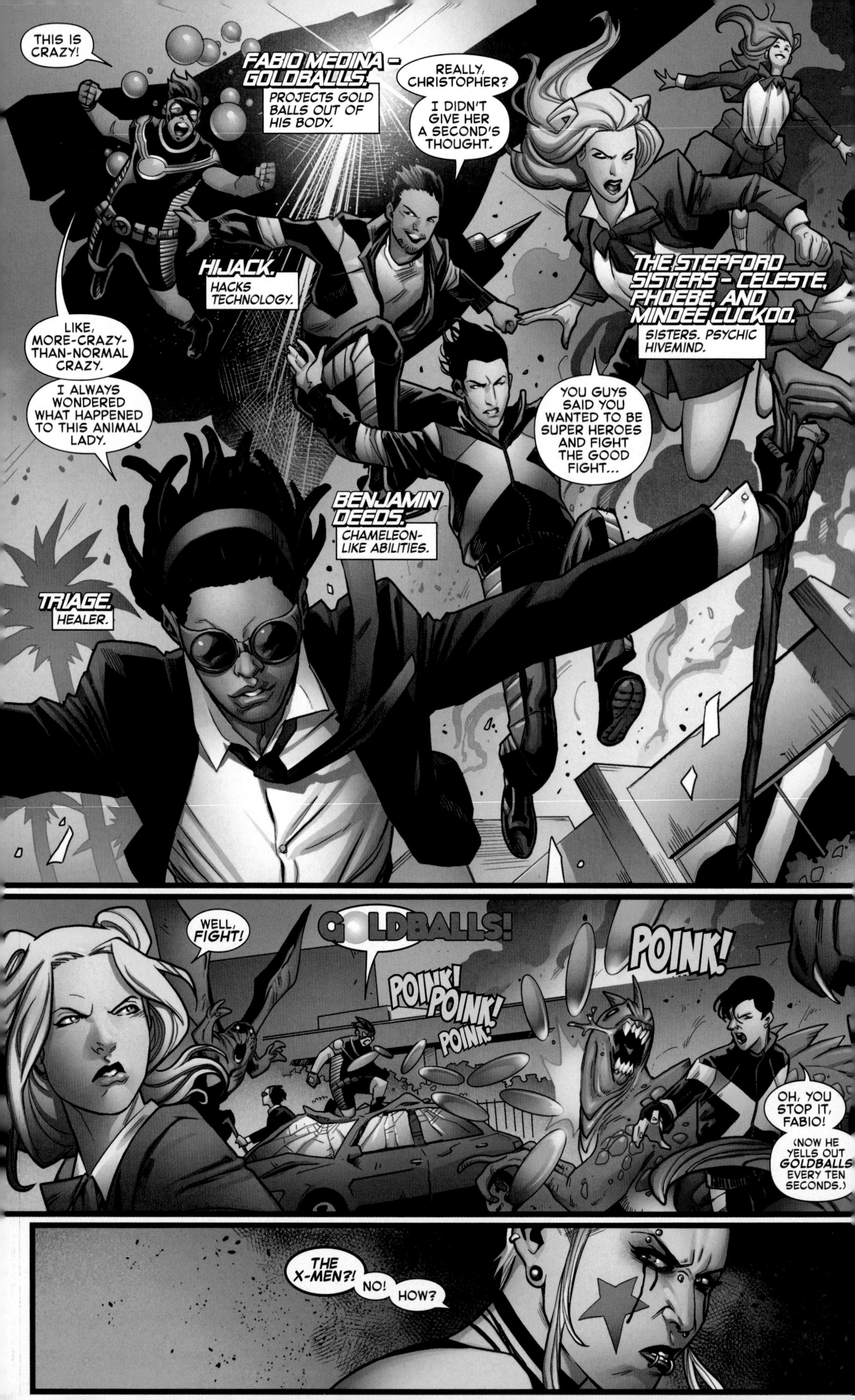
THIS IS CRAZY!
FABIO MEDINA - GOLDBALLS.
PROJECTS GOLD BALLS OUT OF HIS BODY.
REALLY, CHRISTOPHER?
I DIDN'T GIVE HER A SECOND'S THOUGHT.
HIJACK.
HACKS TECHNOLOGY.
THE STEPFORD SISTERS - CELESTE, PHOEBE, AND MINDEE CUCKOO.
SISTERS. PSYCHIC HIVEMIND.
LIKE, MORE-CRAZY-THAN-NORMAL CRAZY.
I ALWAYS WONDERED WHAT HAPPENED TO THIS ANIMAL LADY.
YOU GUYS SAID YOU WANTED TO BE SUPER HEROES AND FIGHT THE GOOD FIGHT...
BENJAMIN DEEDS.
CHAMELEON-LIKE ABILITIES.
TRIAGE.
HEALER.
WELL, FIGHT!
GOLDBALLS!
POINK!
POINK!
POINK!
POINK!
OH, YOU STOP IT, FABIO!
(NOW HE YELLS OUT GOLDBALLS EVERY TEN SECONDS.)
THE X-MEN?!
NO!
HOW?

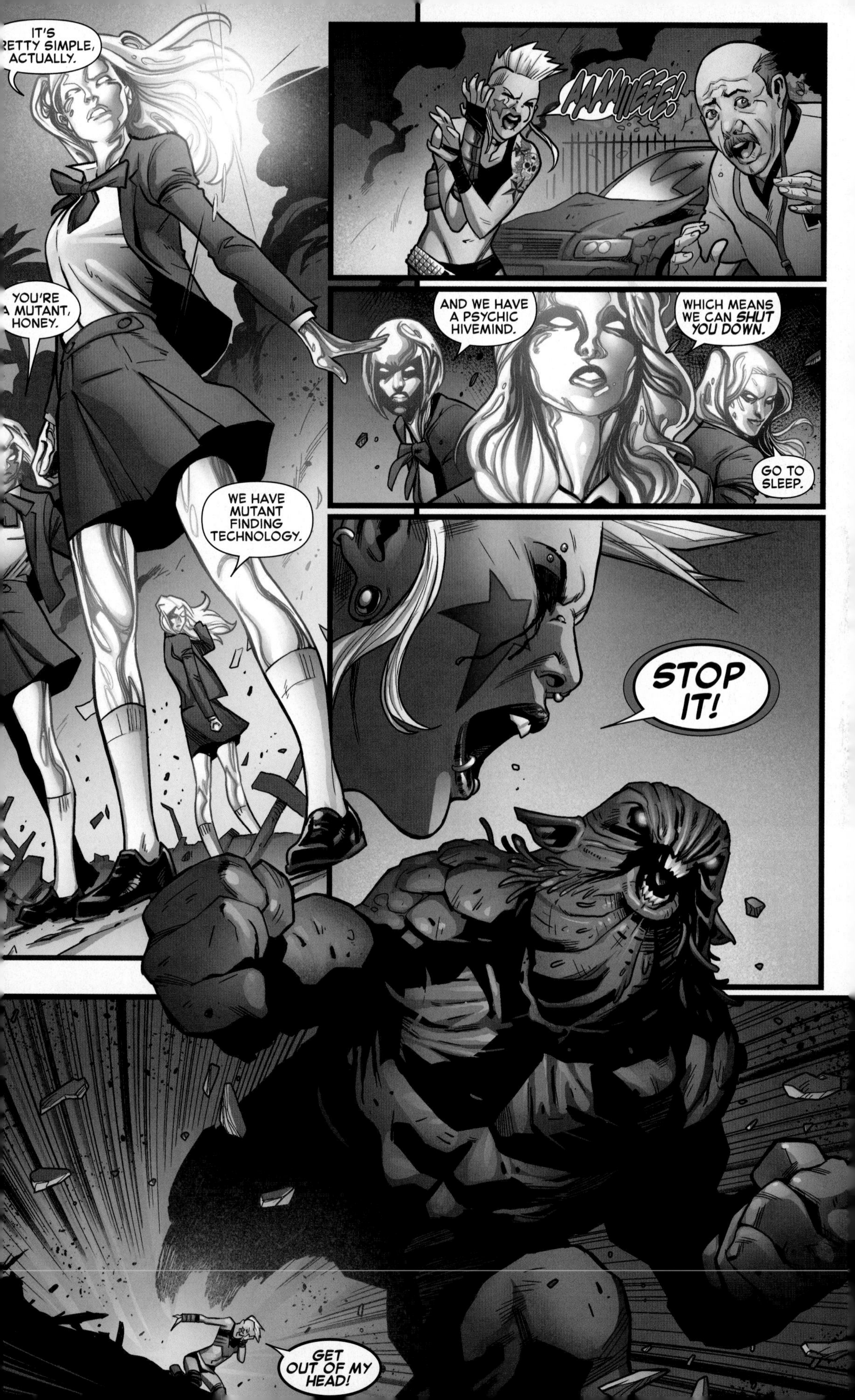
IT'S RETTY SIMPLE, ACTUALLY.
YOU'RE A MUTANT, HONEY.
WE HAVE MUTANT FINDING TECHNOLOGY.
AAAIIIEEE!
AND WE HAVE A PSYCHIC HIVEMIND.
WHICH MEANS WE CAN *SHUT YOU DOWN.*
GO TO SLEEP.
STOP IT!
GET OUT OF MY HEAD!

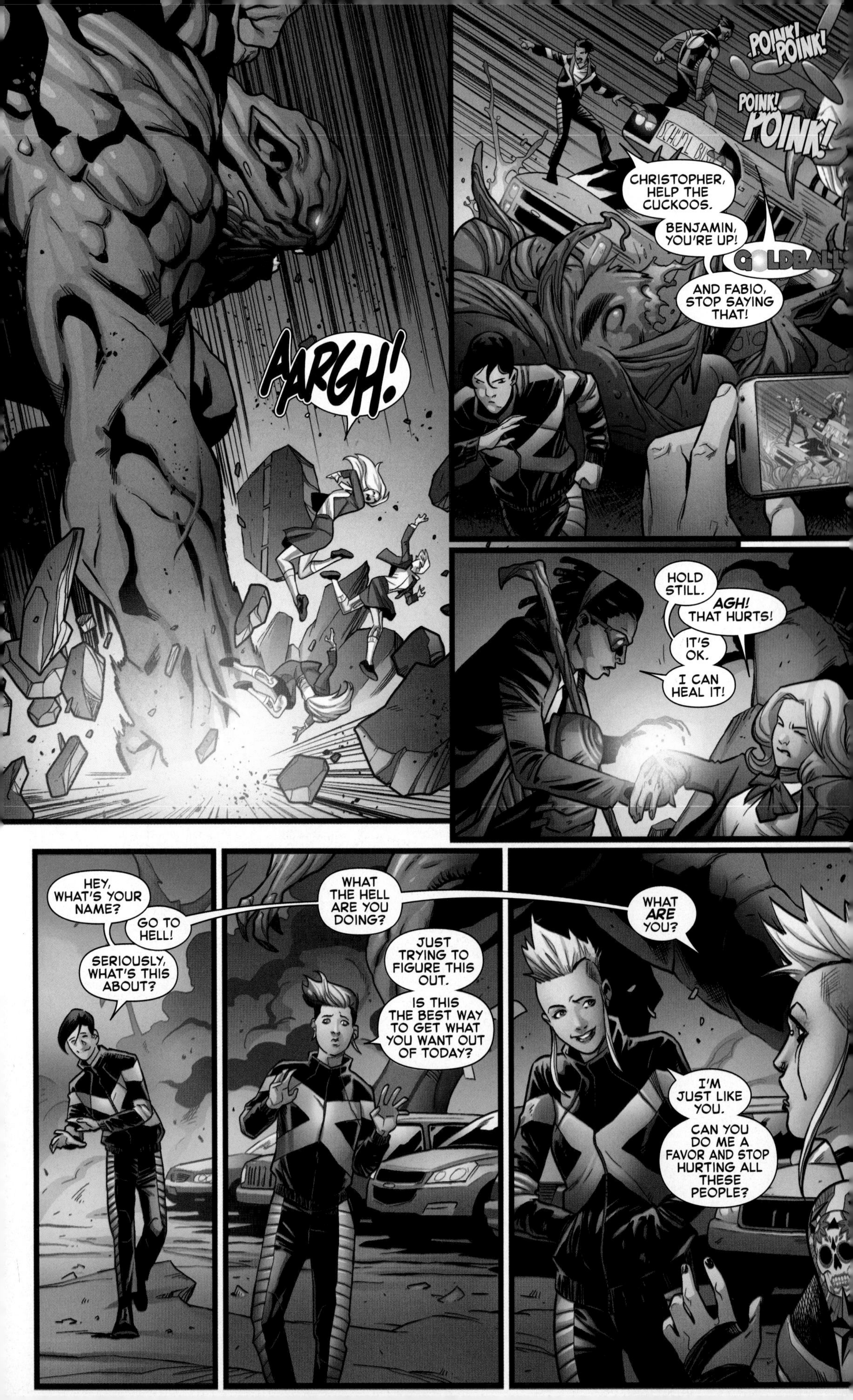
AARGH!
POINK! POINK!
POINK! POINK!
CHRISTOPHER, HELP THE CUCKOOS.
BENJAMIN, YOU'RE UP!
GOLDBALL
AND FABIO, STOP SAYING THAT!
HOLD STILL.
AGH! THAT HURTS!
IT'S OK.
I CAN HEAL IT!
HEY, WHAT'S YOUR NAME?
GO TO HELL!
SERIOUSLY, WHAT'S THIS ABOUT?
WHAT THE HELL ARE YOU DOING?
JUST TRYING TO FIGURE THIS OUT.
IS THIS THE BEST WAY TO GET WHAT YOU WANT OUT OF TODAY?
WHAT ARE YOU?
I'M JUST LIKE YOU.
CAN YOU DO ME A FAVOR AND STOP HURTING ALL THESE PEOPLE?

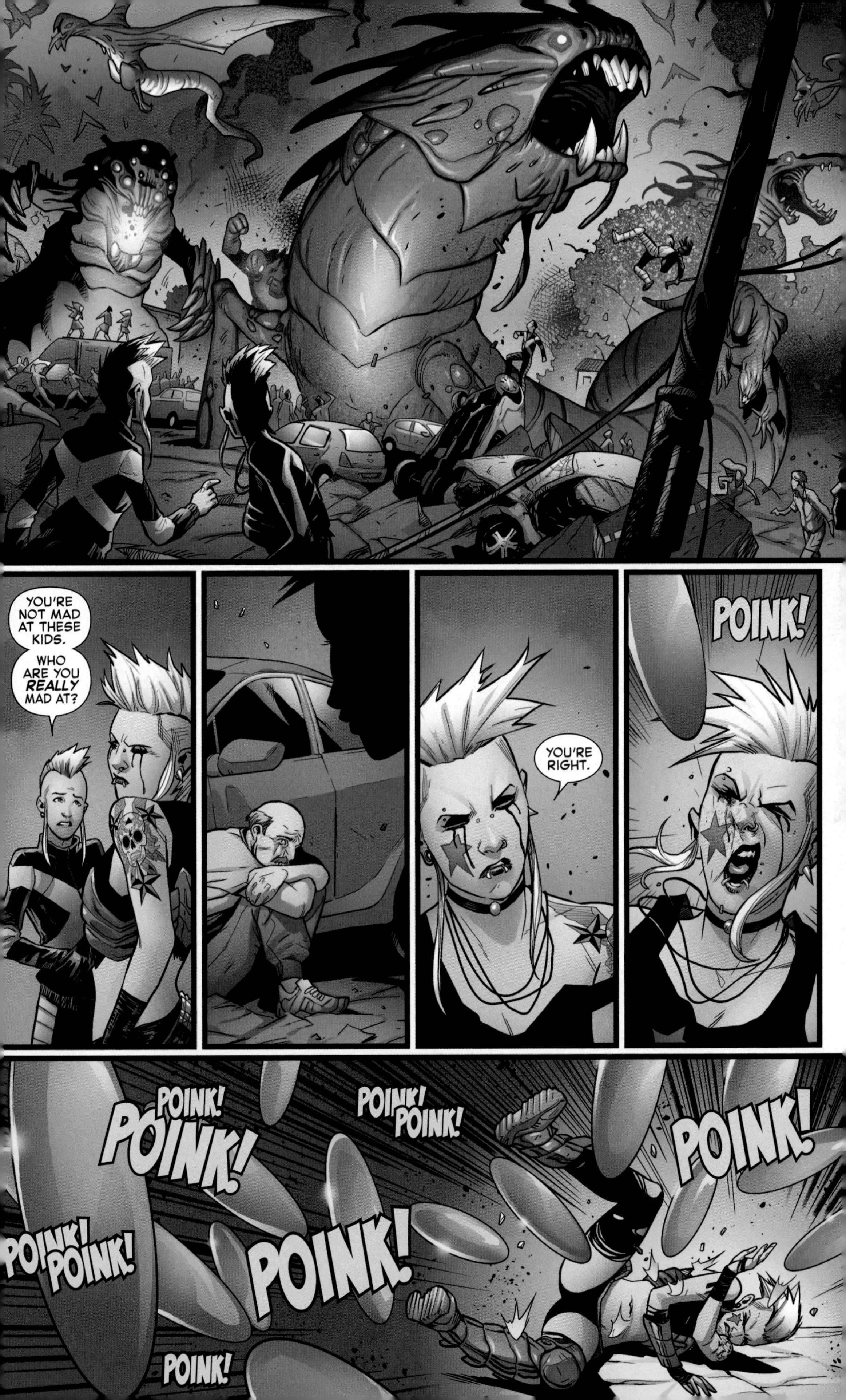
YOU'RE NOT MAD AT THESE KIDS.
WHO ARE YOU *REALLY* MAD AT?
YOU'RE RIGHT.
POINK!
POINK!
POINK!
POINK!
POINK!
POINK!
POINK!
POINK!
POINK!
POINK!

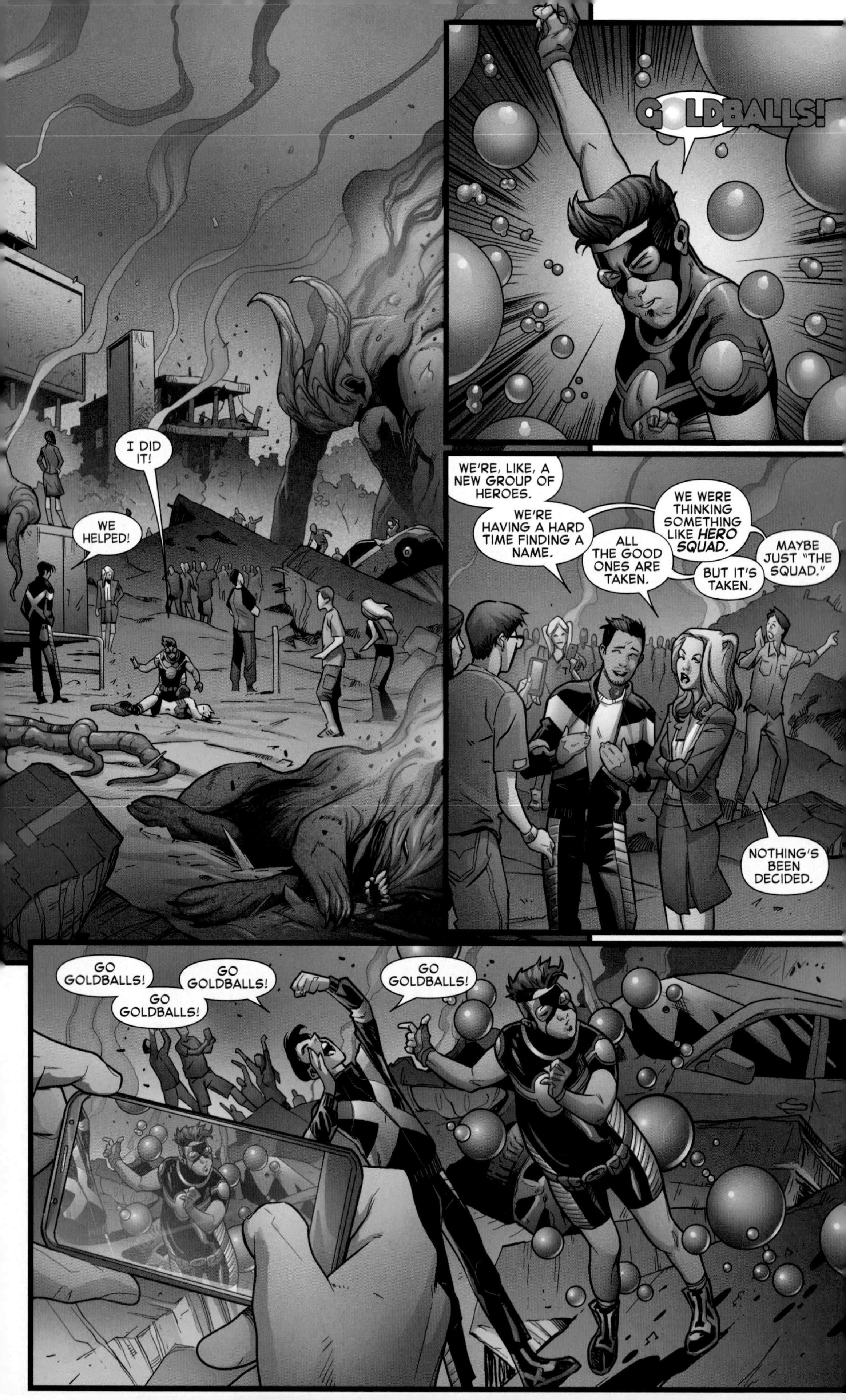
I DID IT!
WE HELPED!
GOLDBALLS!
WE'RE, LIKE, A NEW GROUP OF HEROES.
WE'RE HAVING A HARD TIME FINDING A NAME.
WE WERE THINKING SOMETHING LIKE HERO SQUAD.
ALL THE GOOD ONES ARE TAKEN.
BUT IT'S TAKEN.
MAYBE JUST "THE SQUAD."
NOTHING'S BEEN DECIDED.
GO GOLDBALLS!
GO GOLDBALLS!
GO GOLDBALLS!
GO GOLDBALLS!

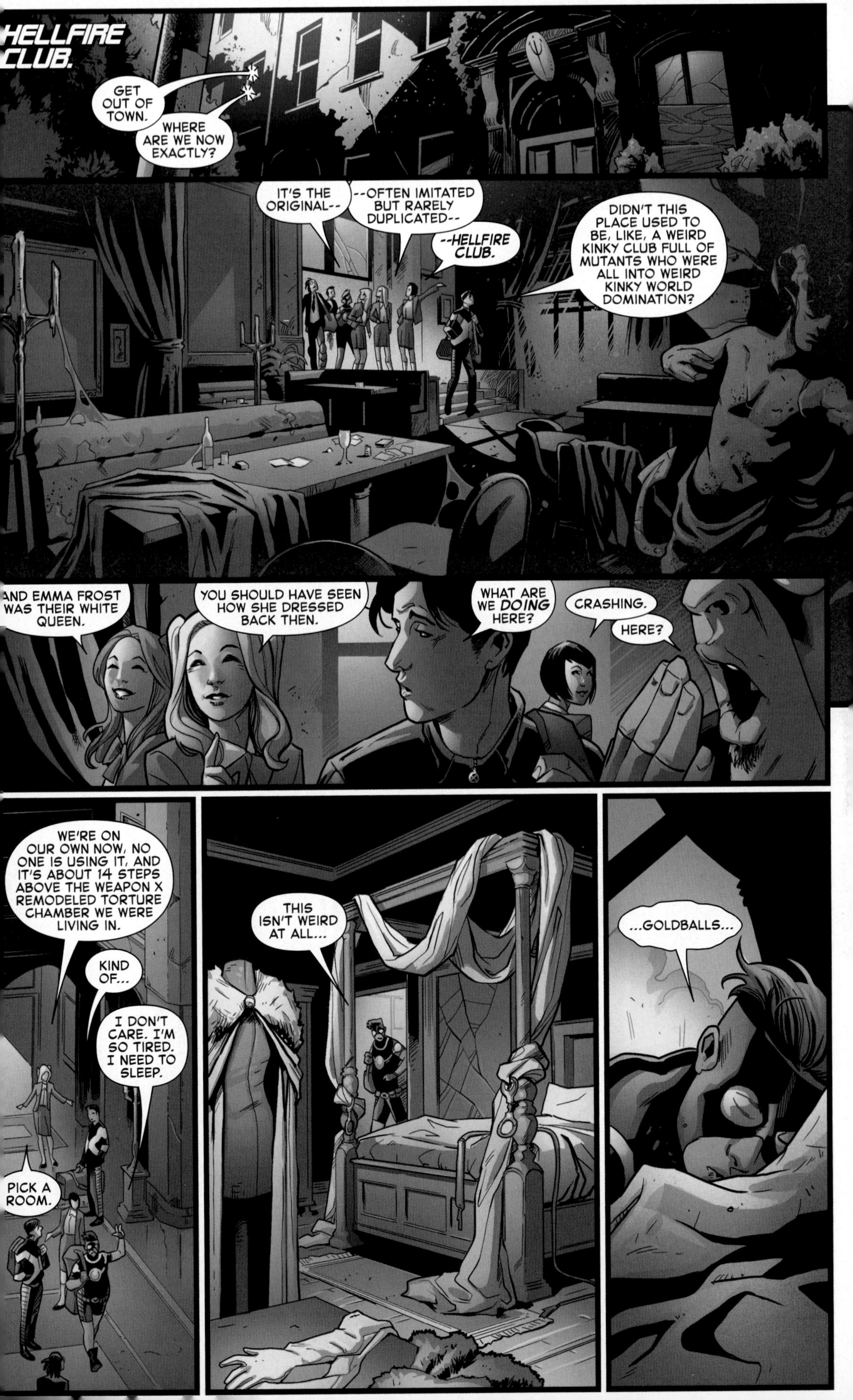
HELLFIRE CLUB.
GET OUT OF TOWN.
WHERE ARE WE NOW EXACTLY?
IT'S THE ORIGINAL--
--OFTEN IMITATED BUT RARELY DUPLICATED--
--HELLFIRE CLUB.
DIDN'T THIS PLACE USED TO BE, LIKE, A WEIRD KINKY CLUB FULL OF MUTANTS WHO WERE ALL INTO WEIRD KINKY WORLD DOMINATION?
AND EMMA FROST WAS THEIR WHITE QUEEN.
YOU SHOULD HAVE SEEN HOW SHE DRESSED BACK THEN.
WHAT ARE WE DOING HERE?
CRASHING.
HERE?
WE'RE ON OUR OWN NOW, NO ONE IS USING IT, AND IT'S ABOUT 14 STEPS ABOVE THE WEAPON X REMODELED TORTURE CHAMBER WE WERE LIVING IN.
KIND OF...
I DON'T CARE. I'M SO TIRED. I NEED TO SLEEP.
PICK A ROOM.
THIS ISN'T WEIRD AT ALL...
...GOLDBALLS...

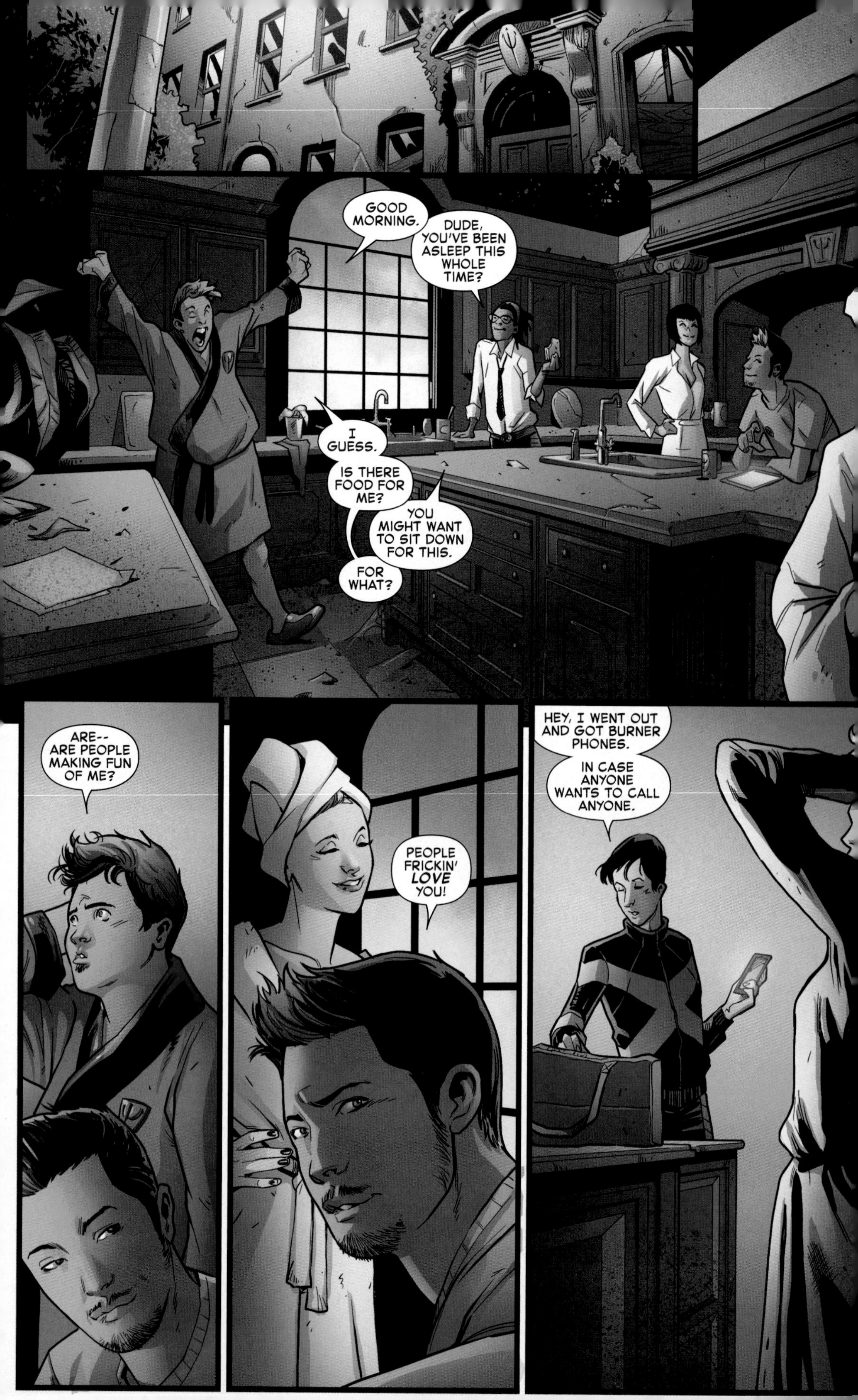
GOOD MORNING.
DUDE, YOU'VE BEEN ASLEEP THIS WHOLE TIME?
I GUESS.
IS THERE FOOD FOR ME?
YOU MIGHT WANT TO SIT DOWN FOR THIS.
FOR WHAT?
ARE-- ARE PEOPLE MAKING FUN OF ME?
PEOPLE FRICKIN' LOVE YOU!
HEY, I WENT OUT AND GOT BURNER PHONES.
IN CASE ANYONE WANTS TO CALL ANYONE.

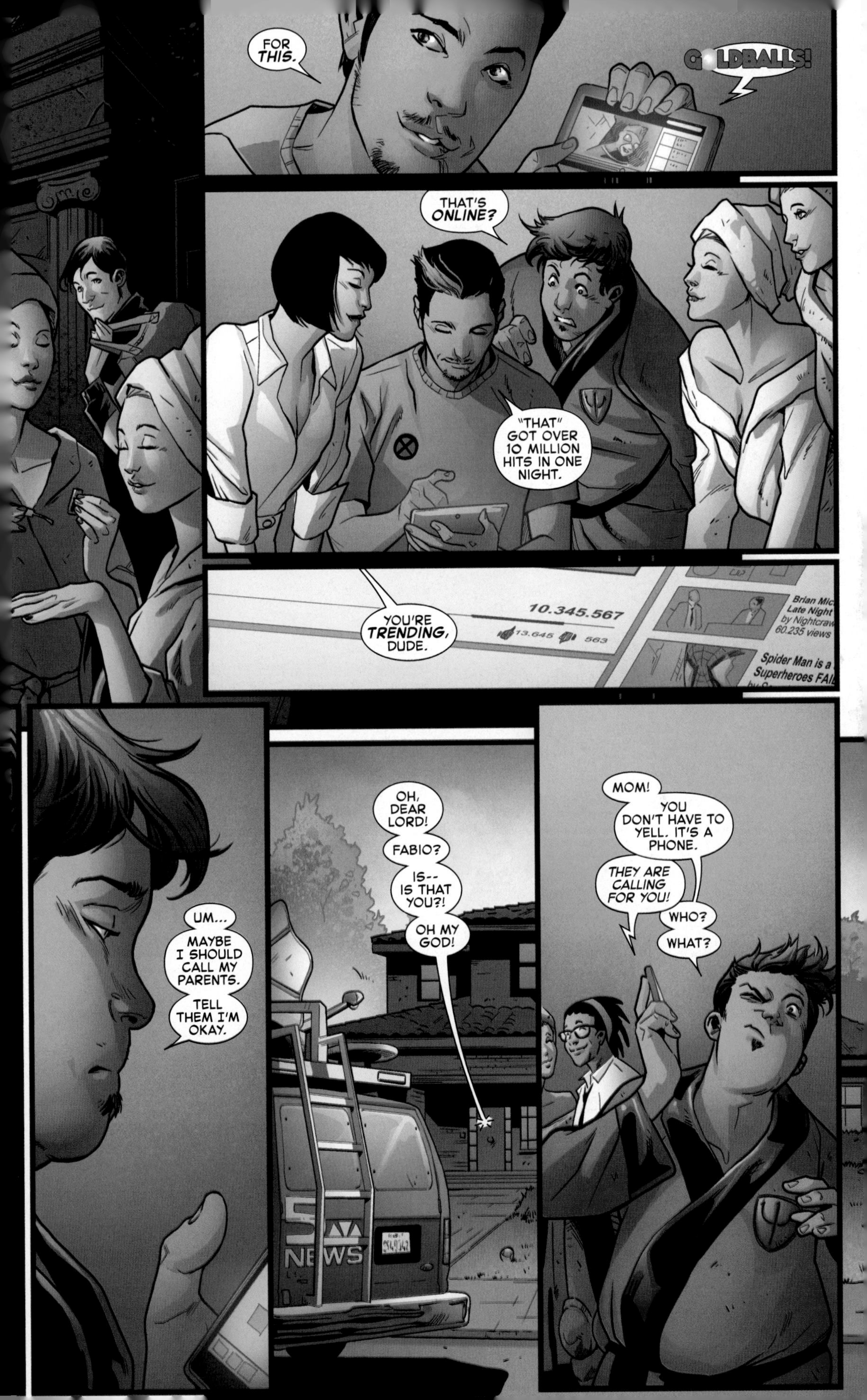

FOR THIS.
GOLDBALLS!
THAT'S ONLINE?
"THAT" GOT OVER 10 MILLION HITS IN ONE NIGHT.
YOU'RE TRENDING, DUDE.
10.345.567
13.645 563
Brian Mic
Late Night
by Nightcraw
60.235 views
Spider Man is a
Superheroes FAIL
UM...
MAYBE I SHOULD CALL MY PARENTS.
TELL THEM I'M OKAY.
OH, DEAR LORD!
FABIO?
IS-- IS THAT YOU?!
OH MY GOD!
5 NEWS
MOM!
YOU DON'T HAVE TO YELL. IT'S A PHONE.
THEY ARE CALLING FOR YOU!
WHO?
WHAT?

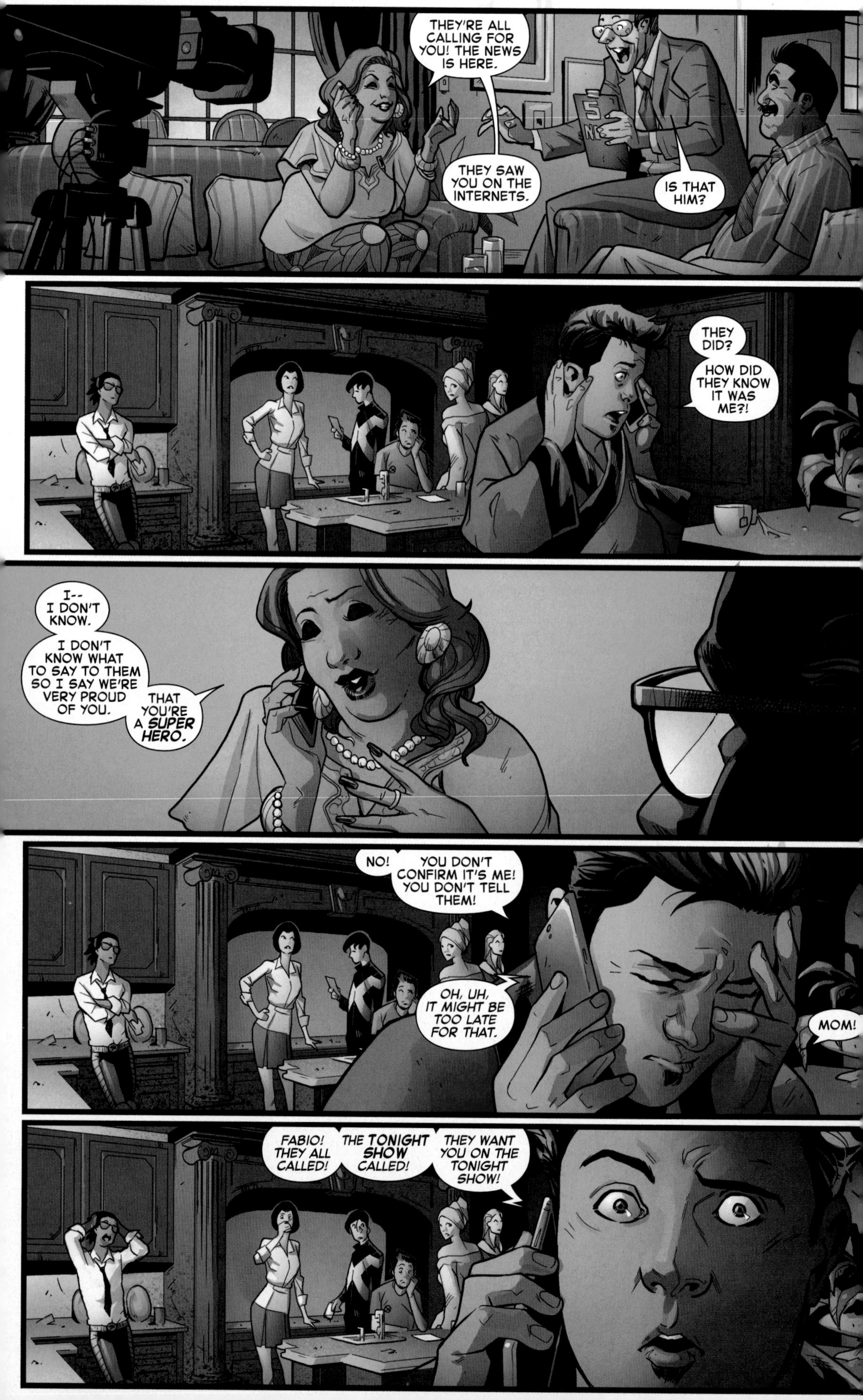
THEY'RE ALL CALLING FOR YOU! THE NEWS IS HERE.
THEY SAW YOU ON THE INTERNETS.
IS THAT HIM?
THEY DID?
HOW DID THEY KNOW IT WAS ME?!
I-- I DON'T KNOW.
I DON'T KNOW WHAT TO SAY TO THEM SO I SAY WE'RE VERY PROUD OF YOU.
THAT YOU'RE A SUPER HERO.
NO!
YOU DON'T CONFIRM IT'S ME! YOU DON'T TELL THEM!
OH, UH, IT MIGHT BE TOO LATE FOR THAT.
MOM!
FABIO! THEY ALL CALLED!
THE TONIGHT SHOW CALLED!
THEY WANT YOU ON THE TONIGHT SHOW!

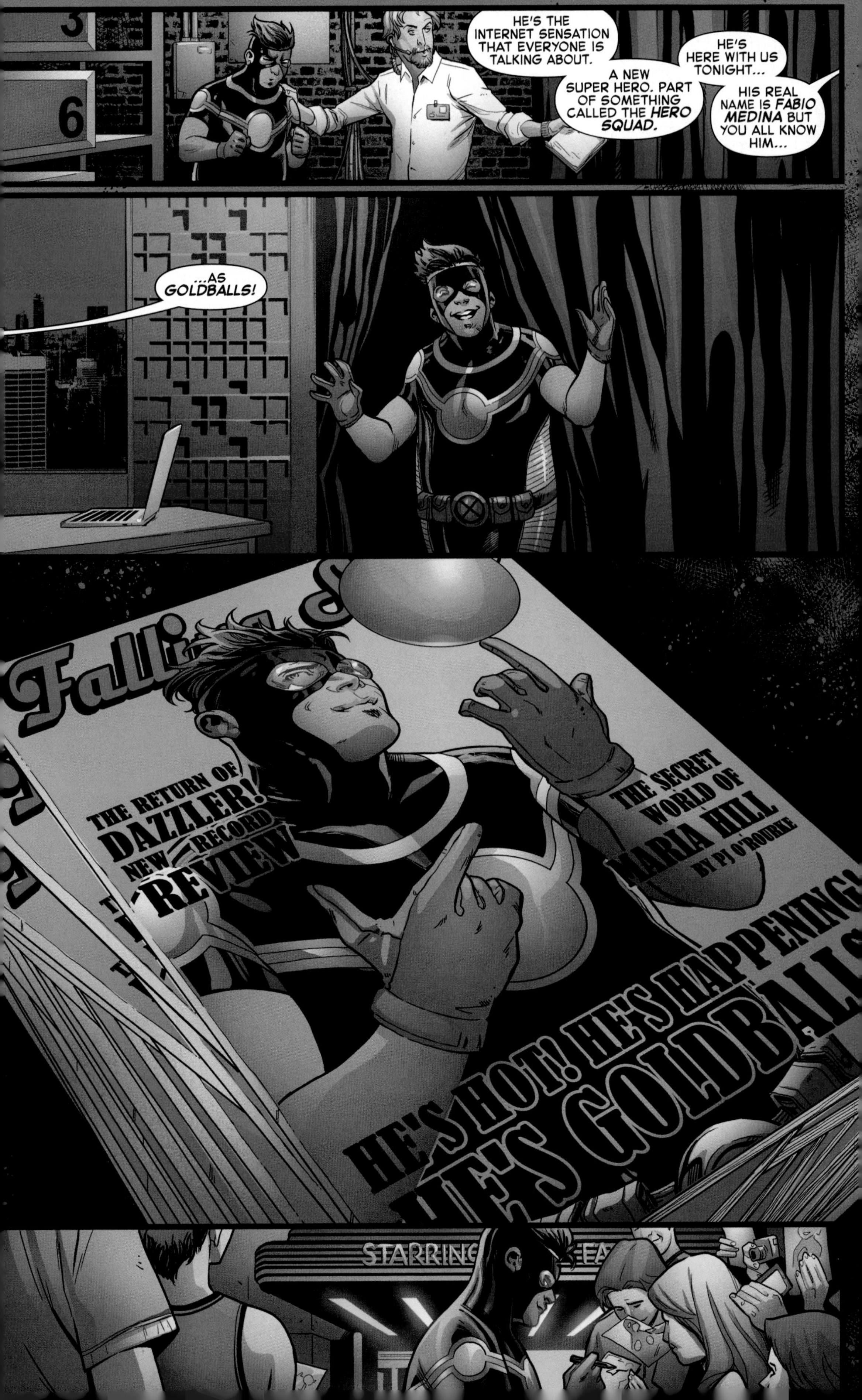
HE'S THE INTERNET SENSATION THAT EVERYONE IS TALKING ABOUT.
A NEW SUPER HERO. PART OF SOMETHING CALLED THE *HERO SQUAD.*
HE'S HERE WITH US TONIGHT...
HIS REAL NAME IS *FABIO MEDINA* BUT YOU ALL KNOW HIM...
...AS *GOLDBALLS!*
THE RETURN OF DAZZLER!
NEW RECORD REVIEW
THE SECRET WORLD OF MARIA HILL
BY PJ O'ROURKE
HE'S HOT! HE'S HAPPENING!

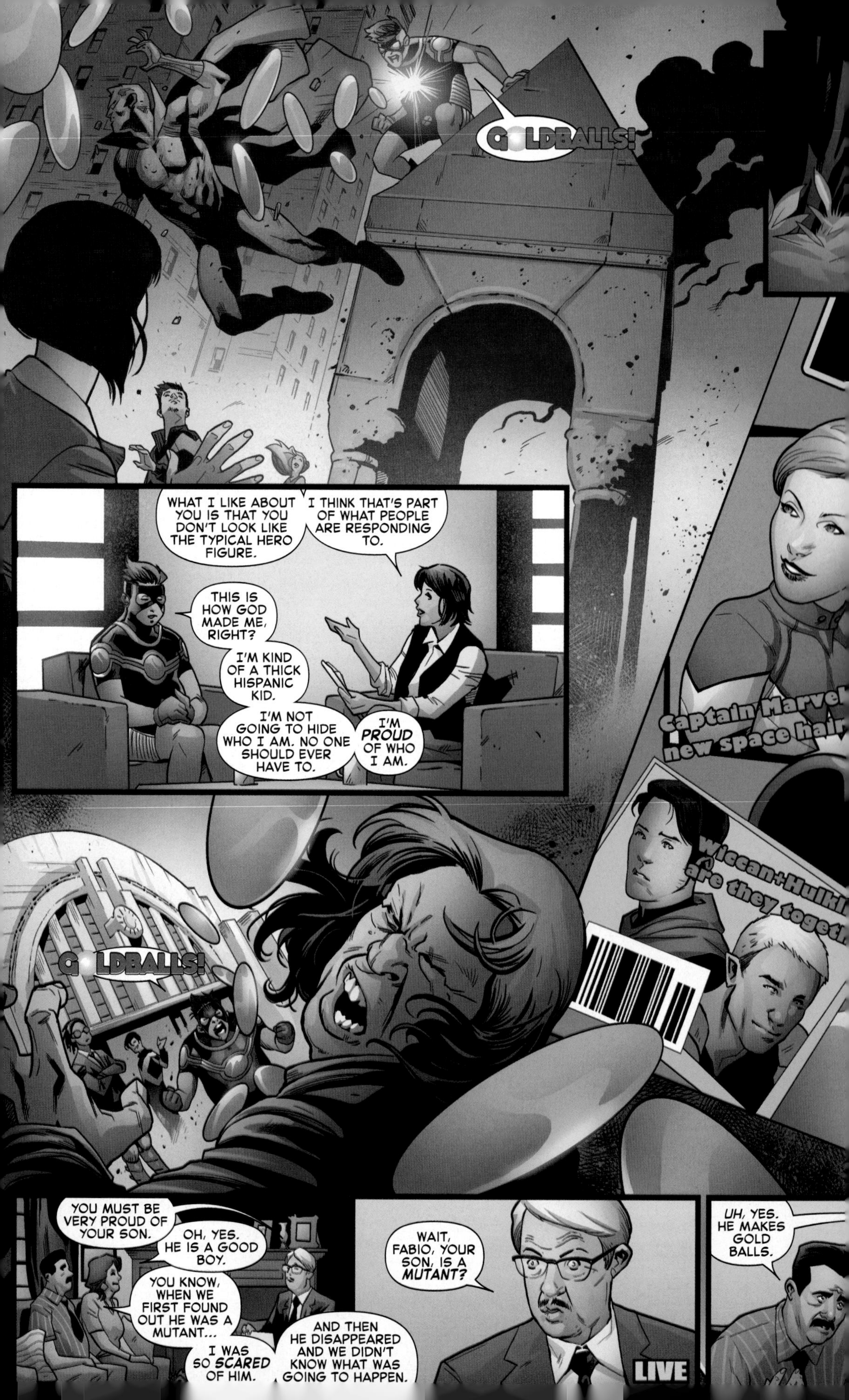
GOLDBALLS!
WHAT I LIKE ABOUT YOU IS THAT YOU DON'T LOOK LIKE THE TYPICAL HERO FIGURE.
I THINK THAT'S PART OF WHAT PEOPLE ARE RESPONDING TO.
THIS IS HOW GOD MADE ME, RIGHT?
I'M KIND OF A THICK HISPANIC KID.
I'M NOT GOING TO HIDE WHO I AM. NO ONE SHOULD EVER HAVE TO.
I'M PROUD OF WHO I AM.
Captain Marvel new space hair
GOLDBALLS!
Wiccan+Hulkl are they togeth
YOU MUST BE VERY PROUD OF YOUR SON.
OH, YES. HE IS A GOOD BOY.
YOU KNOW, WHEN WE FIRST FOUND OUT HE WAS A MUTANT...
I WAS SO SCARED OF HIM.
AND THEN HE DISAPPEARED AND WE DIDN'T KNOW WHAT WAS GOING TO HAPPEN.
WAIT, FABIO, YOUR SON, IS A MUTANT?
LIVE
UH, YES. HE MAKES GOLD BALLS.

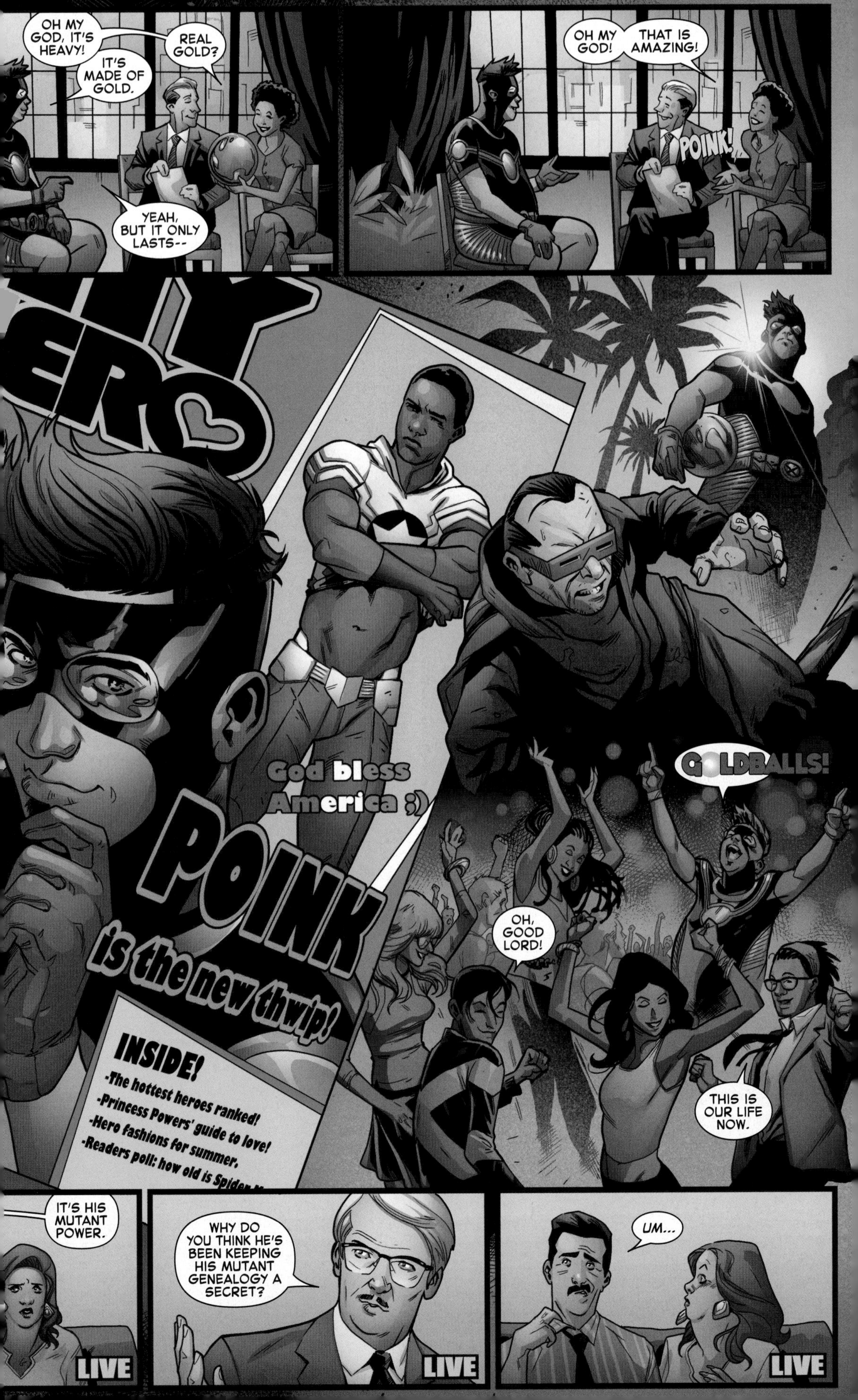
OH MY GOD, IT'S HEAVY!
REAL GOLD?
IT'S MADE OF GOLD.
YEAH, BUT IT ONLY LASTS--
OH MY GOD!
THAT IS AMAZING!
POINK!
ERO
God bless America ;)
POINK is the new thwip!
INSIDE!
-The hottest heroes ranked!
-Princess Powers' guide to love!
-Hero fashions for summer,
-Readers poll: how old is Spider
GOLDBALLS!
OH, GOOD LORD!
THIS IS OUR LIFE NOW.
IT'S HIS MUTANT POWER.
LIVE
WHY DO YOU THINK HE'S BEEN KEEPING HIS MUTANT GENEALOGY A SECRET?
LIVE
UM...
LIVE

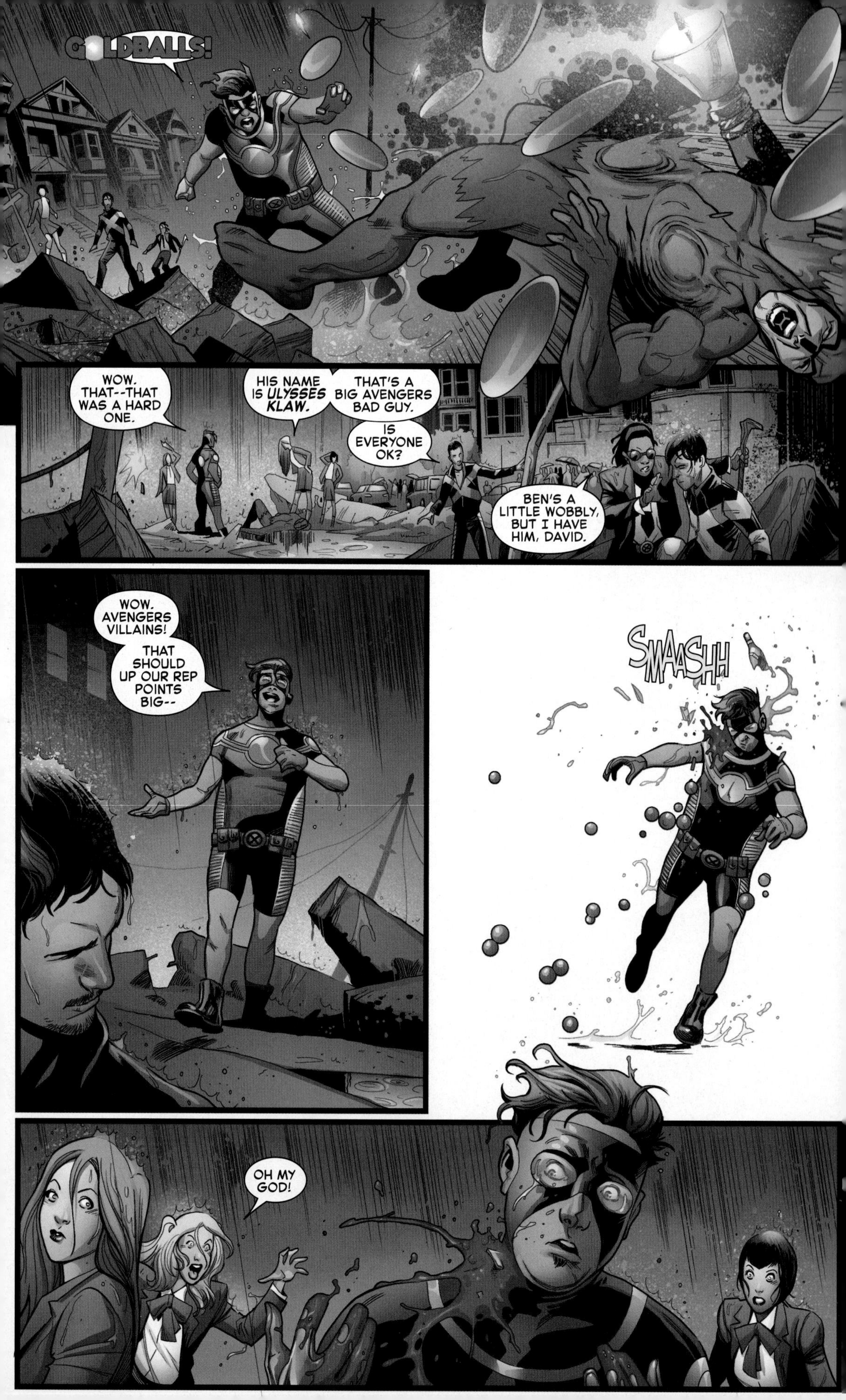
GOLDBALLS!
WOW. THAT--THAT WAS A HARD ONE.
HIS NAME IS ULYSSES KLAW.
THAT'S A BIG AVENGERS BAD GUY.
IS EVERYONE OK?
BEN'S A LITTLE WOBBLY, BUT I HAVE HIM, DAVID.
WOW. AVENGERS VILLAINS!
THAT SHOULD UP OUR REP POINTS BIG--
SMAASHH
OH MY GOD!

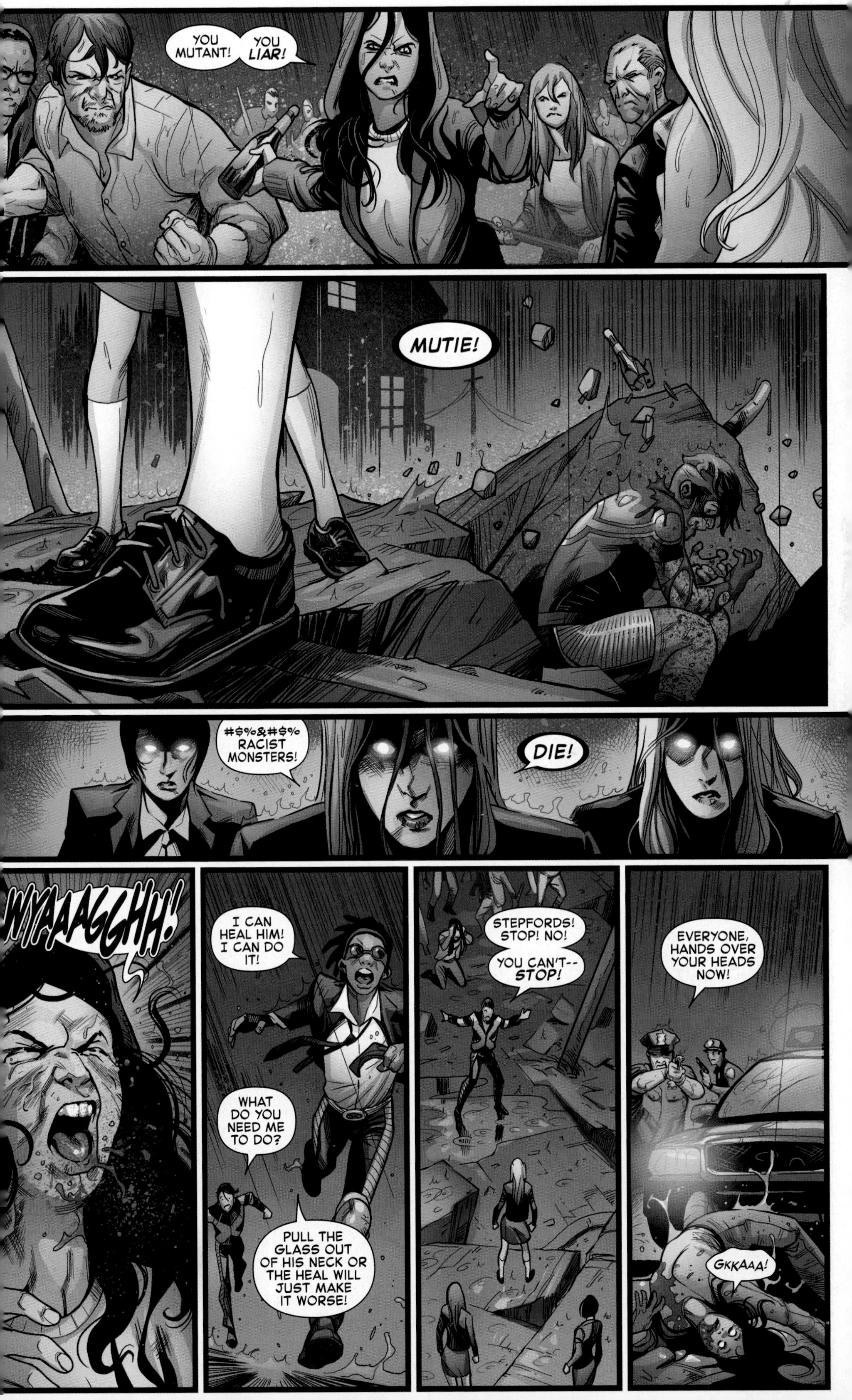
YOU MUTANT!
YOU LIAR!
MUTIE!
#$%&#$% RACIST MONSTERS!
DIE!
WYAAAGGHH!
I CAN HEAL HIM! I CAN DO IT!
WHAT DO YOU NEED ME TO DO?
PULL THE GLASS OUT OF HIS NECK OR THE HEAL WILL JUST MAKE IT WORSE!
STEPFORDS! STOP! NO!
YOU CAN'T-- STOP!
EVERYONE, HANDS OVER YOUR HEADS NOW!
GKKAAA!

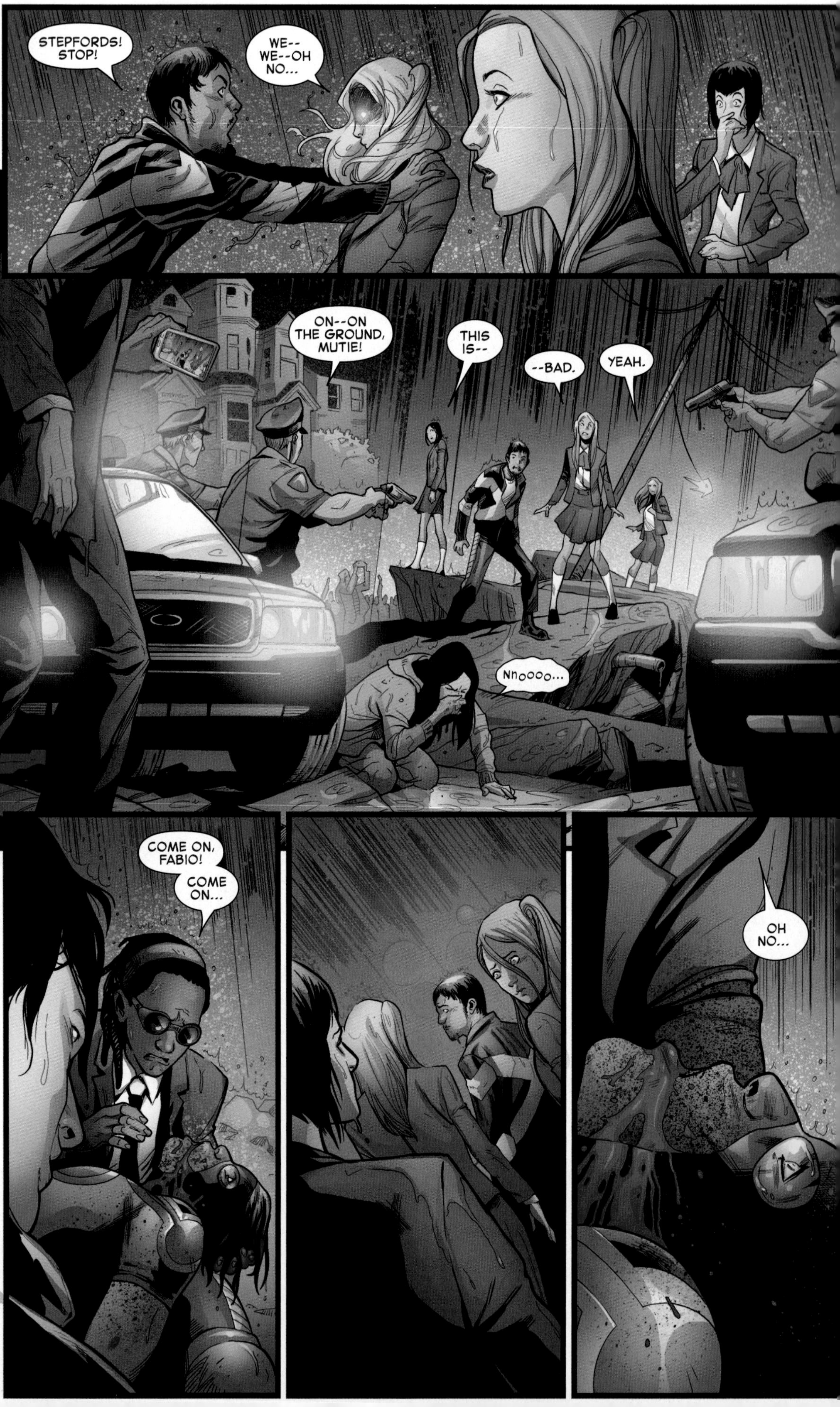
STEPFORDS! STOP!
WE-- WE--OH NO...
ON--ON THE GROUND, MUTIE!
THIS IS--
--BAD.
YEAH.
Nnoooo...
COME ON, FABIO!
COME ON...
OH NO...

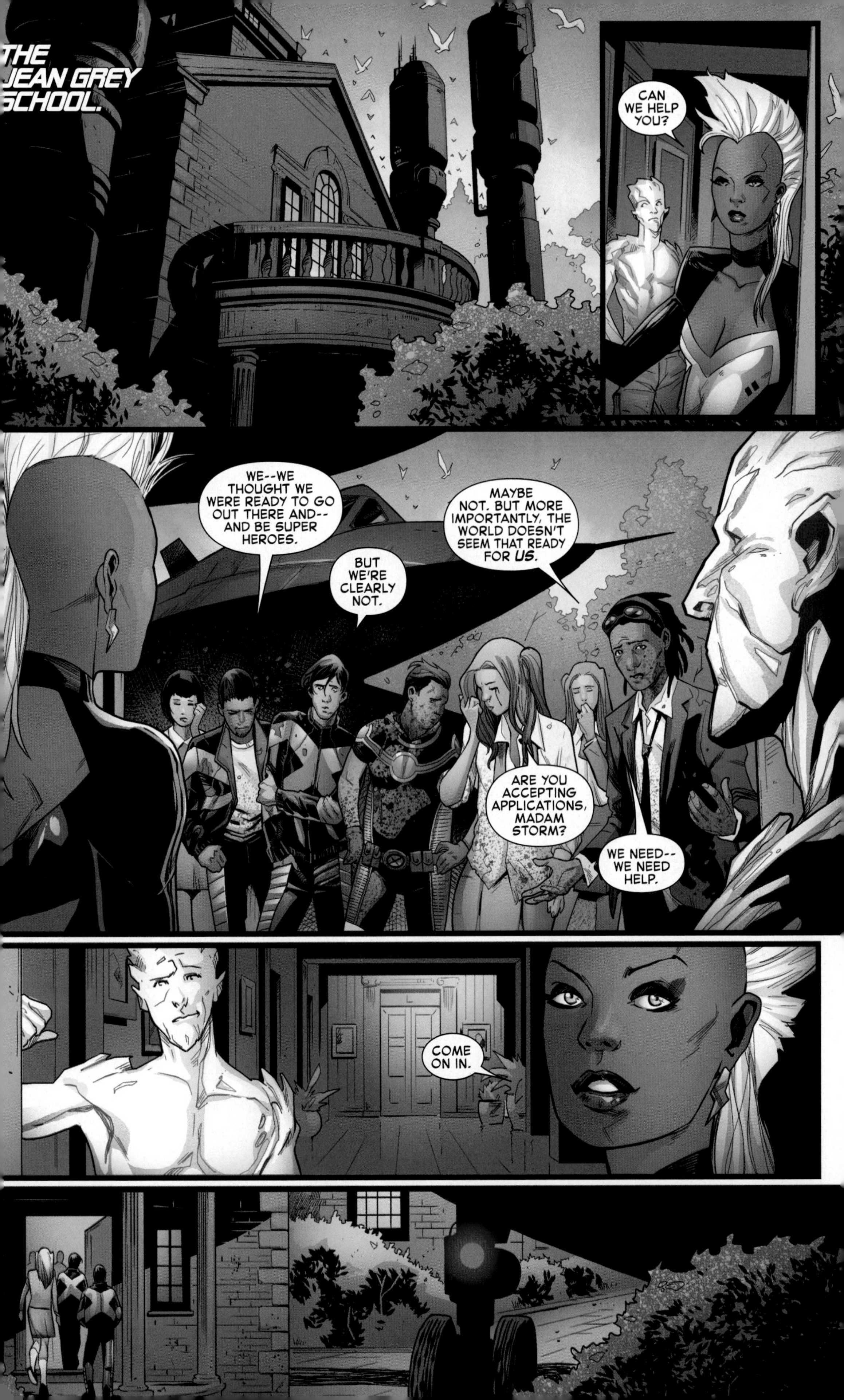
THE JEAN GREY SCHOOL.
CAN WE HELP YOU?
WE--WE THOUGHT WE WERE READY TO GO OUT THERE AND--AND BE SUPER HEROES.
BUT WE'RE CLEARLY NOT.
MAYBE NOT. BUT MORE IMPORTANTLY, THE WORLD DOESN'T SEEM THAT READY FOR US.
ARE YOU ACCEPTING APPLICATIONS, MADAM STORM?
WE NEED--WE NEED HELP.
COME ON IN.

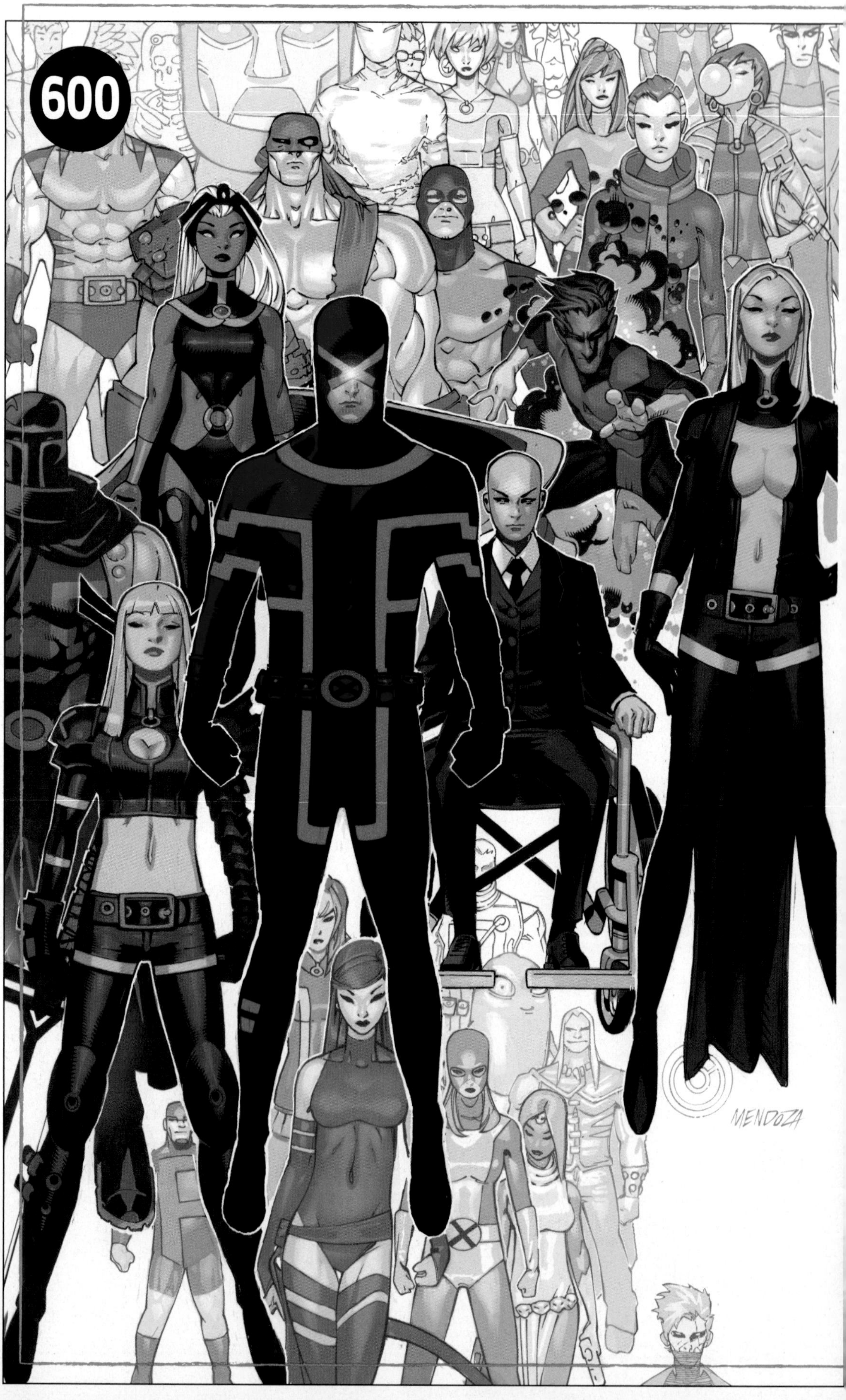
600
MENDOZA

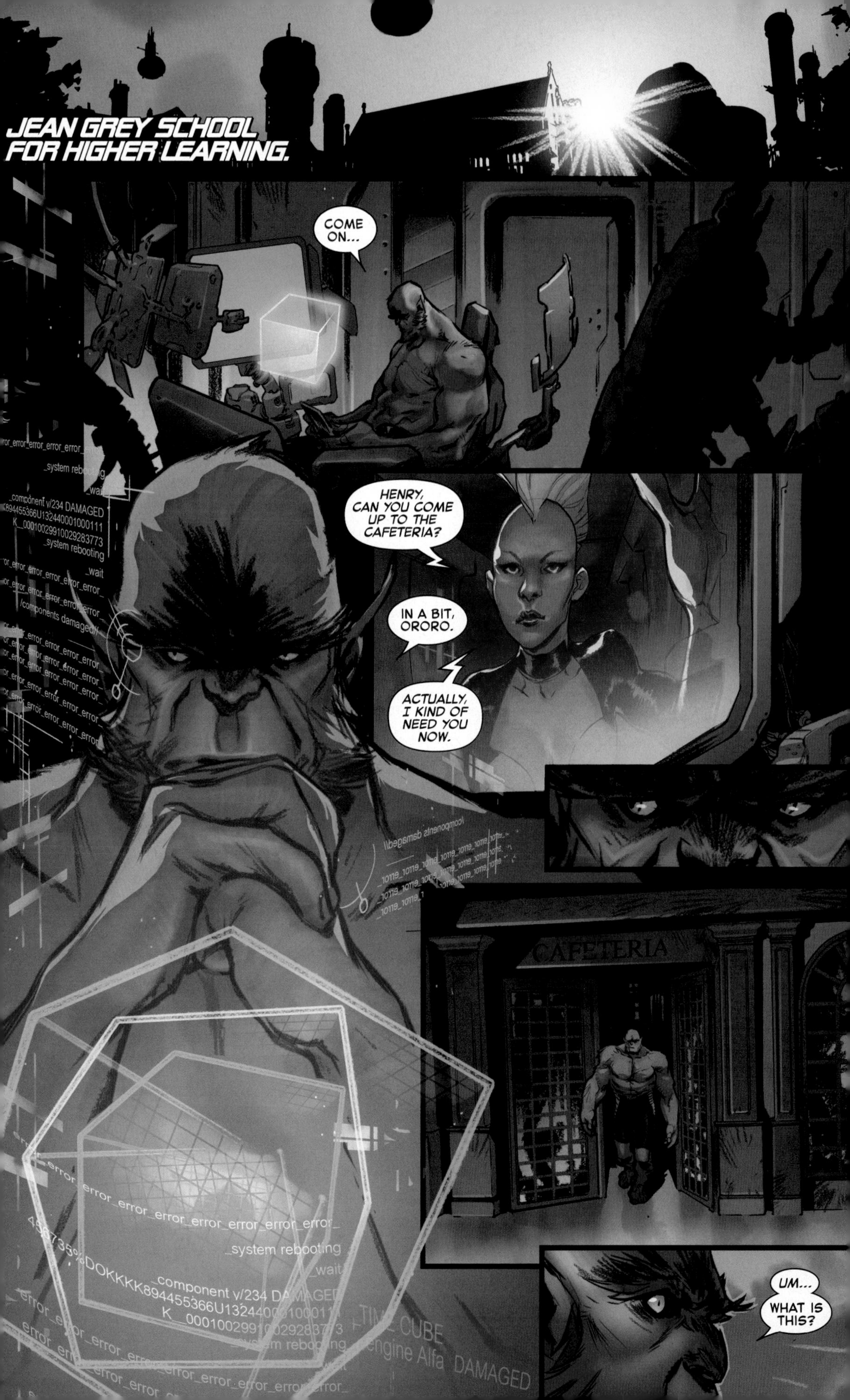
JEAN GREY SCHOOL FOR HIGHER LEARNING.
COME ON...
HENRY, CAN YOU COME UP TO THE CAFETERIA?
IN A BIT, ORORO.
ACTUALLY, I KIND OF NEED YOU NOW.
CAFETERIA
UM... WHAT IS THIS?

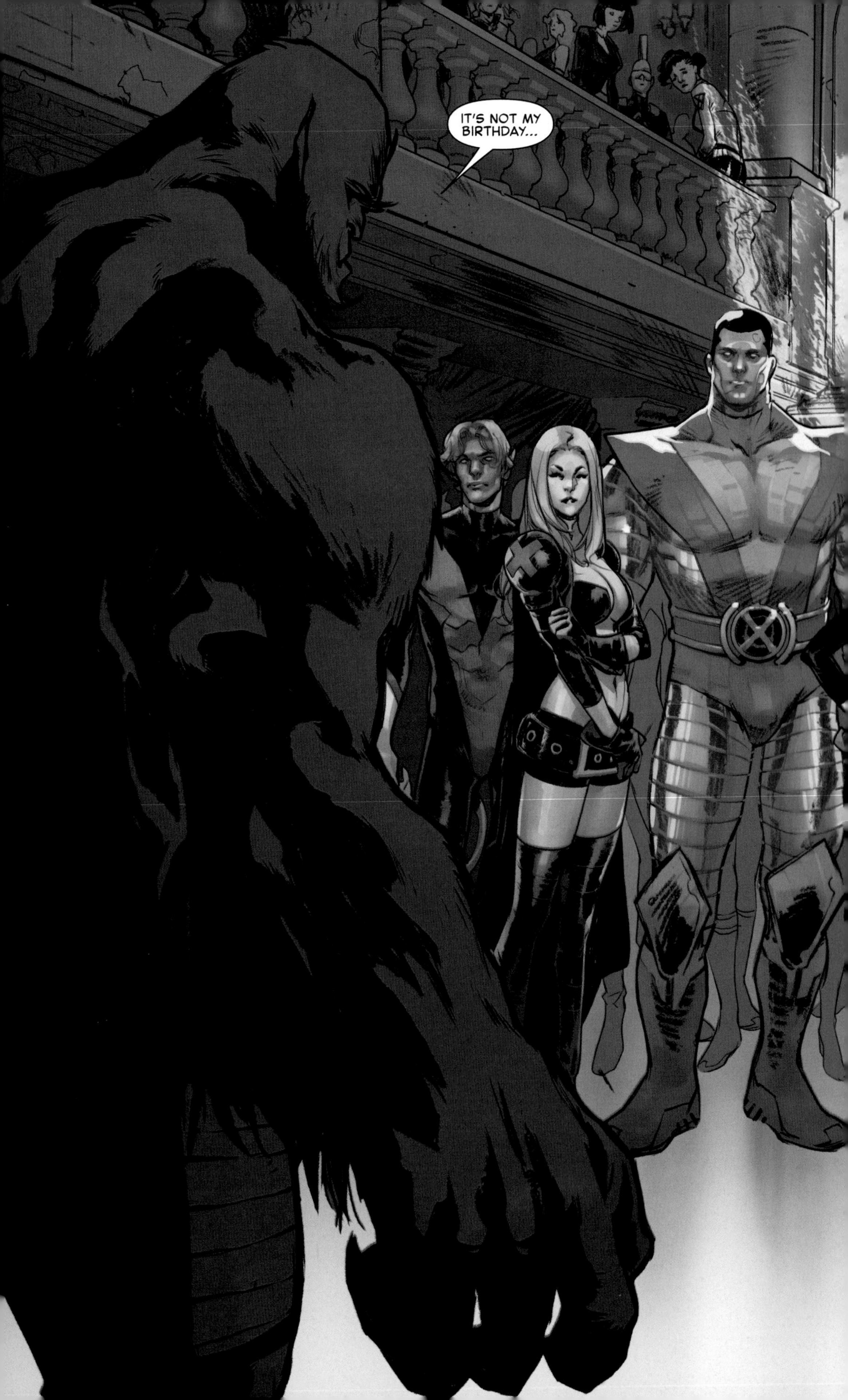
IT'S NOT MY BIRTHDAY...

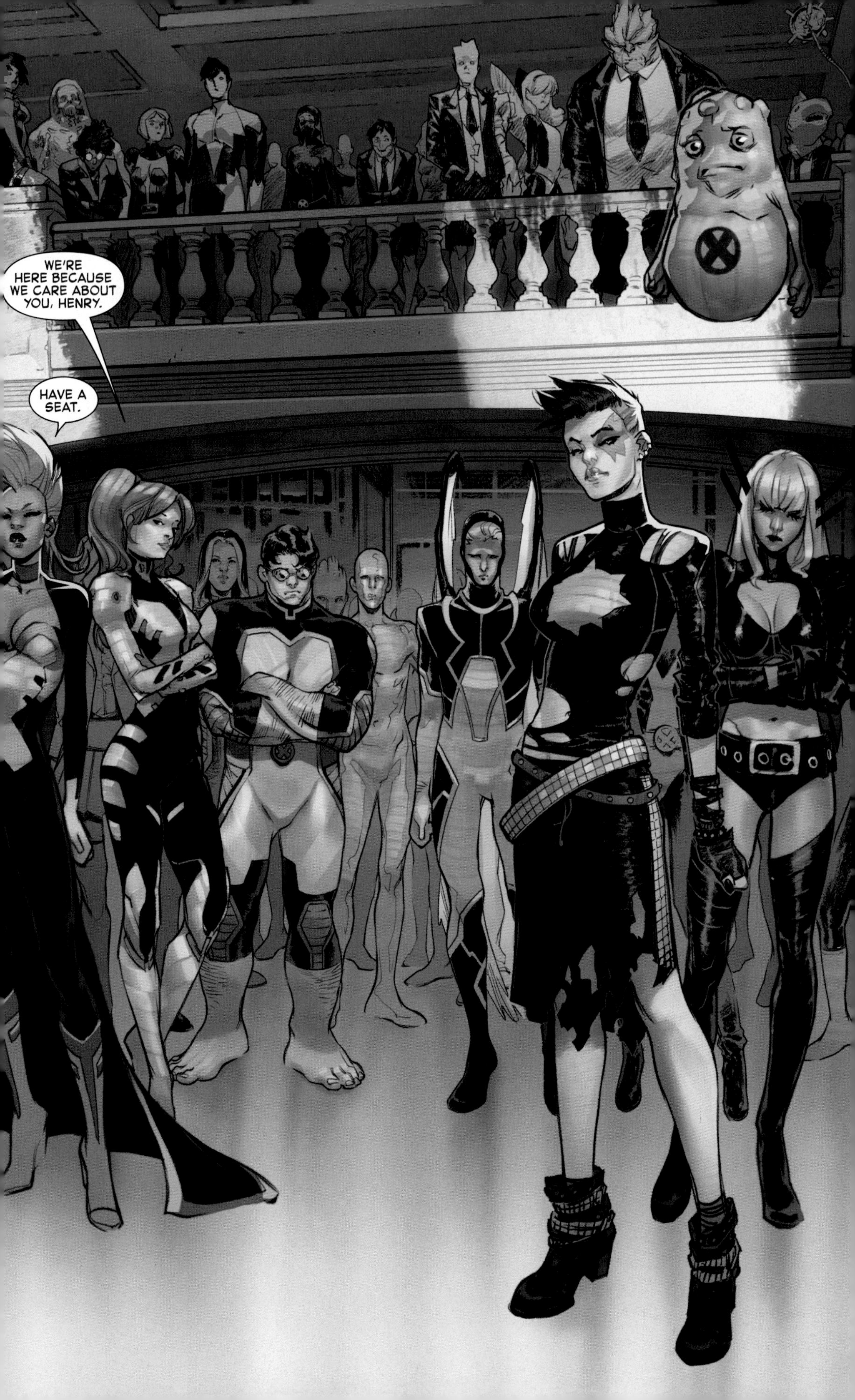
WE'RE HERE BECAUSE WE CARE ABOUT YOU, HENRY.
HAVE A SEAT.

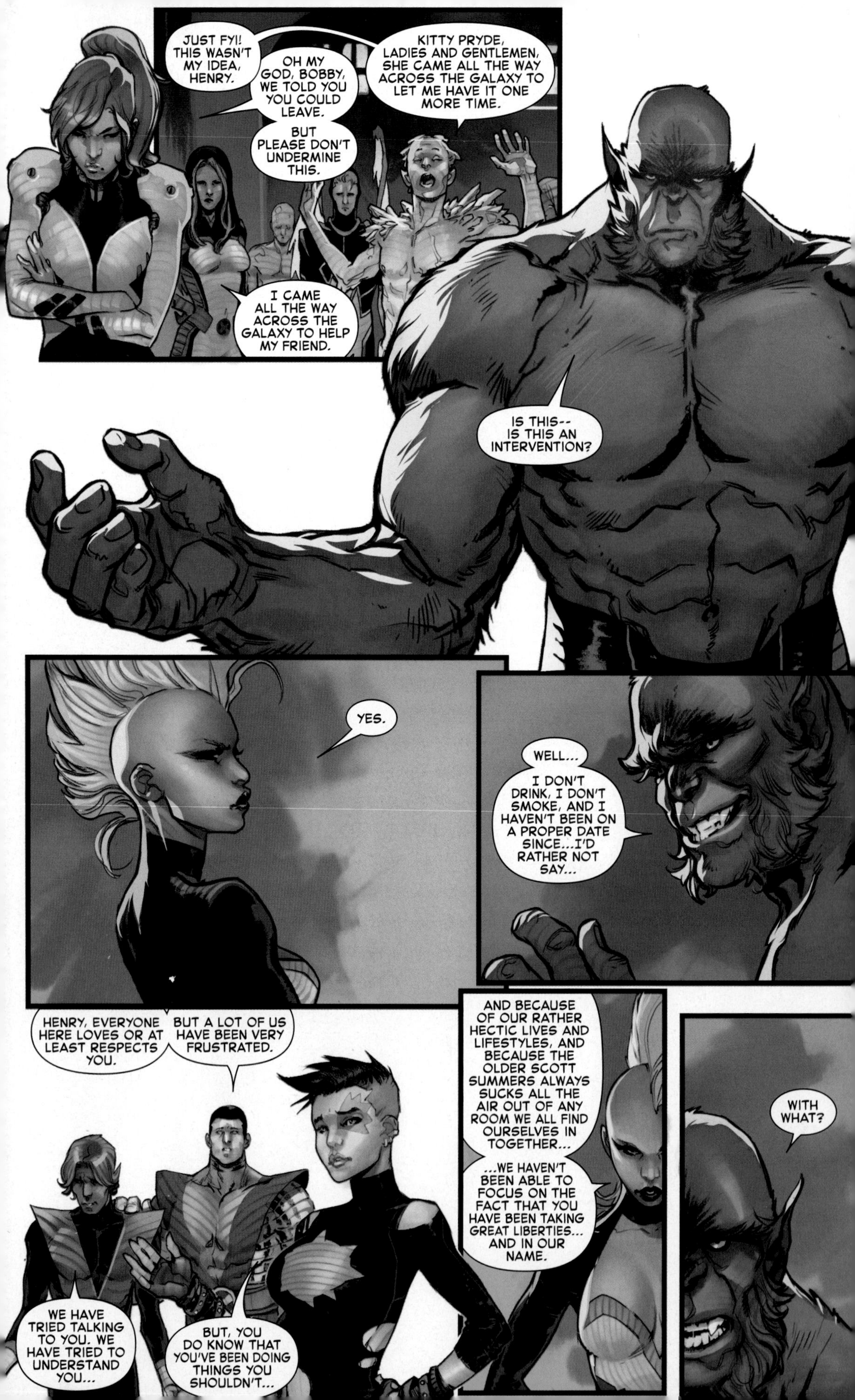
JUST FYI! THIS WASN'T MY IDEA, HENRY.
OH MY GOD, BOBBY, WE TOLD YOU YOU COULD LEAVE.
BUT PLEASE DON'T UNDERMINE THIS.
KITTY PRYDE, LADIES AND GENTLEMEN, SHE CAME ALL THE WAY ACROSS THE GALAXY TO LET ME HAVE IT ONE MORE TIME.
I CAME ALL THE WAY ACROSS THE GALAXY TO HELP MY FRIEND.
IS THIS-- IS THIS AN INTERVENTION?
YES.
WELL...
I DON'T DRINK, I DON'T SMOKE, AND I HAVEN'T BEEN ON A PROPER DATE SINCE...I'D RATHER NOT SAY...
HENRY, EVERYONE HERE LOVES OR AT LEAST RESPECTS YOU.
BUT A LOT OF US HAVE BEEN VERY FRUSTRATED.
WE HAVE TRIED TALKING TO YOU. WE HAVE TRIED TO UNDERSTAND YOU...
BUT, YOU DO KNOW THAT YOU'VE BEEN DOING THINGS YOU SHOULDN'T...
AND BECAUSE OF OUR RATHER HECTIC LIVES AND LIFESTYLES, AND BECAUSE THE OLDER SCOTT SUMMERS ALWAYS SUCKS ALL THE AIR OUT OF ANY ROOM WE ALL FIND OURSELVES IN TOGETHER...
...WE HAVEN'T BEEN ABLE TO FOCUS ON THE FACT THAT YOU HAVE BEEN TAKING GREAT LIBERTIES... AND IN OUR NAME.
WITH WHAT?

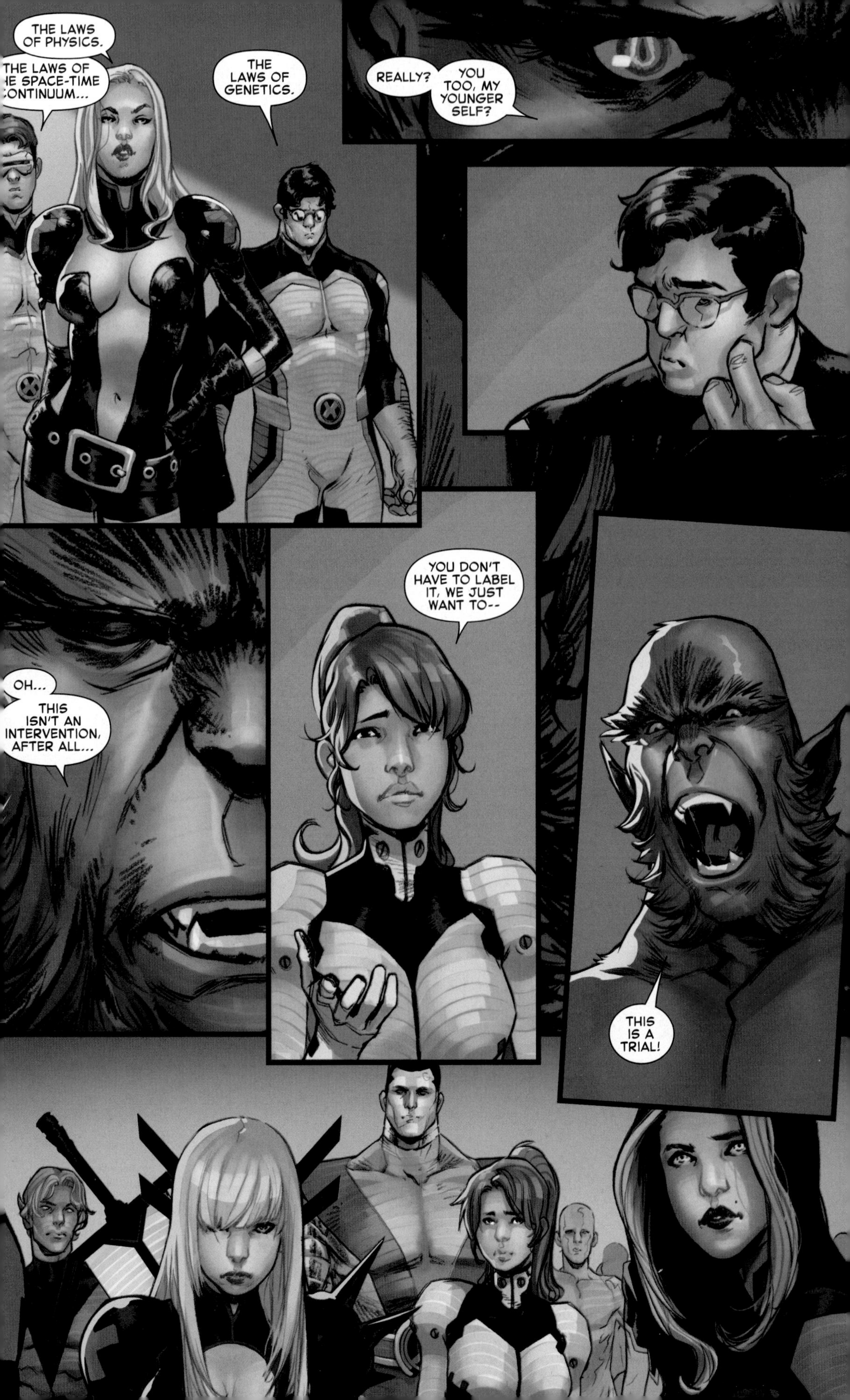
THE LAWS OF PHYSICS.
THE LAWS OF HE SPACE-TIME CONTINUUM...
THE LAWS OF GENETICS.
REALLY?
YOU TOO, MY YOUNGER SELF?
OH...
THIS ISN'T AN INTERVENTION, AFTER ALL...
YOU DON'T HAVE TO LABEL IT, WE JUST WANT TO--
THIS IS A TRIAL!

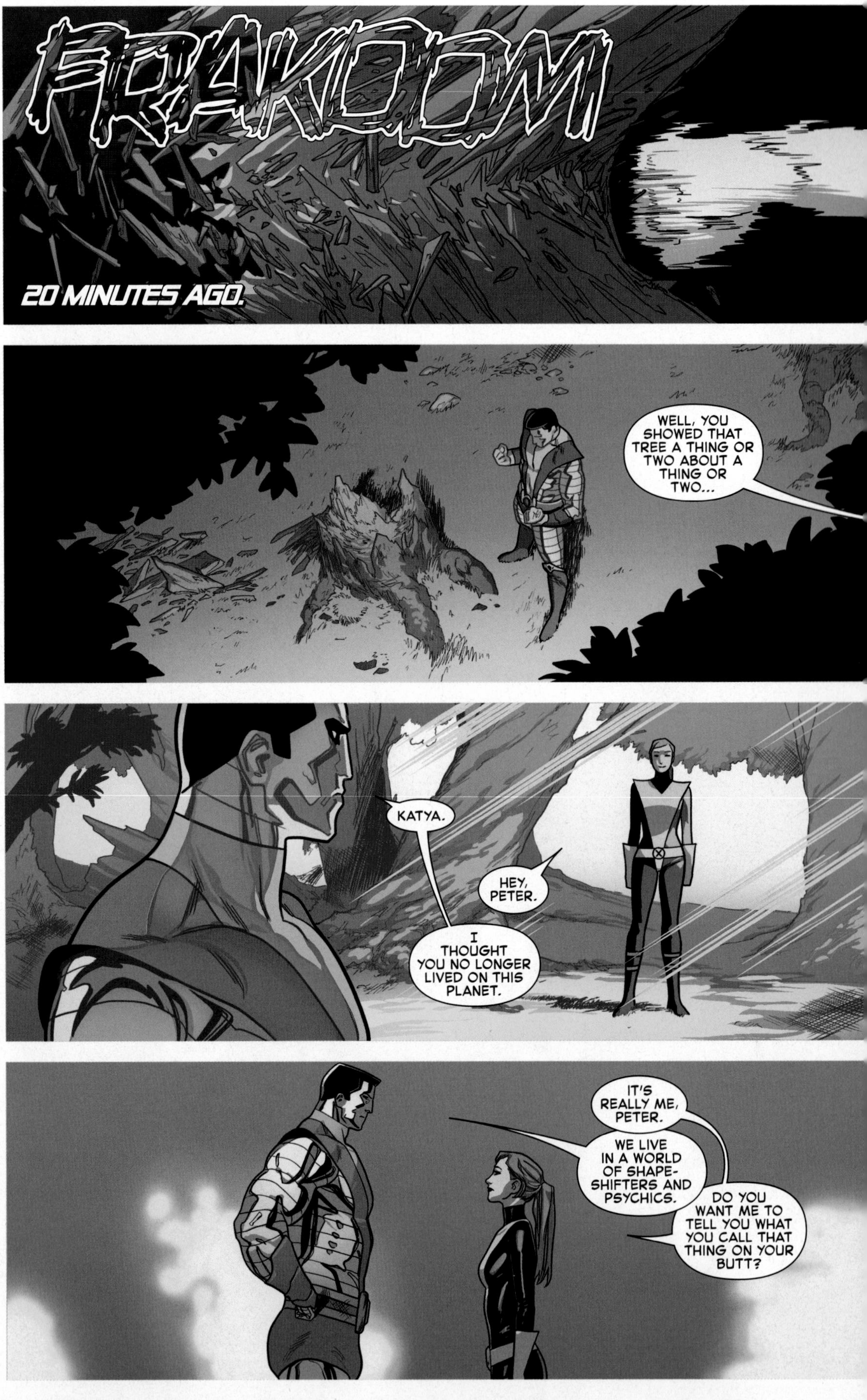
FRAKOOM
20 MINUTES AGO.
WELL, YOU SHOWED THAT TREE A THING OR TWO ABOUT A THING OR TWO...
KATYA.
HEY, PETER.
I THOUGHT YOU NO LONGER LIVED ON THIS PLANET.
IT'S REALLY ME, PETER.
WE LIVE IN A WORLD OF SHAPE-SHIFTERS AND PSYCHICS.
DO YOU WANT ME TO TELL YOU WHAT YOU CALL THAT THING ON YOUR BUTT?

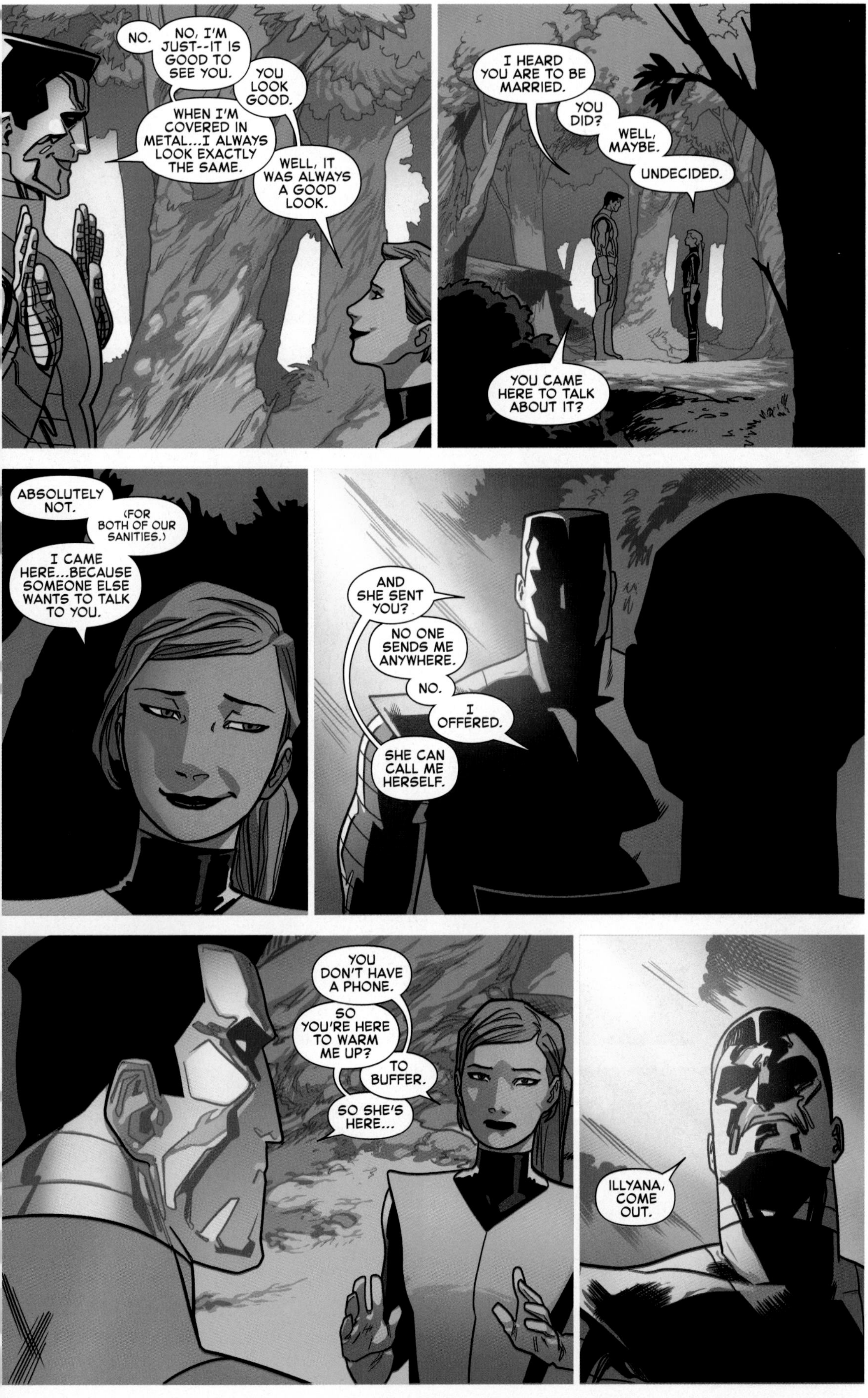
NO.
NO, I'M JUST--IT IS GOOD TO SEE YOU.
YOU LOOK GOOD.
WHEN I'M COVERED IN METAL...I ALWAYS LOOK EXACTLY THE SAME.
WELL, IT WAS ALWAYS A GOOD LOOK.
I HEARD YOU ARE TO BE MARRIED.
YOU DID?
WELL, MAYBE.
UNDECIDED.
YOU CAME HERE TO TALK ABOUT IT?
ABSOLUTELY NOT.
(FOR BOTH OF OUR SANITIES.)
I CAME HERE...BECAUSE SOMEONE ELSE WANTS TO TALK TO YOU.
AND SHE SENT YOU?
NO ONE SENDS ME ANYWHERE.
NO.
I OFFERED.
SHE CAN CALL ME HERSELF.
YOU DON'T HAVE A PHONE.
SO YOU'RE HERE TO WARM ME UP?
TO BUFFER.
SO SHE'S HERE...
ILLYANA, COME OUT.

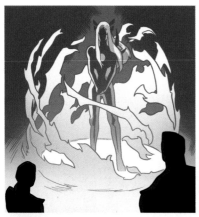

YOU LOOK EXACTLY THE SAME, BROTHER.

THAT'S EXACTLY WHAT I SAID.

YOU LOOK QUITE DIFFERENT.

I AM DIFFERENT. I HAVE BEEN TEACHING, AND I HAVE BEEN TRAINING WITH DOCTOR STRANGE.

REALLY?

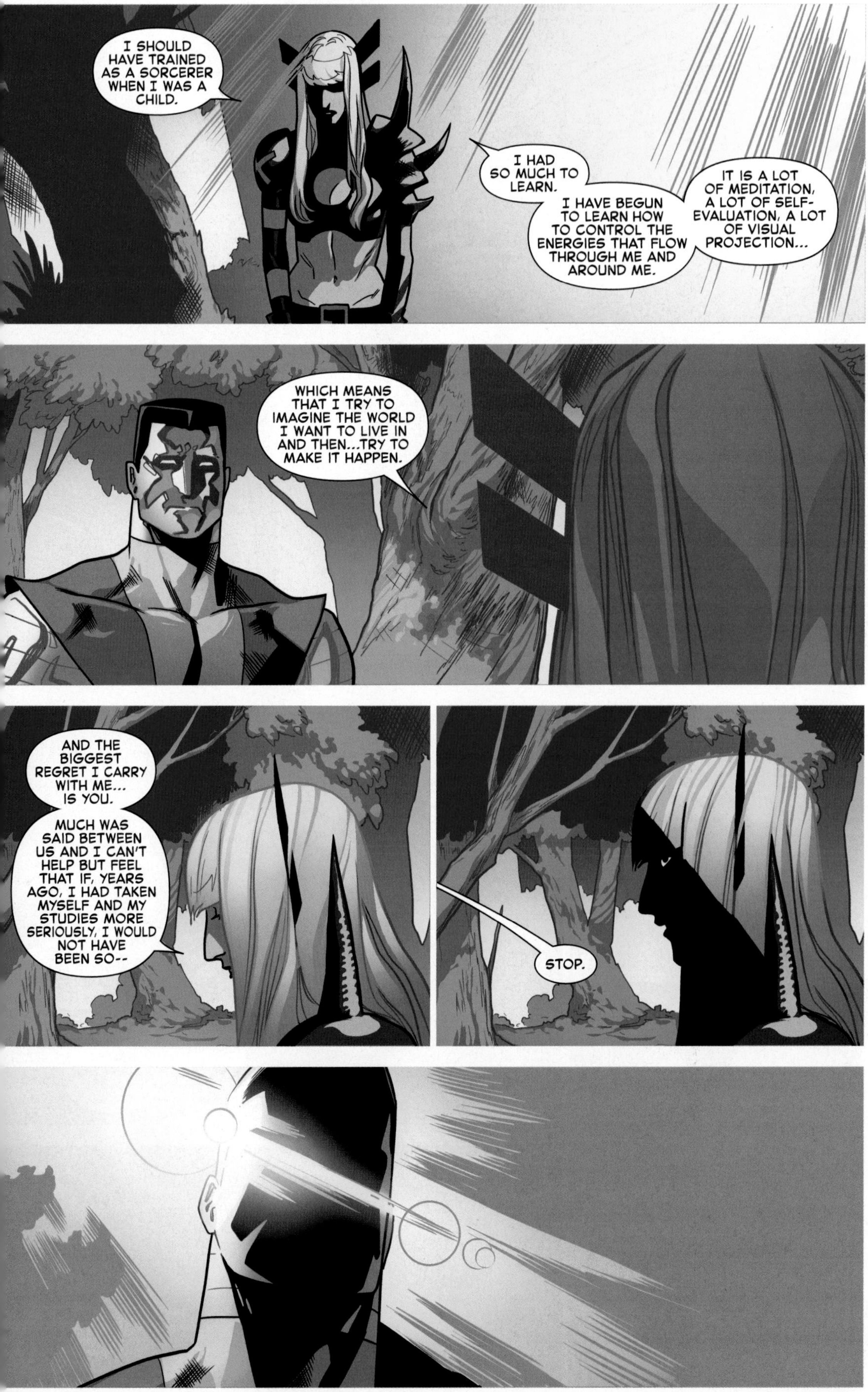
I SHOULD HAVE TRAINED AS A SORCERER WHEN I WAS A CHILD.
I HAD SO MUCH TO LEARN.
I HAVE BEGUN TO LEARN HOW TO CONTROL THE ENERGIES THAT FLOW THROUGH ME AND AROUND ME.
IT IS A LOT OF MEDITATION, A LOT OF SELF-EVALUATION, A LOT OF VISUAL PROJECTION...
WHICH MEANS THAT I TRY TO IMAGINE THE WORLD I WANT TO LIVE IN AND THEN...TRY TO MAKE IT HAPPEN.
AND THE BIGGEST REGRET I CARRY WITH ME... IS YOU.
MUCH WAS SAID BETWEEN US AND I CAN'T HELP BUT FEEL THAT IF, YEARS AGO, I HAD TAKEN MYSELF AND MY STUDIES MORE SERIOUSLY, I WOULD NOT HAVE BEEN SO--
STOP.

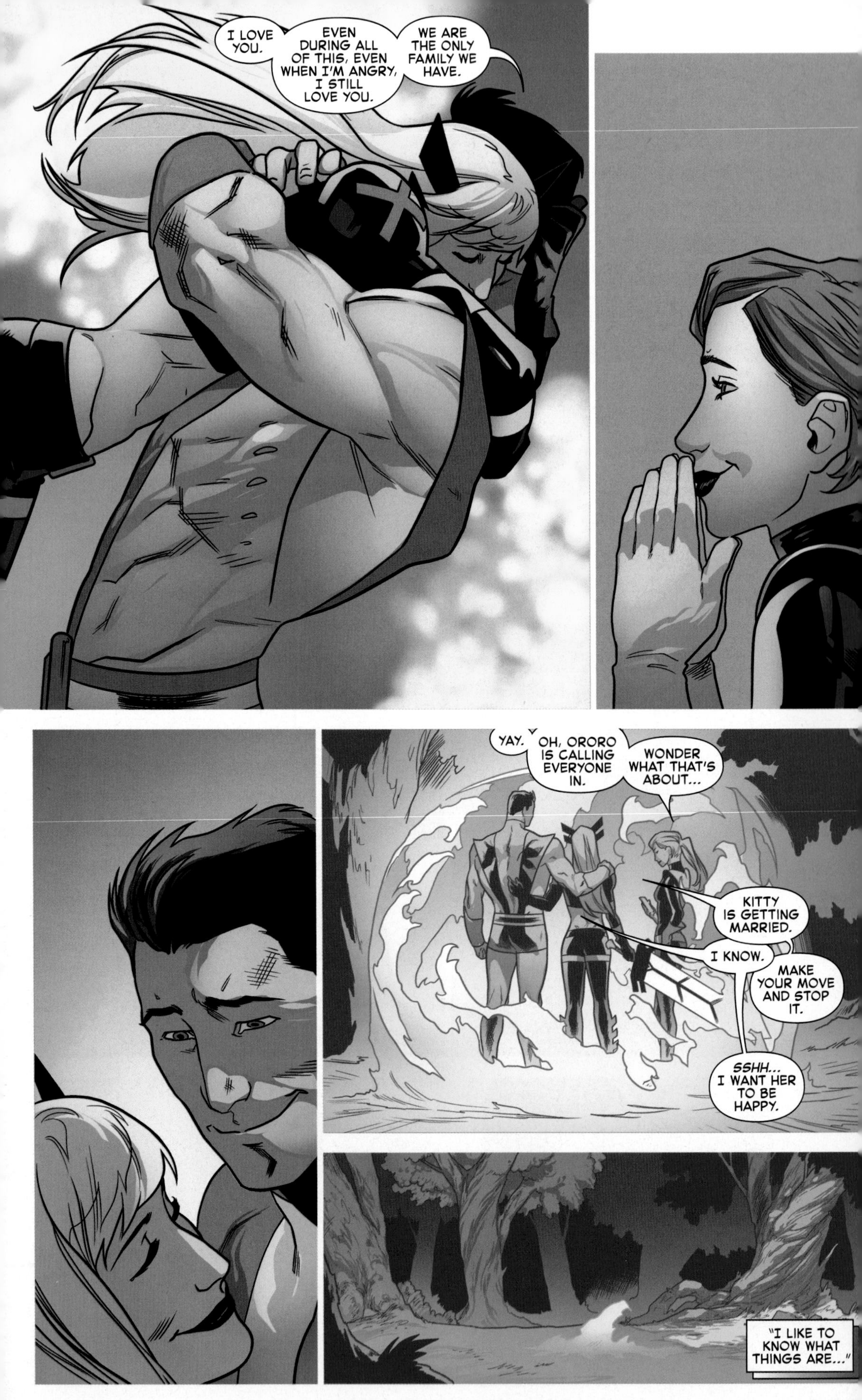
I LOVE YOU.
EVEN DURING ALL OF THIS, EVEN WHEN I'M ANGRY, I STILL LOVE YOU.
WE ARE THE ONLY FAMILY WE HAVE.
YAY.
OH, ORORO IS CALLING EVERYONE IN.
WONDER WHAT THAT'S ABOUT...
KITTY IS GETTING MARRIED.
I KNOW.
MAKE YOUR MOVE AND STOP IT.
SSHH... I WANT HER TO BE HAPPY.
"I LIKE TO KNOW WHAT THINGS ARE..."

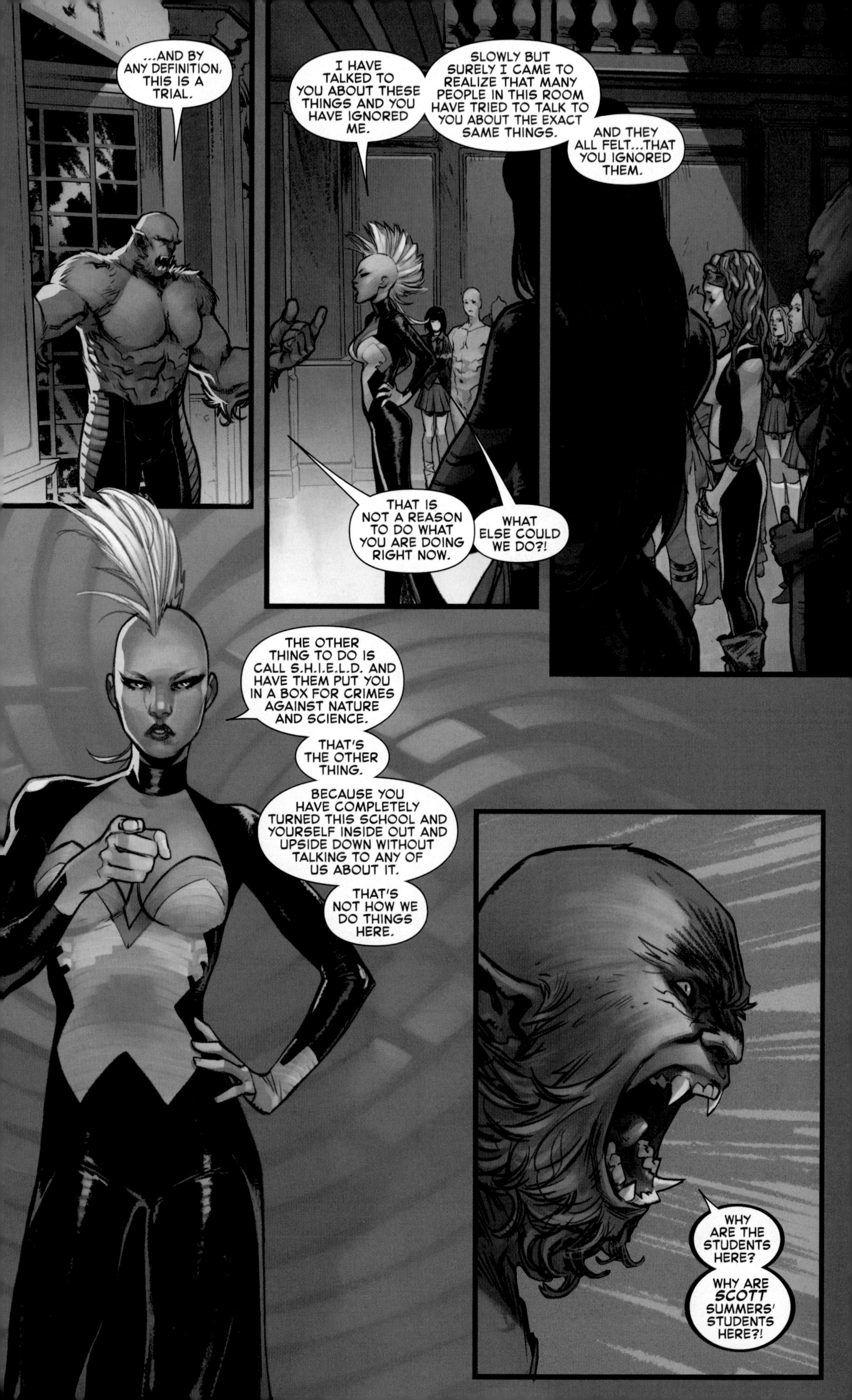
...AND BY ANY DEFINITION, THIS IS A TRIAL.
I HAVE TALKED TO YOU ABOUT THESE THINGS AND YOU HAVE IGNORED ME.
SLOWLY BUT SURELY I CAME TO REALIZE THAT MANY PEOPLE IN THIS ROOM HAVE TRIED TO TALK TO YOU ABOUT THE EXACT SAME THINGS.
AND THEY ALL FELT...THAT YOU IGNORED THEM.
THAT IS NOT A REASON TO DO WHAT YOU ARE DOING RIGHT NOW.
WHAT ELSE COULD WE DO?!
THE OTHER THING TO DO IS CALL S.H.I.E.L.D. AND HAVE THEM PUT YOU IN A BOX FOR CRIMES AGAINST NATURE AND SCIENCE.
THAT'S THE OTHER THING.
BECAUSE YOU HAVE COMPLETELY TURNED THIS SCHOOL AND YOURSELF INSIDE OUT AND UPSIDE DOWN WITHOUT TALKING TO ANY OF US ABOUT IT.
THAT'S NOT HOW WE DO THINGS HERE.
WHY ARE THE STUDENTS HERE?
WHY ARE *SCOTT* SUMMERS' STUDENTS HERE?!

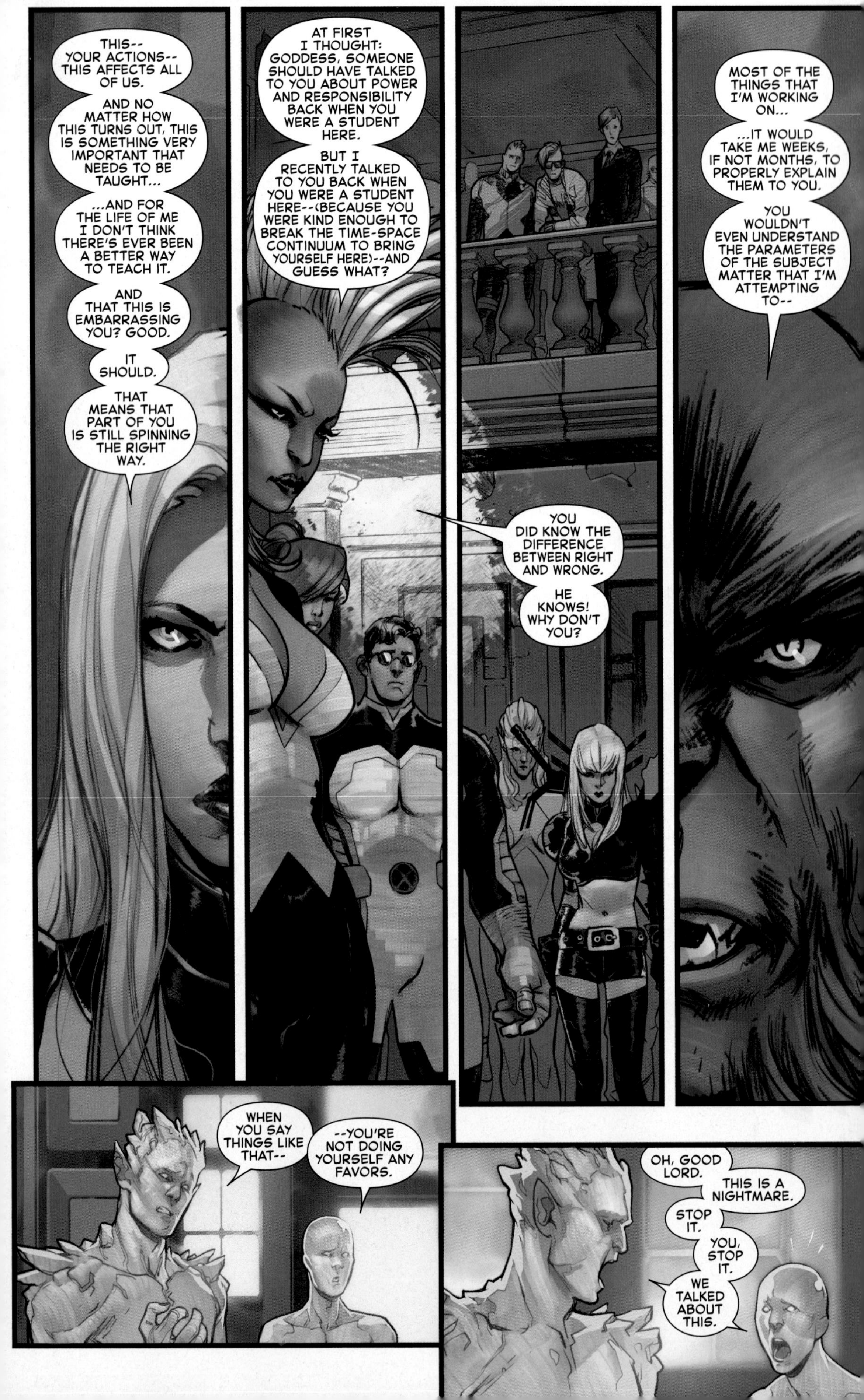
THIS-- YOUR ACTIONS-- THIS AFFECTS ALL OF US.
AND NO MATTER HOW THIS TURNS OUT, THIS IS SOMETHING VERY IMPORTANT THAT NEEDS TO BE TAUGHT...
...AND FOR THE LIFE OF ME I DON'T THINK THERE'S EVER BEEN A BETTER WAY TO TEACH IT.
AND THAT THIS IS EMBARRASSING YOU? GOOD.
IT SHOULD.
THAT MEANS THAT PART OF YOU IS STILL SPINNING THE RIGHT WAY.
AT FIRST I THOUGHT: GODDESS, SOMEONE SHOULD HAVE TALKED TO YOU ABOUT POWER AND RESPONSIBILITY BACK WHEN YOU WERE A STUDENT HERE.
BUT I RECENTLY TALKED TO YOU BACK WHEN YOU WERE A STUDENT HERE--(BECAUSE YOU WERE KIND ENOUGH TO BREAK THE TIME-SPACE CONTINUUM TO BRING YOURSELF HERE)--AND GUESS WHAT?
YOU DID KNOW THE DIFFERENCE BETWEEN RIGHT AND WRONG.
HE KNOWS! WHY DON'T YOU?
MOST OF THE THINGS THAT I'M WORKING ON...
...IT WOULD TAKE ME WEEKS, IF NOT MONTHS, TO PROPERLY EXPLAIN THEM TO YOU.
YOU WOULDN'T EVEN UNDERSTAND THE PARAMETERS OF THE SUBJECT MATTER THAT I'M ATTEMPTING TO--
WHEN YOU SAY THINGS LIKE THAT--
--YOU'RE NOT DOING YOURSELF ANY FAVORS.
OH, GOOD LORD.
THIS IS A NIGHTMARE.
STOP IT.
YOU, STOP IT.
WE TALKED ABOUT THIS.

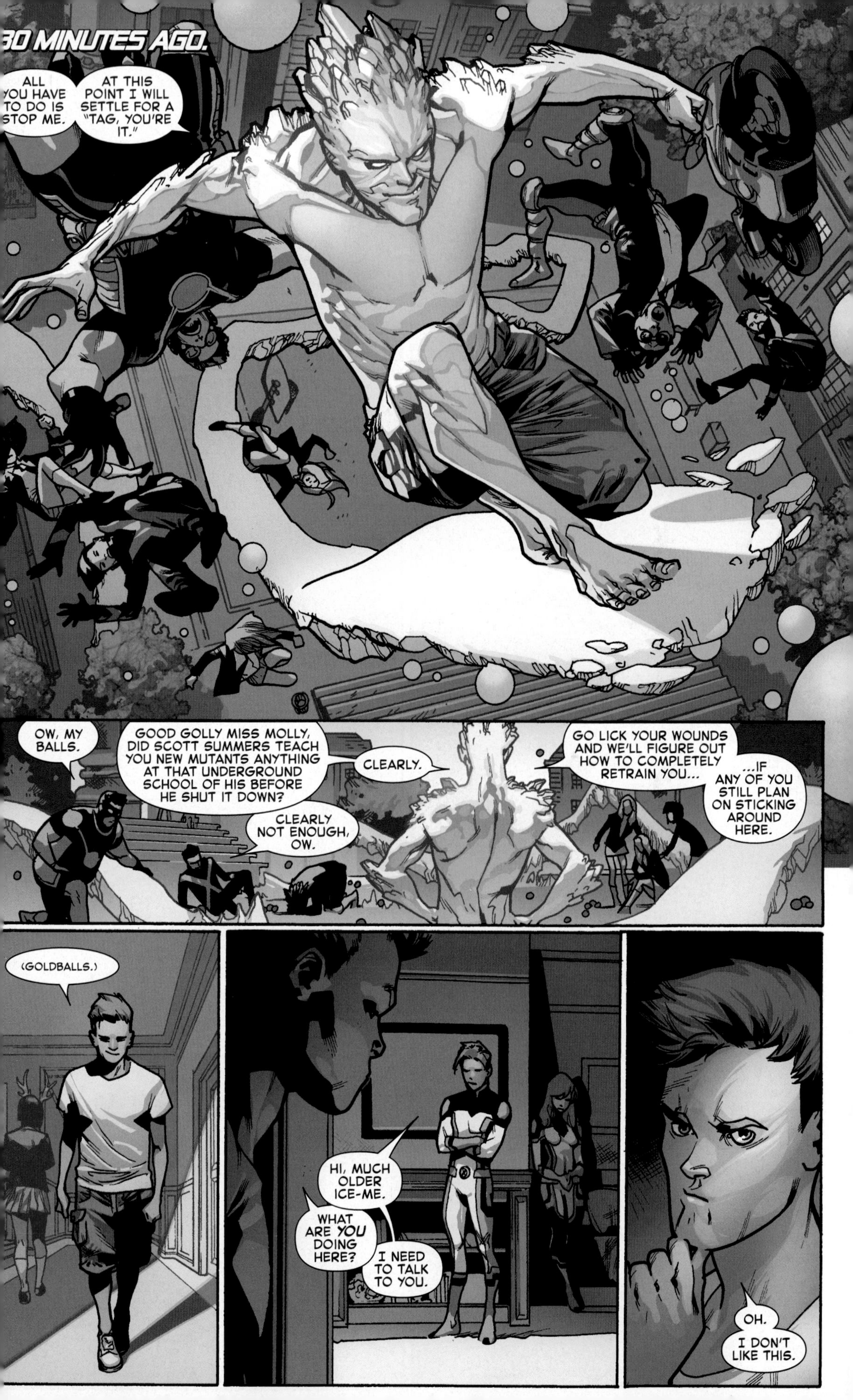
30 MINUTES AGO.
ALL YOU HAVE TO DO IS STOP ME.
AT THIS POINT I WILL SETTLE FOR A "TAG, YOU'RE IT."
OW, MY BALLS.
GOOD GOLLY MISS MOLLY, DID SCOTT SUMMERS TEACH YOU NEW MUTANTS ANYTHING AT THAT UNDERGROUND SCHOOL OF HIS BEFORE HE SHUT IT DOWN?
CLEARLY.
CLEARLY NOT ENOUGH, OW.
GO LICK YOUR WOUNDS AND WE'LL FIGURE OUT HOW TO COMPLETELY RETRAIN YOU...
...IF ANY OF YOU STILL PLAN ON STICKING AROUND HERE.
(GOLDBALLS.)
HI, MUCH OLDER ICE-ME.
WHAT ARE *YOU* DOING HERE?
I NEED TO TALK TO YOU.
OH.
I DON'T LIKE THIS.

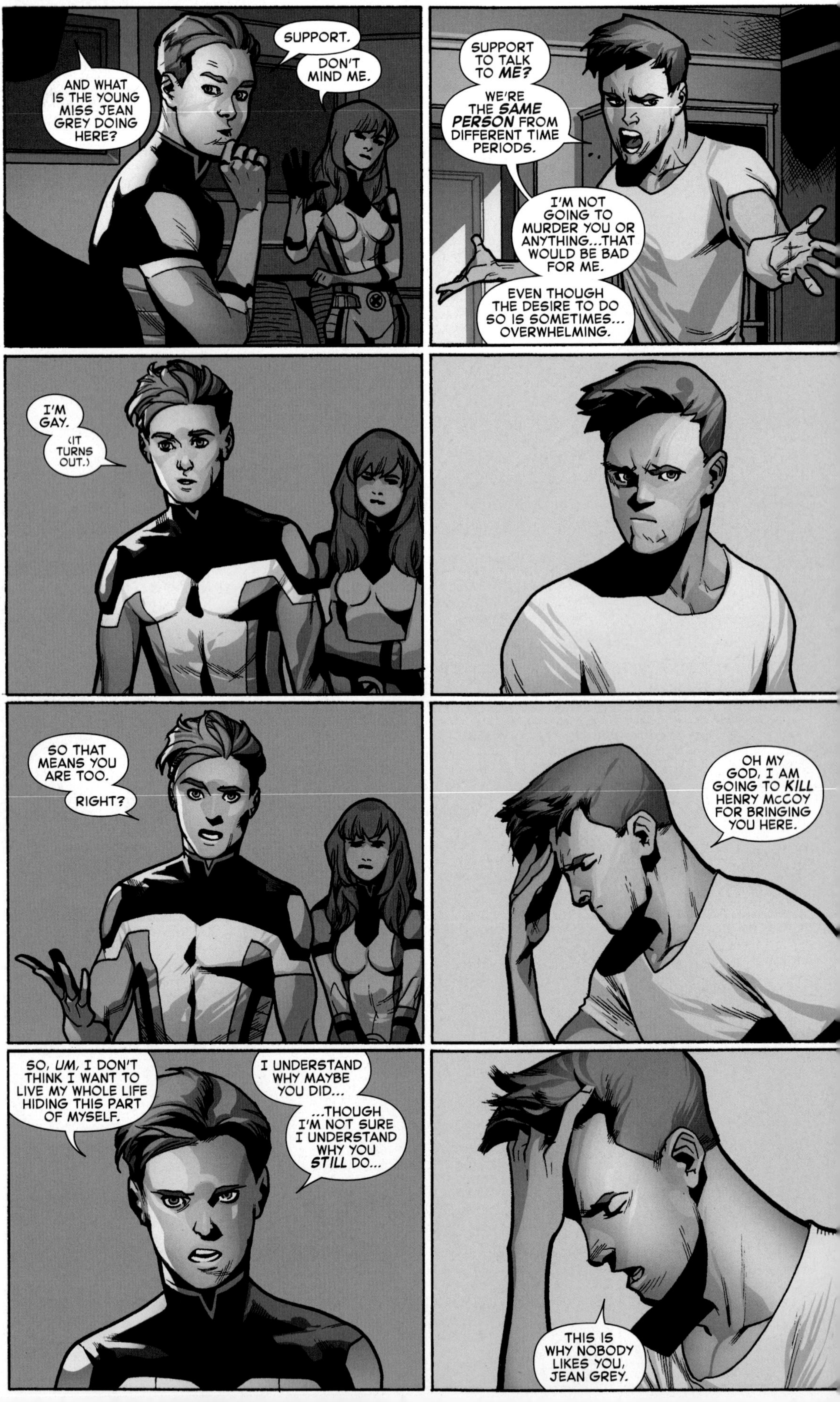
AND WHAT IS THE YOUNG MISS JEAN GREY DOING HERE?
SUPPORT.
DON'T MIND ME.
SUPPORT TO TALK TO *ME?*
WE'RE THE *SAME PERSON* FROM DIFFERENT TIME PERIODS.
I'M NOT GOING TO MURDER YOU OR ANYTHING...THAT WOULD BE BAD FOR ME.
EVEN THOUGH THE DESIRE TO DO SO IS SOMETIMES... OVERWHELMING.
I'M GAY.
(IT TURNS OUT.)
SO THAT MEANS YOU ARE TOO.
RIGHT?
OH MY GOD, I AM GOING TO *KILL* HENRY McCOY FOR BRINGING YOU HERE.
SO, *UM,* I DON'T THINK I WANT TO LIVE MY WHOLE LIFE HIDING THIS PART OF MYSELF.
I UNDERSTAND WHY MAYBE YOU DID...
...THOUGH I'M NOT SURE I UNDERSTAND WHY YOU *STILL* DO...
THIS IS WHY NOBODY LIKES YOU, JEAN GREY.

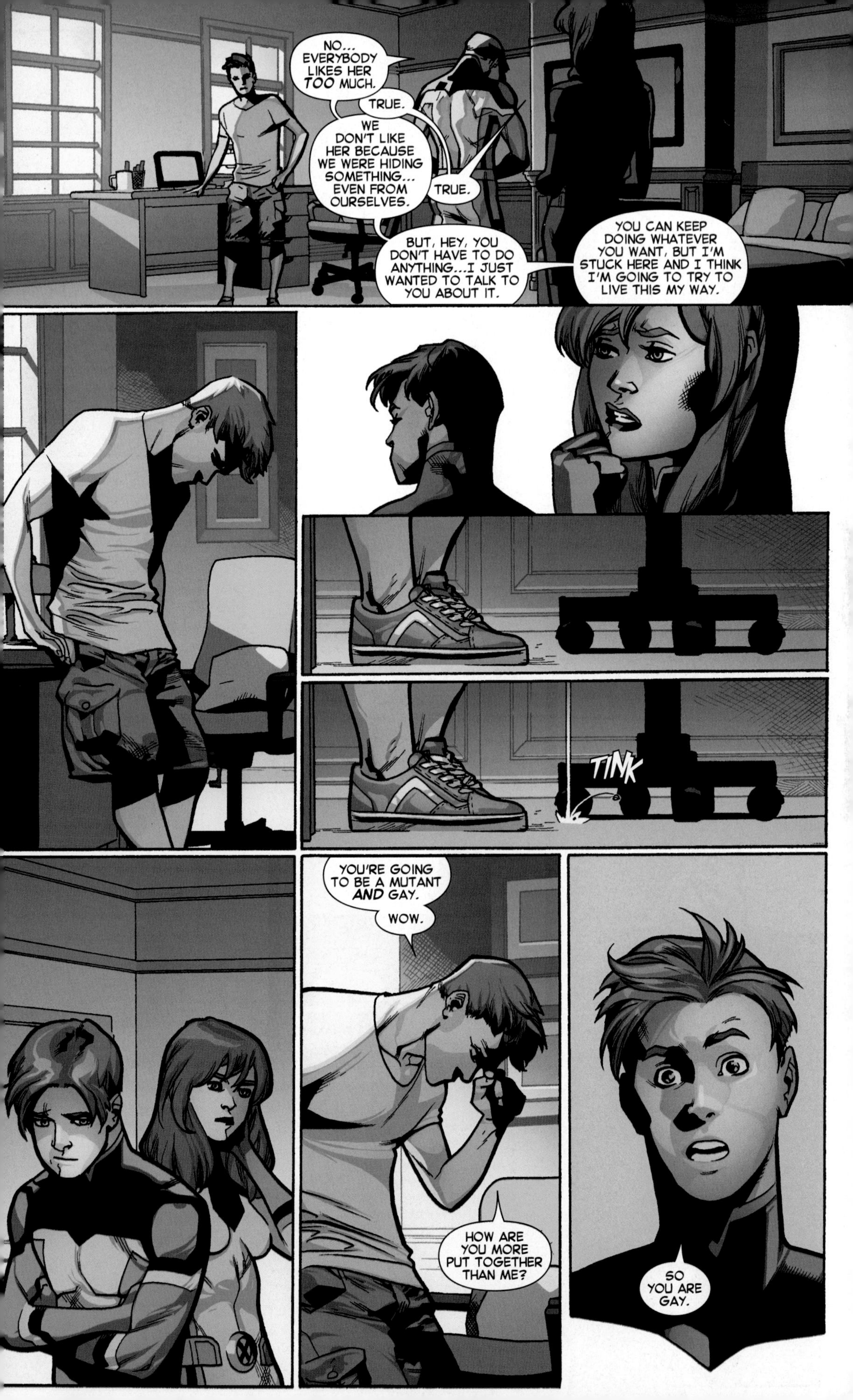
NO... EVERYBODY LIKES HER *TOO* MUCH.
TRUE.
WE DON'T LIKE HER BECAUSE WE WERE HIDING SOMETHING... EVEN FROM OURSELVES.
TRUE.
BUT, HEY, YOU DON'T HAVE TO DO ANYTHING...I JUST WANTED TO TALK TO YOU ABOUT IT.
YOU CAN KEEP DOING WHATEVER YOU WANT, BUT I'M STUCK HERE AND I THINK I'M GOING TO TRY TO LIVE THIS MY WAY.
TINK
YOU'RE GOING TO BE A MUTANT **AND** GAY.
WOW.
HOW ARE YOU MORE PUT TOGETHER THAN ME?
SO YOU ARE GAY.

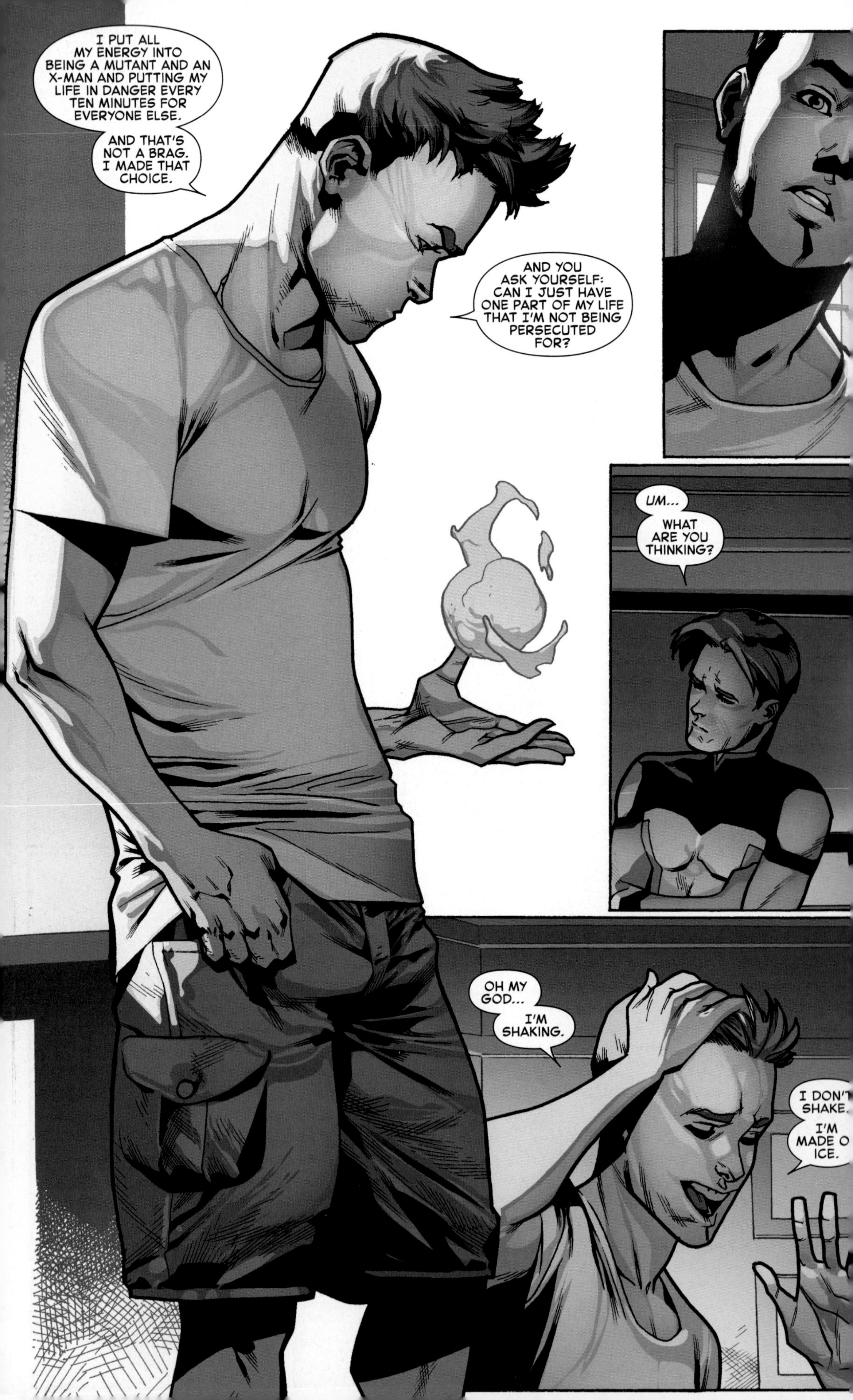
I PUT ALL MY ENERGY INTO BEING A MUTANT AND AN X-MAN AND PUTTING MY LIFE IN DANGER EVERY TEN MINUTES FOR EVERYONE ELSE.
AND THAT'S NOT A BRAG. I MADE THAT CHOICE.
AND YOU ASK YOURSELF: CAN I JUST HAVE ONE PART OF MY LIFE THAT I'M NOT BEING PERSECUTED FOR?
UM...
WHAT ARE YOU THINKING?
OH MY GOD...
I'M SHAKING.
I DON'T SHAKE.
I'M MADE O ICE.

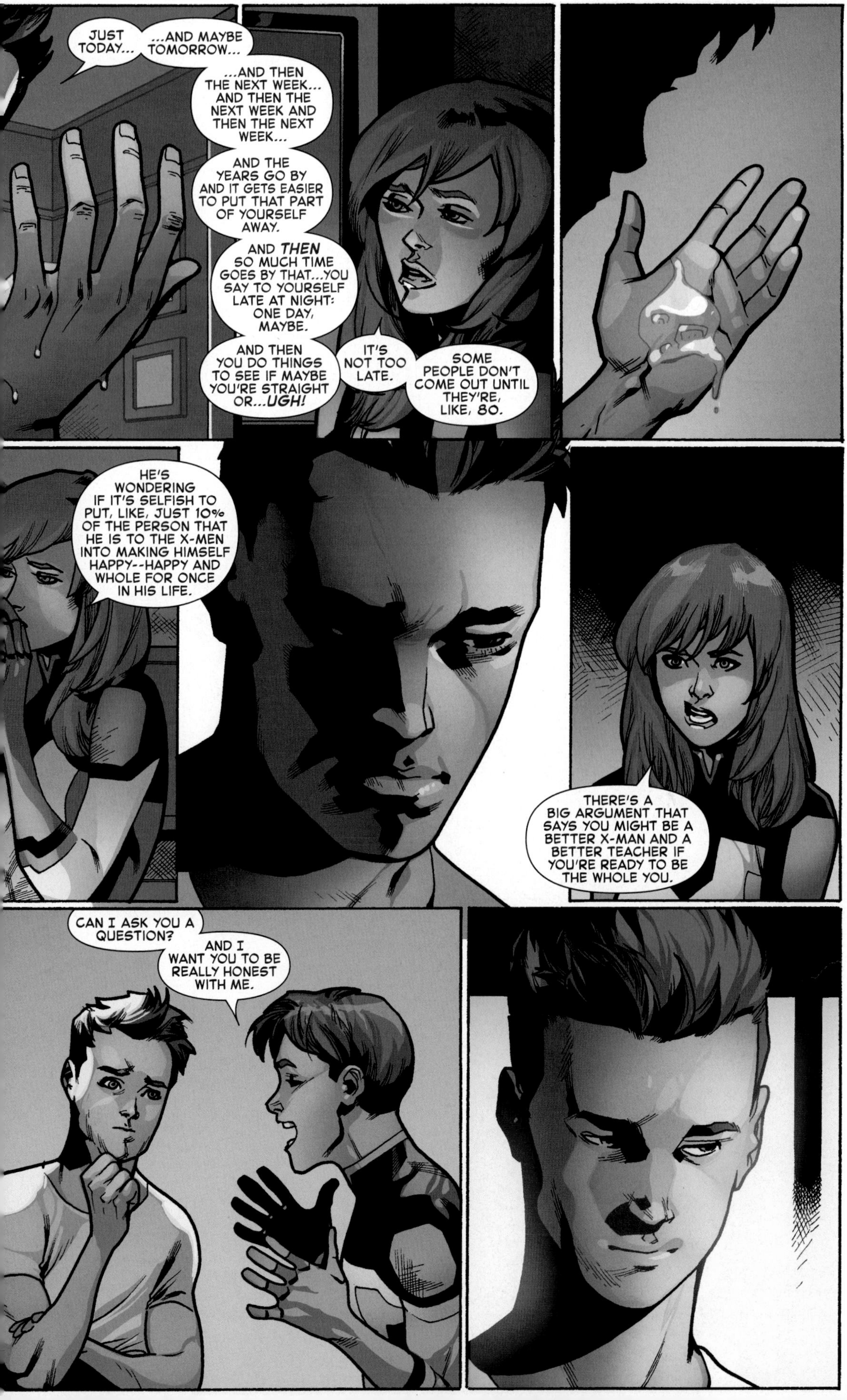
JUST TODAY...
...AND MAYBE TOMORROW...
...AND THEN THE NEXT WEEK... AND THEN THE NEXT WEEK AND THEN THE NEXT WEEK...
AND THE YEARS GO BY AND IT GETS EASIER TO PUT THAT PART OF YOURSELF AWAY.
AND *THEN* SO MUCH TIME GOES BY THAT...YOU SAY TO YOURSELF LATE AT NIGHT: ONE DAY, MAYBE.
AND THEN YOU DO THINGS TO SEE IF MAYBE YOU'RE STRAIGHT OR...*UGH!*
IT'S NOT TOO LATE.
SOME PEOPLE DON'T COME OUT UNTIL THEY'RE, LIKE, 80.
HE'S WONDERING IF IT'S SELFISH TO PUT, LIKE, JUST 10% OF THE PERSON THAT HE IS TO THE X-MEN INTO MAKING HIMSELF HAPPY--HAPPY AND WHOLE FOR ONCE IN HIS LIFE.
THERE'S A BIG ARGUMENT THAT SAYS YOU MIGHT BE A BETTER X-MAN AND A BETTER TEACHER IF YOU'RE READY TO BE THE WHOLE YOU.
CAN I ASK YOU A QUESTION?
AND I WANT YOU TO BE REALLY HONEST WITH ME.

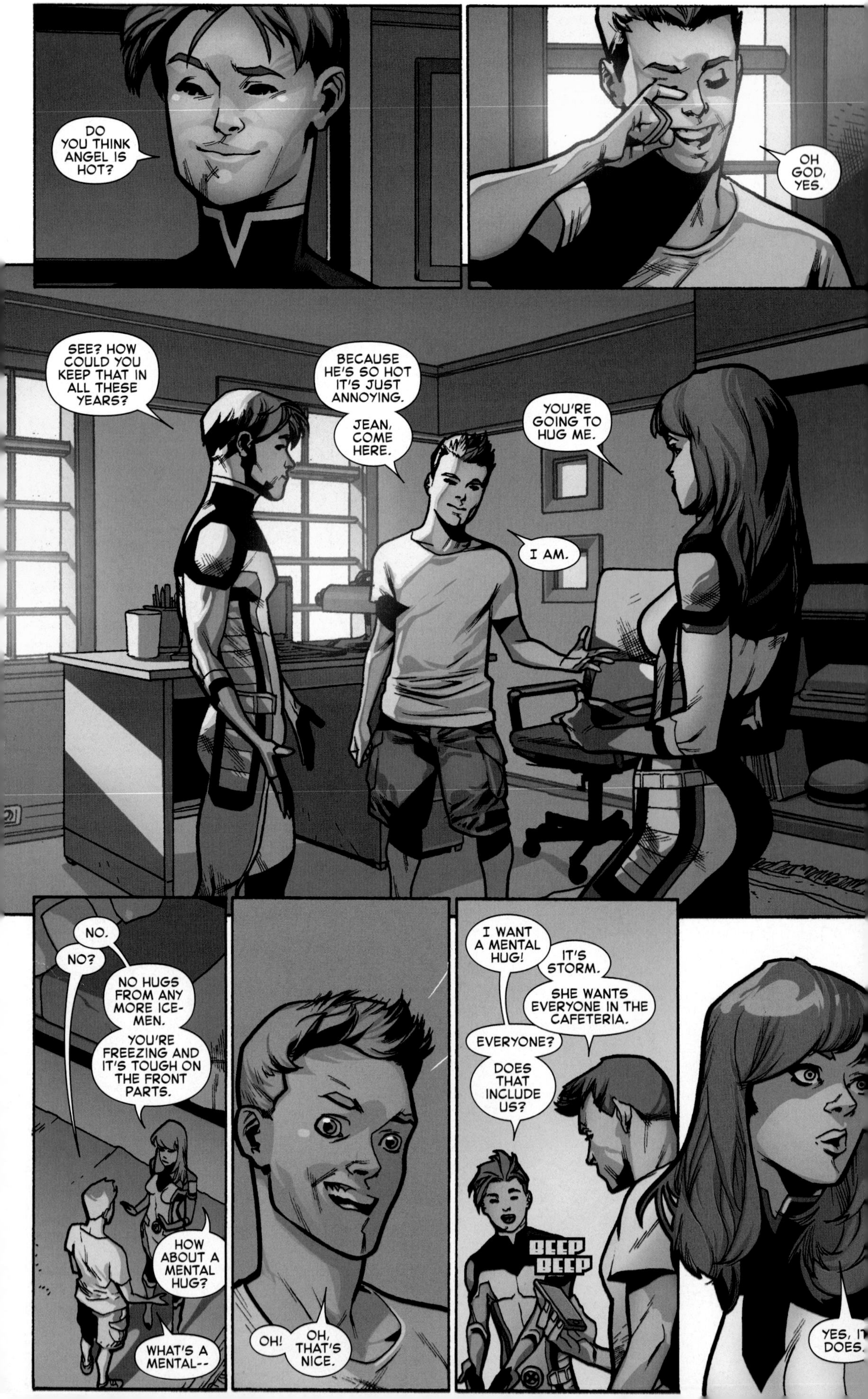
DO YOU THINK ANGEL IS HOT?
OH GOD, YES.
SEE? HOW COULD YOU KEEP THAT IN ALL THESE YEARS?
BECAUSE HE'S SO HOT IT'S JUST ANNOYING.
JEAN, COME HERE.
YOU'RE GOING TO HUG ME.
I AM.
NO.
NO?
NO HUGS FROM ANY MORE ICE-MEN.
YOU'RE FREEZING AND IT'S TOUGH ON THE FRONT PARTS.
HOW ABOUT A MENTAL HUG?
WHAT'S A MENTAL--
OH!
OH, THAT'S NICE.
I WANT A MENTAL HUG!
IT'S STORM.
SHE WANTS EVERYONE IN THE CAFETERIA.
EVERYONE?
DOES THAT INCLUDE US?
BEEP BEEP
YES, IT DOES.

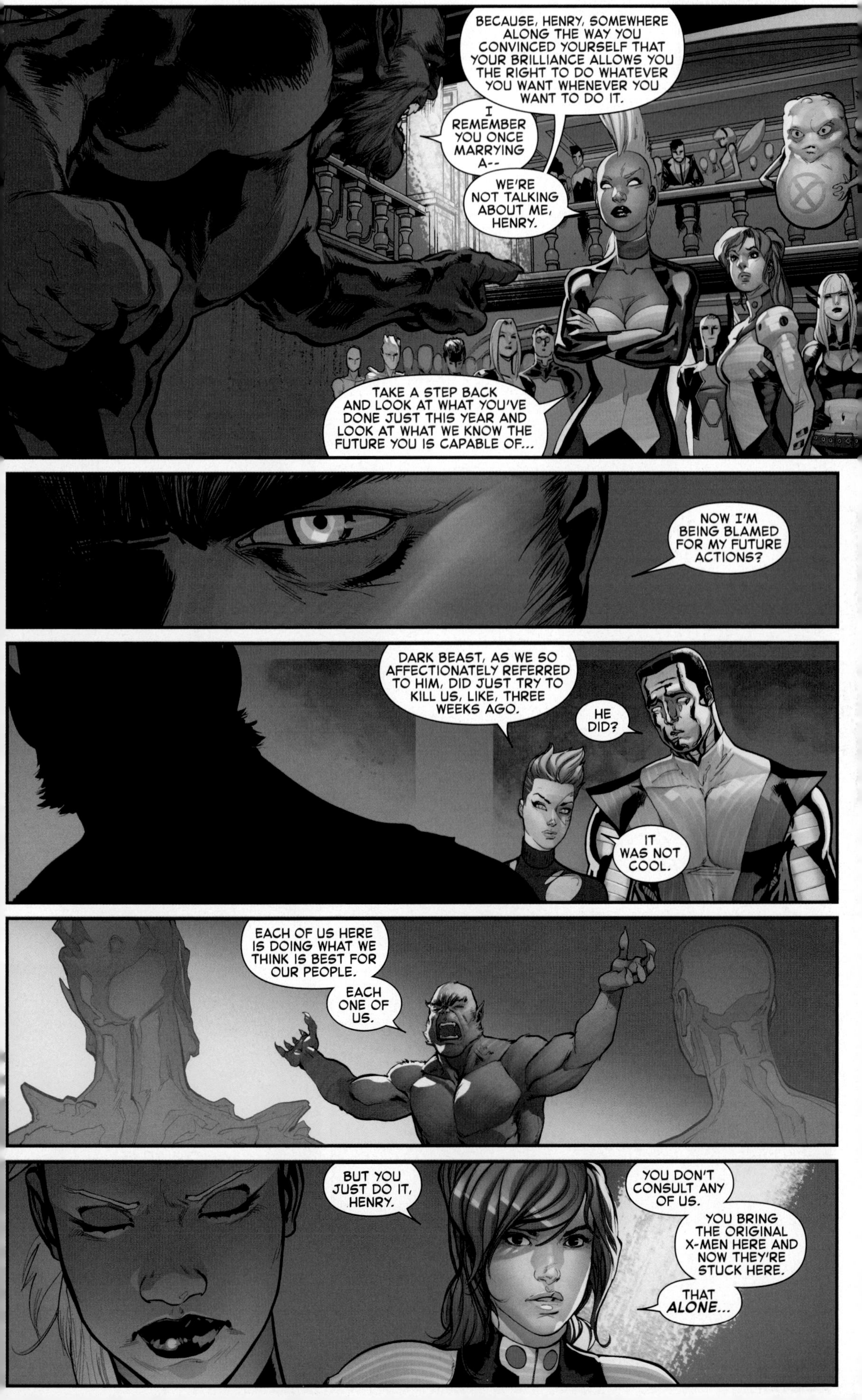
BECAUSE, HENRY, SOMEWHERE ALONG THE WAY YOU CONVINCED YOURSELF THAT YOUR BRILLIANCE ALLOWS YOU THE RIGHT TO DO WHATEVER YOU WANT WHENEVER YOU WANT TO DO IT.
I REMEMBER YOU ONCE MARRYING A--
WE'RE NOT TALKING ABOUT ME, HENRY.
TAKE A STEP BACK AND LOOK AT WHAT YOU'VE DONE JUST THIS YEAR AND LOOK AT WHAT WE KNOW THE FUTURE YOU IS CAPABLE OF...
NOW I'M BEING BLAMED FOR MY FUTURE ACTIONS?
DARK BEAST, AS WE SO AFFECTIONATELY REFERRED TO HIM, DID JUST TRY TO KILL US, LIKE, THREE WEEKS AGO.
HE DID?
IT WAS NOT COOL.
EACH OF US HERE IS DOING WHAT WE THINK IS BEST FOR OUR PEOPLE.
EACH ONE OF US.
BUT YOU JUST DO IT, HENRY.
YOU DON'T CONSULT ANY OF US.
YOU BRING THE ORIGINAL X-MEN HERE AND NOW THEY'RE STUCK HERE.
THAT *ALONE*...

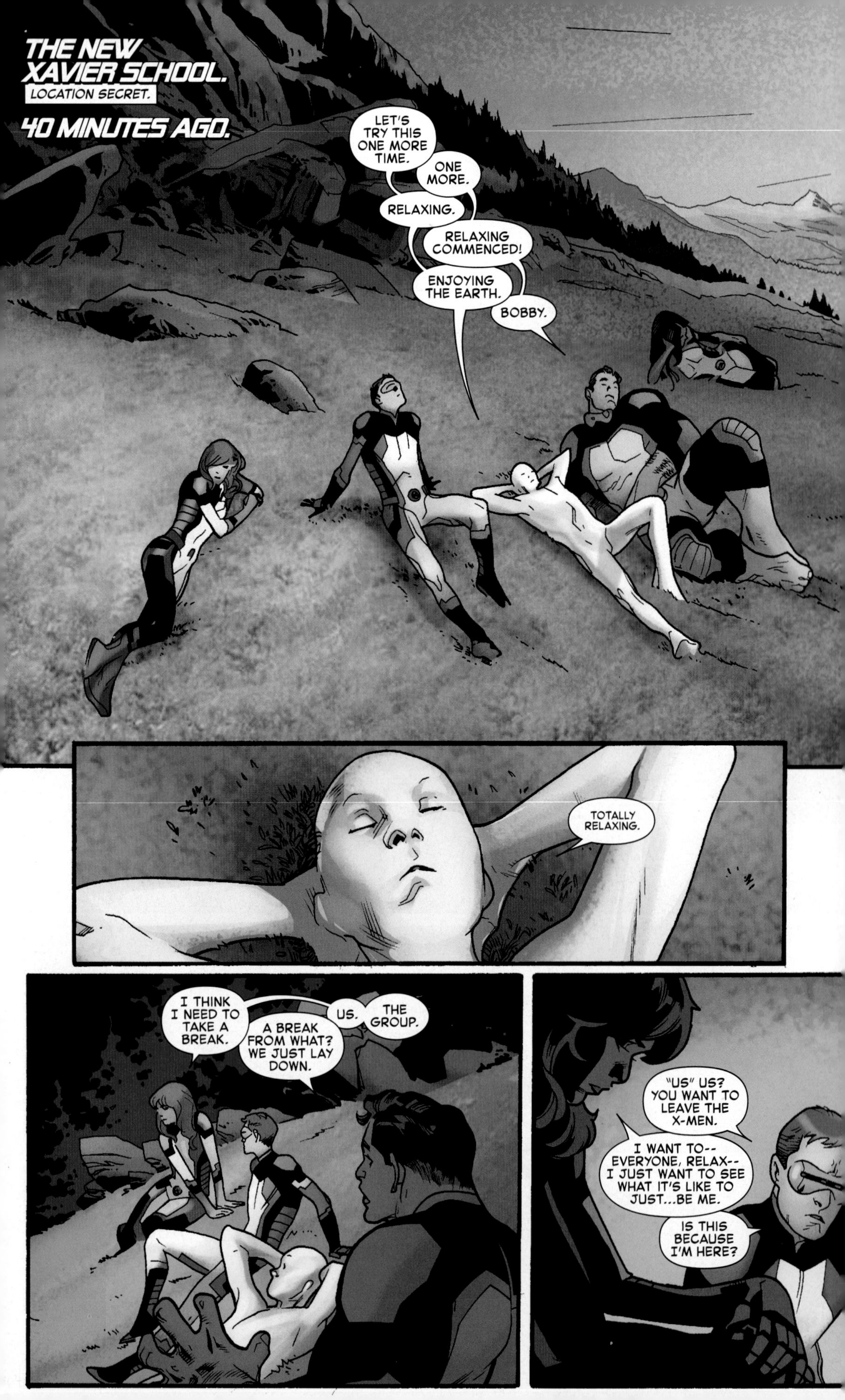
THE NEW XAVIER SCHOOL.
LOCATION SECRET.
40 MINUTES AGO.
LET'S TRY THIS ONE MORE TIME.
ONE MORE.
RELAXING.
RELAXING COMMENCED!
ENJOYING THE EARTH.
BOBBY.
TOTALLY RELAXING.
I THINK I NEED TO TAKE A BREAK.
A BREAK FROM WHAT? WE JUST LAY DOWN.
US.
THE GROUP.
"US" US? YOU WANT TO LEAVE THE X-MEN.
I WANT TO-- EVERYONE, RELAX-- I JUST WANT TO SEE WHAT IT'S LIKE TO JUST...BE ME.
IS THIS BECAUSE I'M HERE?

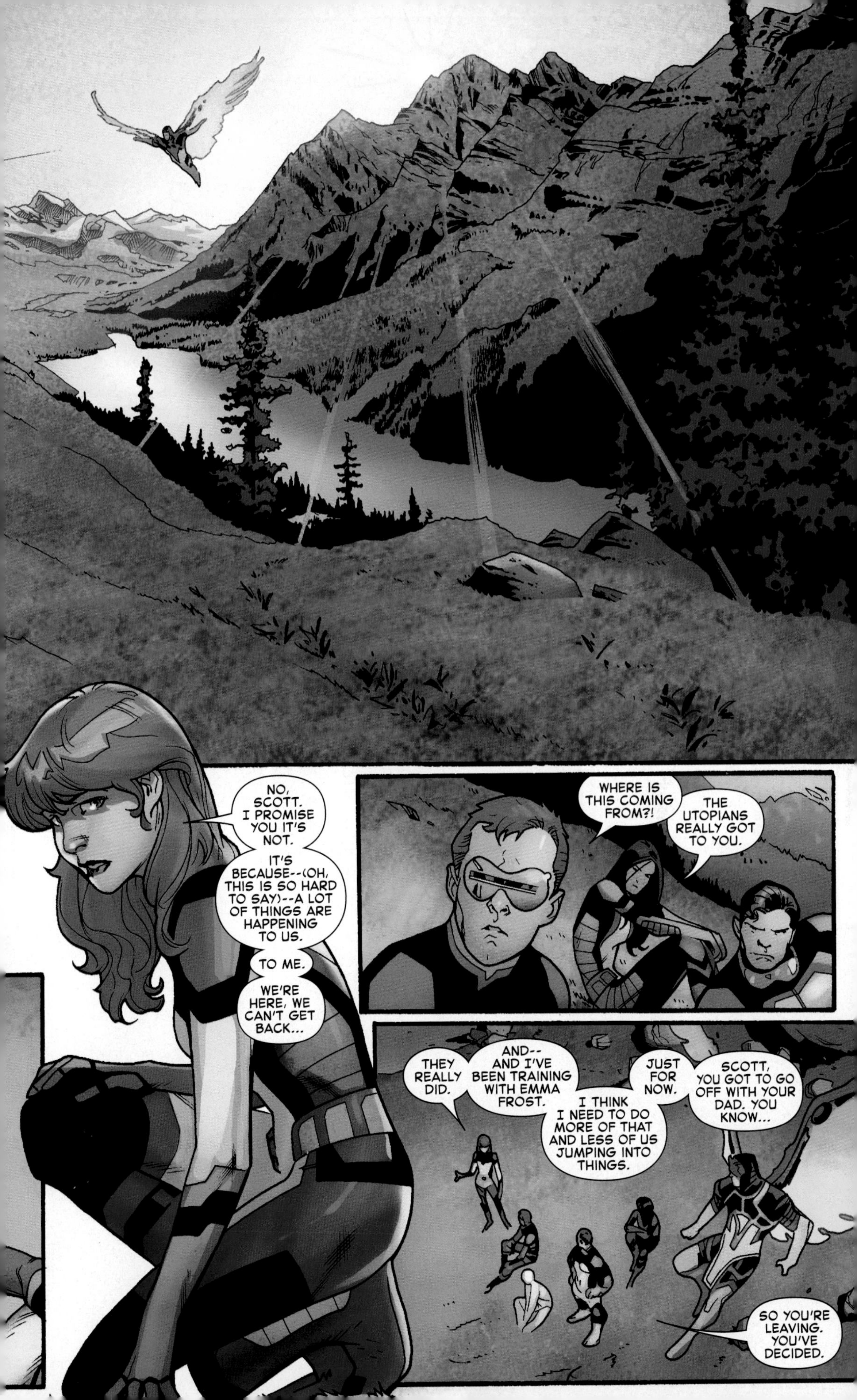

NO, SCOTT. I PROMISE YOU IT'S NOT.
IT'S BECAUSE--(OH, THIS IS SO HARD TO SAY)--A LOT OF THINGS ARE HAPPENING TO US.
TO ME.
WE'RE HERE, WE CAN'T GET BACK...
WHERE IS THIS COMING FROM?!
THE UTOPIANS REALLY GOT TO YOU.
THEY REALLY DID.
AND-- AND I'VE BEEN TRAINING WITH EMMA FROST.
I THINK I NEED TO DO MORE OF THAT AND LESS OF US JUMPING INTO THINGS.
JUST FOR NOW.
SCOTT, YOU GOT TO GO OFF WITH YOUR DAD. YOU KNOW...
SO YOU'RE LEAVING. YOU'VE DECIDED.

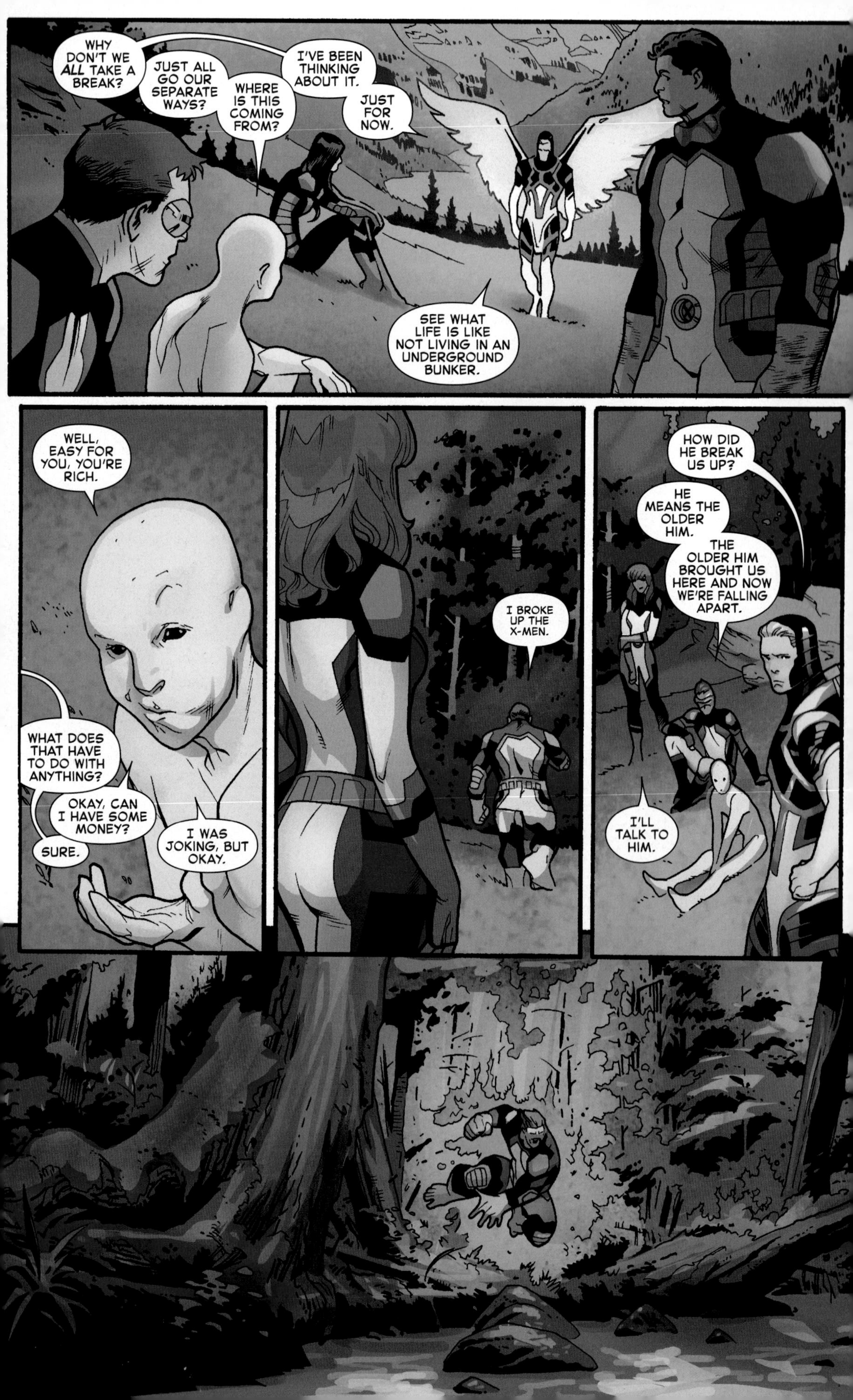
WHY DON'T WE ALL TAKE A BREAK?
JUST ALL GO OUR SEPARATE WAYS?
WHERE IS THIS COMING FROM?
I'VE BEEN THINKING ABOUT IT.
JUST FOR NOW.
SEE WHAT LIFE IS LIKE NOT LIVING IN AN UNDERGROUND BUNKER.
WELL, EASY FOR YOU, YOU'RE RICH.
WHAT DOES THAT HAVE TO DO WITH ANYTHING?
OKAY, CAN I HAVE SOME MONEY?
SURE.
I WAS JOKING, BUT OKAY.
I BROKE UP THE X-MEN.
HOW DID HE BREAK US UP?
HE MEANS THE OLDER HIM.
THE OLDER HIM BROUGHT US HERE AND NOW WE'RE FALLING APART.
I'LL TALK TO HIM.

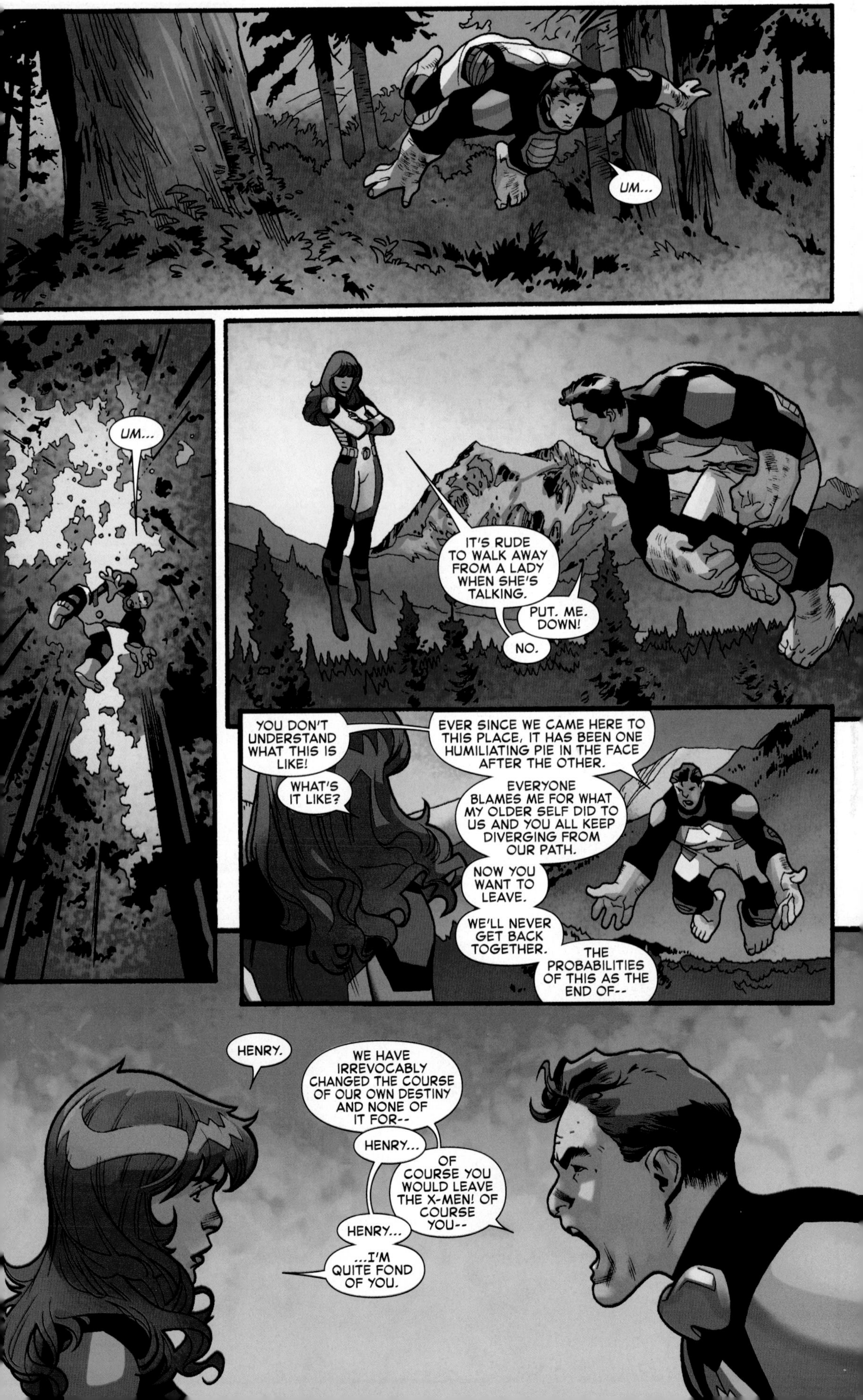
UM...
UM...
IT'S RUDE TO WALK AWAY FROM A LADY WHEN SHE'S TALKING.
PUT. ME. DOWN!
NO.
YOU DON'T UNDERSTAND WHAT THIS IS LIKE!
WHAT'S IT LIKE?
EVER SINCE WE CAME HERE TO THIS PLACE, IT HAS BEEN ONE HUMILIATING PIE IN THE FACE AFTER THE OTHER.
EVERYONE BLAMES ME FOR WHAT MY OLDER SELF DID TO US AND YOU ALL KEEP DIVERGING FROM OUR PATH.
NOW YOU WANT TO LEAVE.
WE'LL NEVER GET BACK TOGETHER.
THE PROBABILITIES OF THIS AS THE END OF--
HENRY.
WE HAVE IRREVOCABLY CHANGED THE COURSE OF OUR OWN DESTINY AND NONE OF IT FOR--
HENRY...
OF COURSE YOU WOULD LEAVE THE X-MEN! OF COURSE YOU--
HENRY...
...I'M QUITE FOND OF YOU.

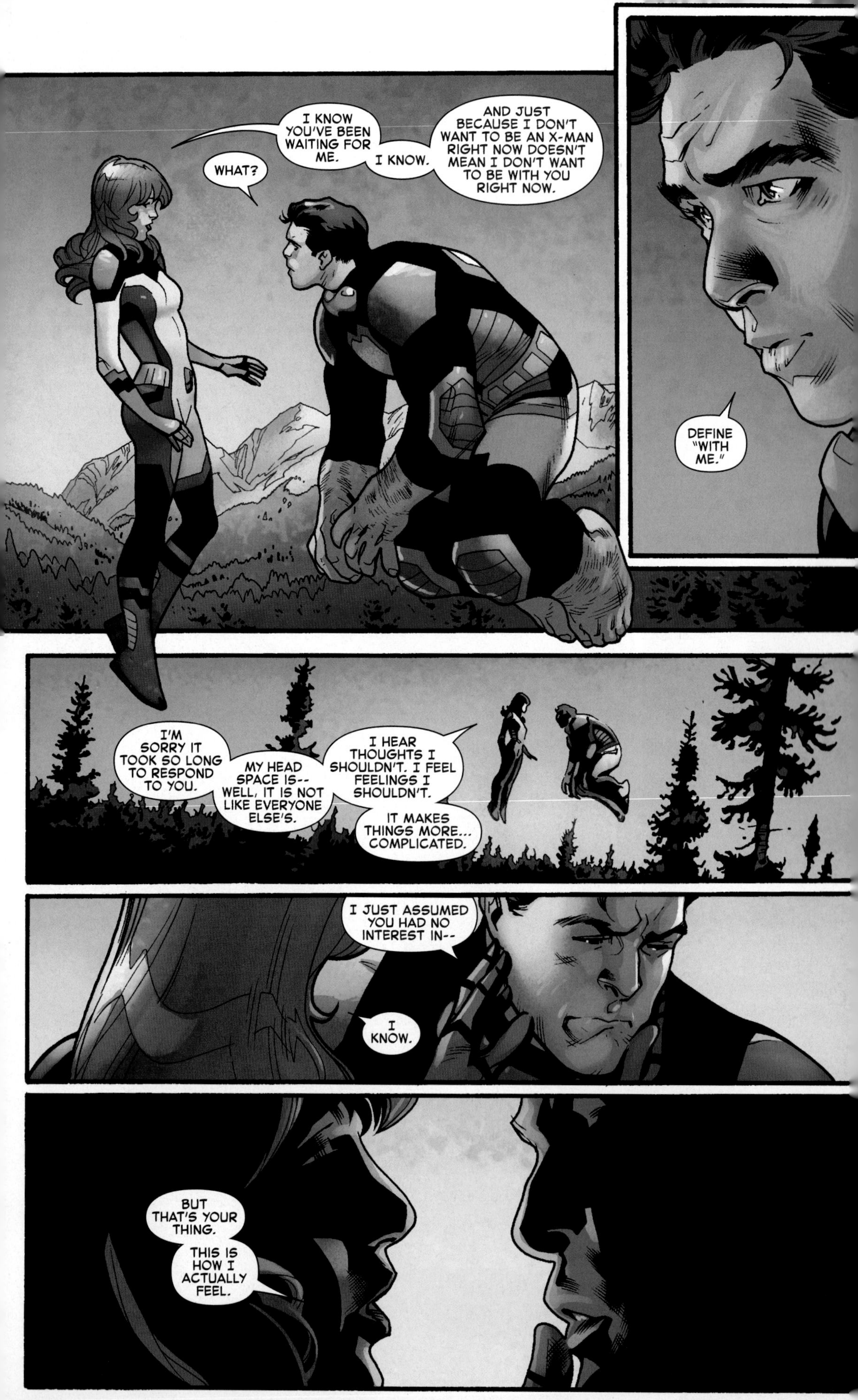
WHAT?
I KNOW YOU'VE BEEN WAITING FOR ME.
I KNOW.
AND JUST BECAUSE I DON'T WANT TO BE AN X-MAN RIGHT NOW DOESN'T MEAN I DON'T WANT TO BE WITH YOU RIGHT NOW.
DEFINE "WITH ME."
I'M SORRY IT TOOK SO LONG TO RESPOND TO YOU.
MY HEAD SPACE IS-- WELL, IT IS NOT LIKE EVERYONE ELSE'S.
I HEAR THOUGHTS I SHOULDN'T. I FEEL FEELINGS I SHOULDN'T.
IT MAKES THINGS MORE... COMPLICATED.
I JUST ASSUMED YOU HAD NO INTEREST IN--
I KNOW.
BUT THAT'S YOUR THING.
THIS IS HOW I ACTUALLY FEEL.

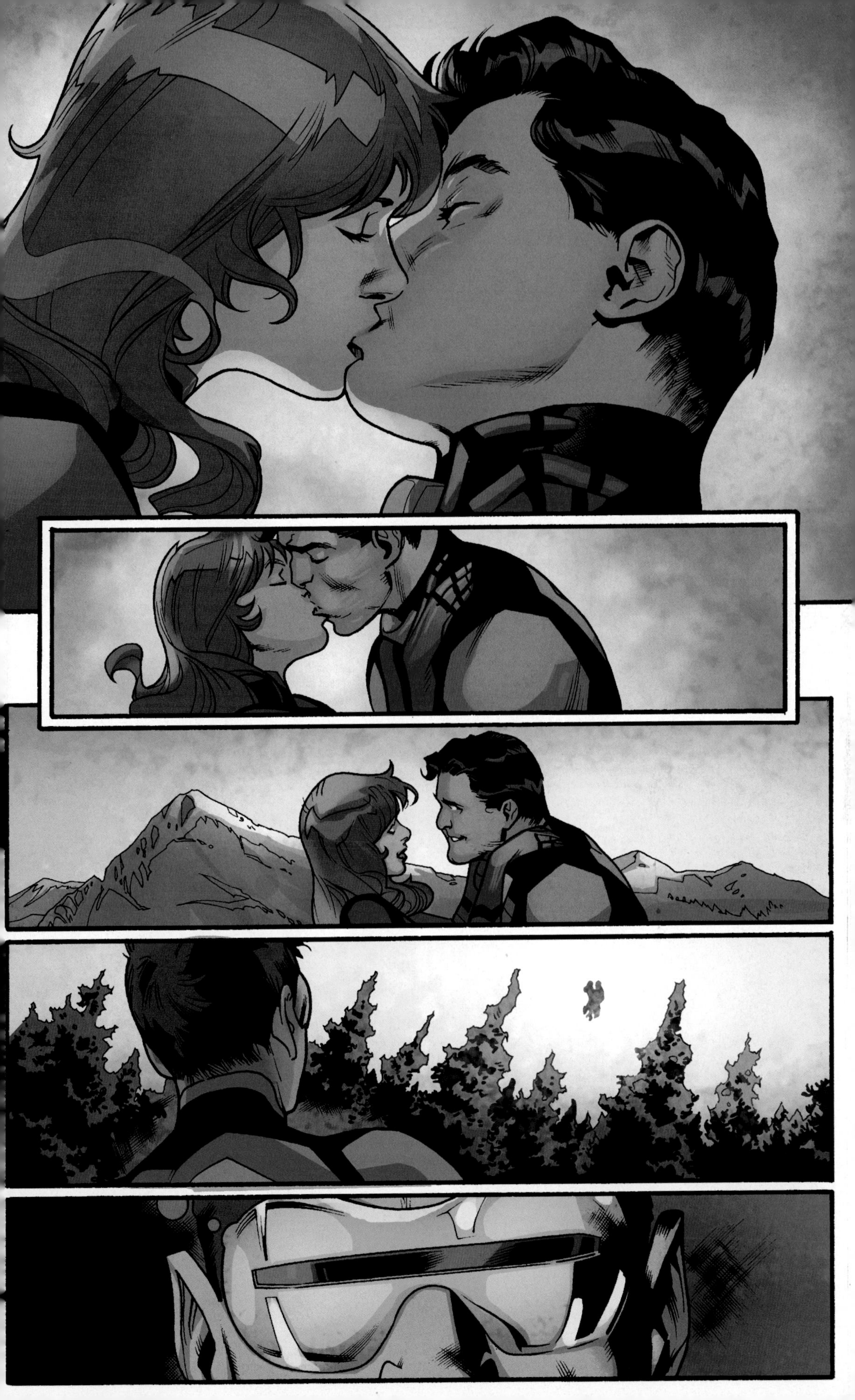

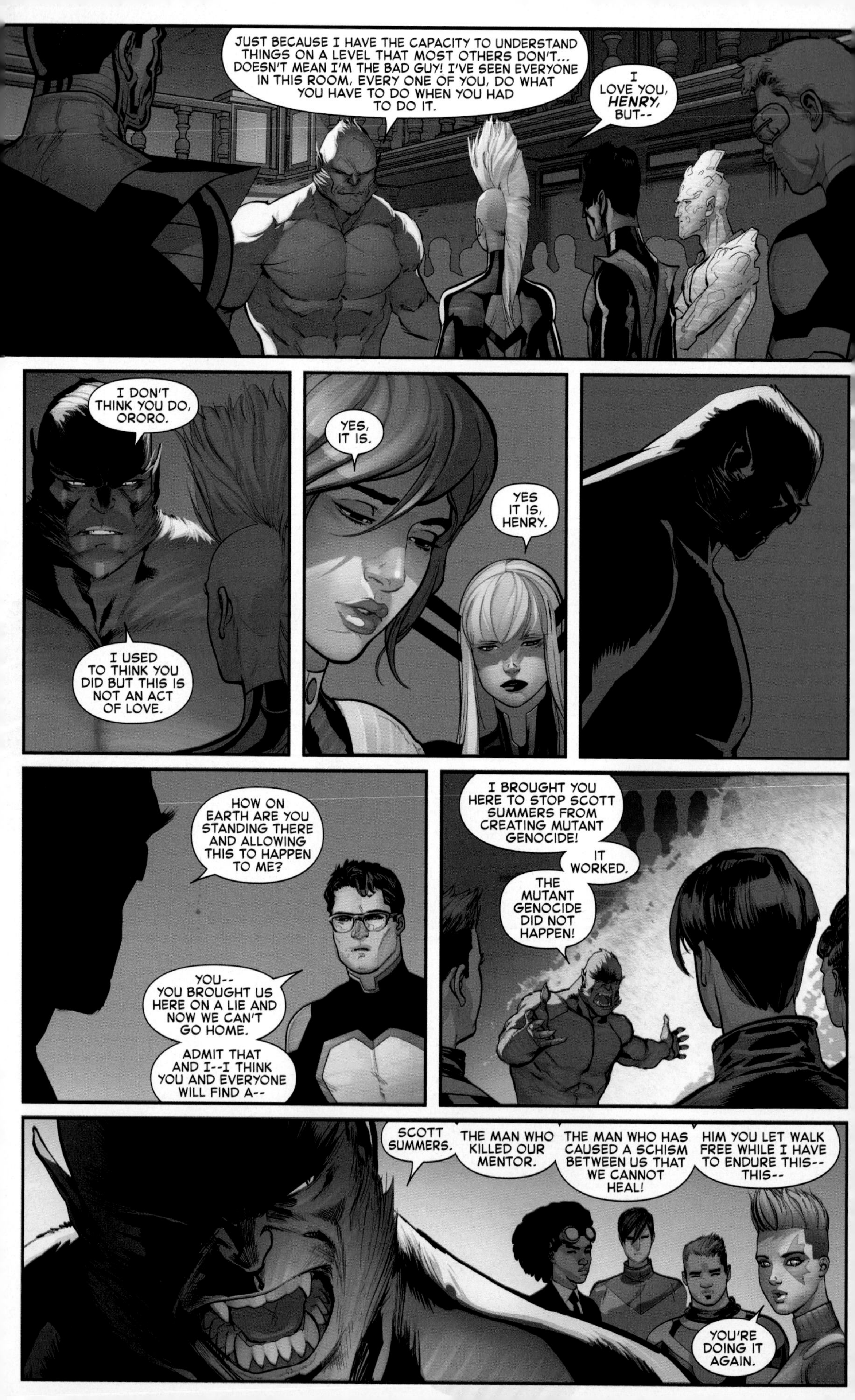
JUST BECAUSE I HAVE THE CAPACITY TO UNDERSTAND THINGS ON A LEVEL THAT MOST OTHERS DON'T... DOESN'T MEAN I'M THE BAD GUY! I'VE SEEN EVERYONE IN THIS ROOM, EVERY ONE OF YOU, DO WHAT YOU HAVE TO DO WHEN YOU HAD TO DO IT.
I LOVE YOU, HENRY, BUT--
I DON'T THINK YOU DO, ORORO.
I USED TO THINK YOU DID BUT THIS IS NOT AN ACT OF LOVE.
YES, IT IS.
YES IT IS, HENRY.
HOW ON EARTH ARE YOU STANDING THERE AND ALLOWING THIS TO HAPPEN TO ME?
YOU-- YOU BROUGHT US HERE ON A LIE AND NOW WE CAN'T GO HOME.
ADMIT THAT AND I--I THINK YOU AND EVERYONE WILL FIND A--
I BROUGHT YOU HERE TO STOP SCOTT SUMMERS FROM CREATING MUTANT GENOCIDE!
IT WORKED.
THE MUTANT GENOCIDE DID NOT HAPPEN!
SCOTT SUMMERS.
THE MAN WHO KILLED OUR MENTOR.
THE MAN WHO HAS CAUSED A SCHISM BETWEEN US THAT WE CANNOT HEAL!
HIM YOU LET WALK FREE WHILE I HAVE TO ENDURE THIS-- THIS--
YOU'RE DOING IT AGAIN.

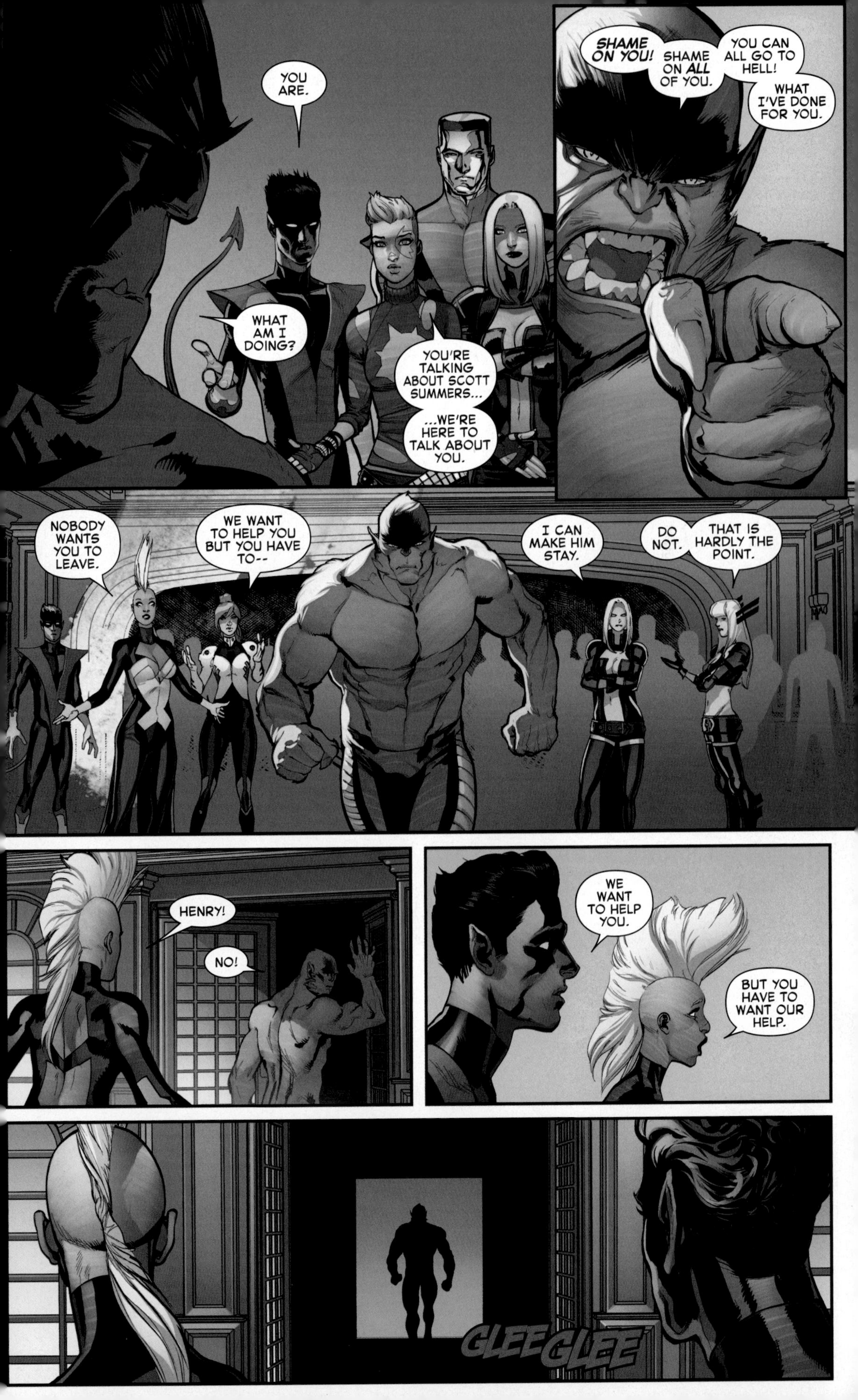

YOU ARE.
WHAT AM I DOING?
YOU'RE TALKING ABOUT SCOTT SUMMERS...
...WE'RE HERE TO TALK ABOUT YOU.
SHAME ON YOU!
SHAME ON ALL OF YOU.
YOU CAN ALL GO TO HELL!
WHAT I'VE DONE FOR YOU.
NOBODY WANTS YOU TO LEAVE.
WE WANT TO HELP YOU BUT YOU HAVE TO--
I CAN MAKE HIM STAY.
DO NOT.
THAT IS HARDLY THE POINT.
HENRY!
NO!
WE WANT TO HELP YOU.
BUT YOU HAVE TO WANT OUR HELP.
GLEE GLEE

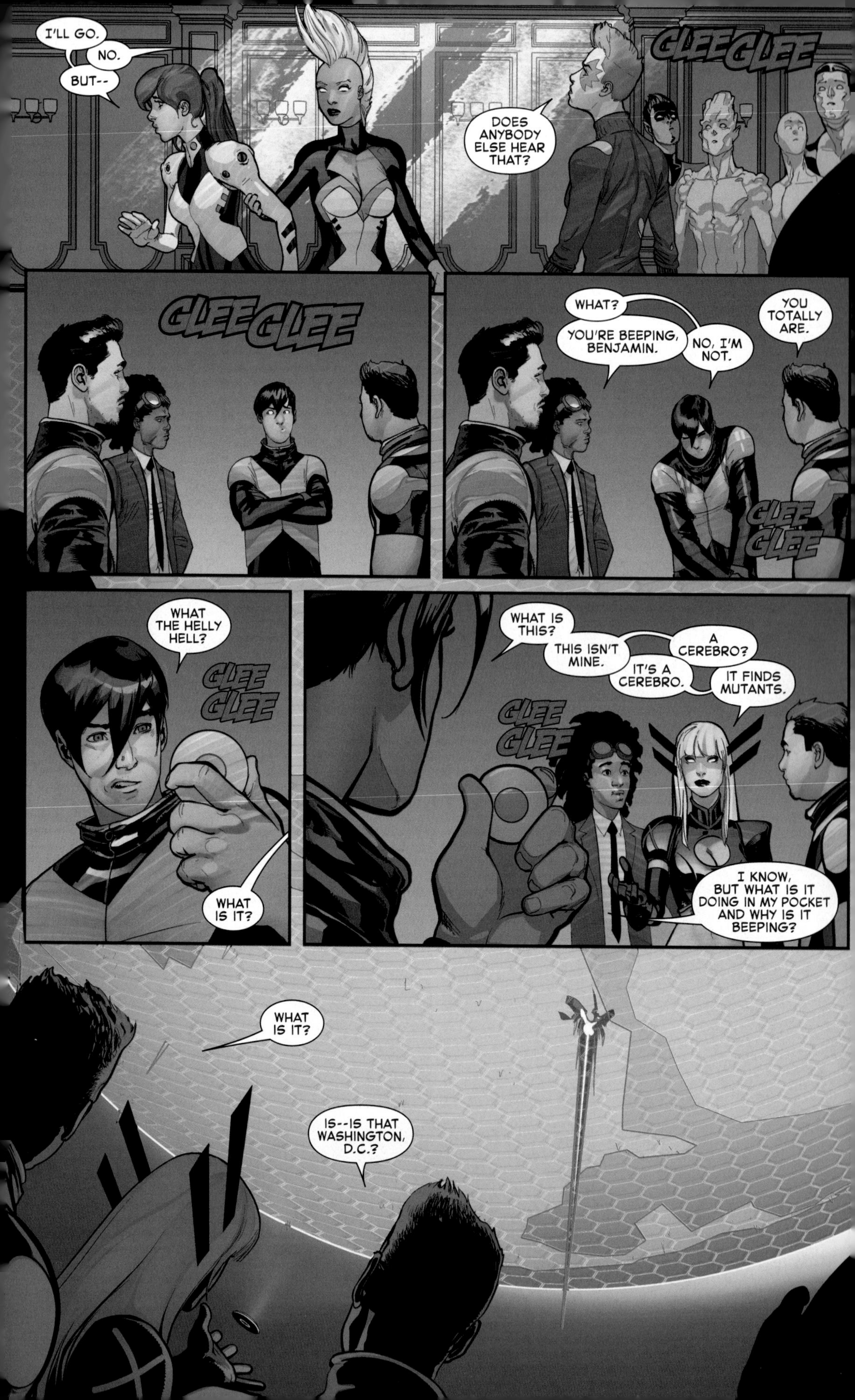
I'LL GO.
NO.
BUT--
DOES ANYBODY ELSE HEAR THAT?
GLEEGLEE
GLEEGLEE
WHAT?
YOU'RE BEEPING, BENJAMIN.
NO, I'M NOT.
YOU TOTALLY ARE.
GLEE GLEE
WHAT THE HELLY HELL?
GLEE GLEE
WHAT IS IT?
WHAT IS THIS?
THIS ISN'T MINE.
IT'S A CEREBRO.
A CEREBRO?
IT FINDS MUTANTS.
GLEE GLEE
I KNOW, BUT WHAT IS IT DOING IN MY POCKET AND WHY IS IT BEEPING?
WHAT IS IT?
IS--IS THAT WASHINGTON, D.C.?

YES. IT'S DEFINITELY WASHINGTON, D.C.

OH...

GODDESS, DAMN HIM!

IS THIS REAL?

WHAT IS IT?

WELL, IT'S REAL. IT'S ALL OVER THE NEWS!

I THINK WE SHOULD GO.

DID YOU KNOW ABOUT THIS?

NO.

I CAN TAKE US THERE.

WOULD YOU?

WHAT IS IT?

THIS. YOU STUDENTS DON'T HAVE TO GO, BUT WE DO.

IT IS COMPLETELY UP TO YOU.

AND THIS IS NOT A TEST.

ACCORDING TO OUR MUTANT HIVE MIND, EVERYBODY IN THIS ROOM REALLY WANTS TO GO.

LET'S JUST DO IT.

HE KNOWS WE'RE COMING.

DOES HE WANT TO FIGHT?

THAT WE ARE NOT GOING TO DO.

HE DOESN'T WANT TO FIGHT.

BUT WHAT DOES HE WANT?

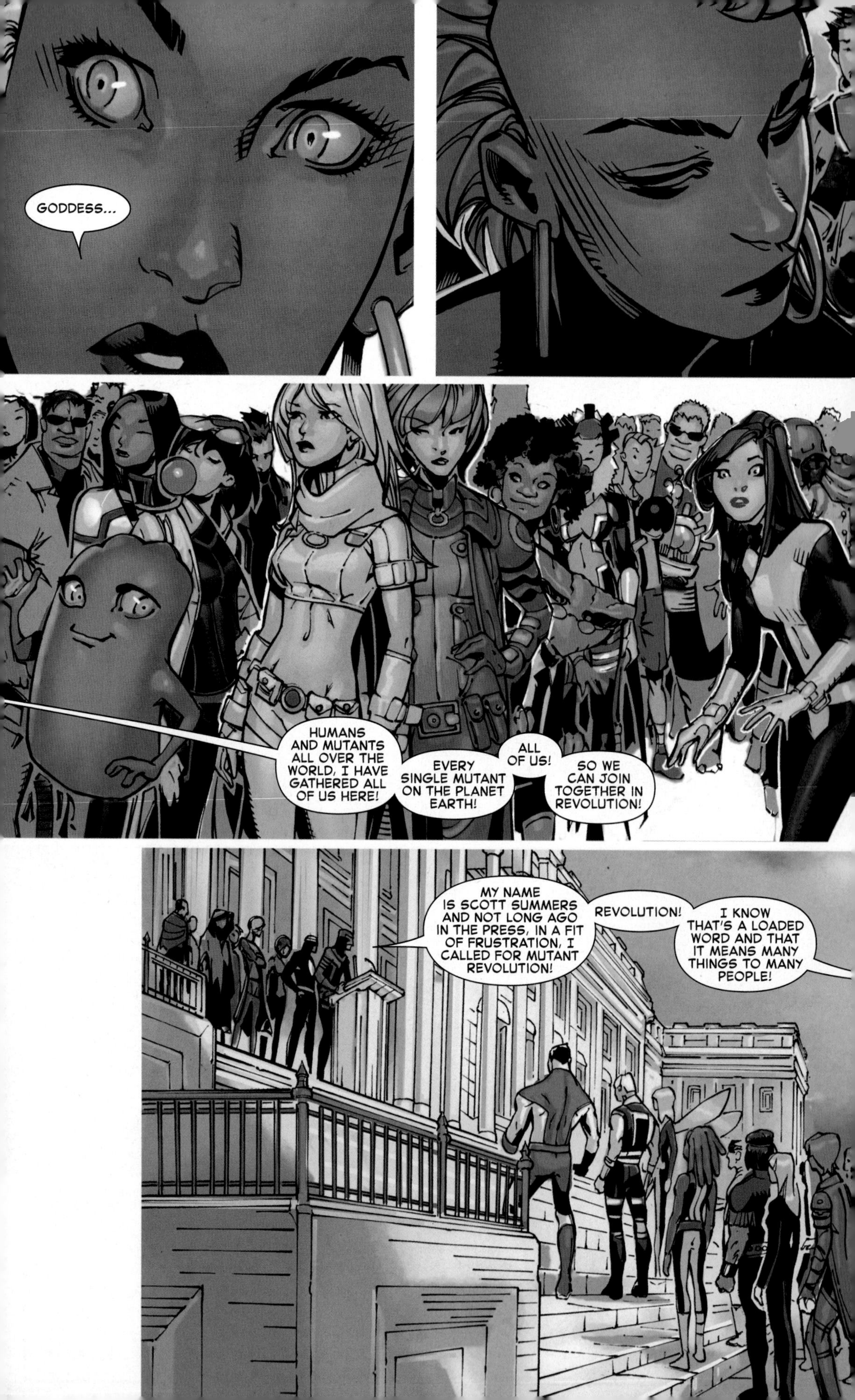
GODDESS...
HUMANS AND MUTANTS ALL OVER THE WORLD, I HAVE GATHERED ALL OF US HERE!
EVERY SINGLE MUTANT ON THE PLANET EARTH!
ALL OF US!
SO WE CAN JOIN TOGETHER IN REVOLUTION!
MY NAME IS SCOTT SUMMERS AND NOT LONG AGO IN THE PRESS, IN A FIT OF FRUSTRATION, I CALLED FOR MUTANT REVOLUTION!
REVOLUTION!
I KNOW THAT'S A LOADED WORD AND THAT IT MEANS MANY THINGS TO MANY PEOPLE!

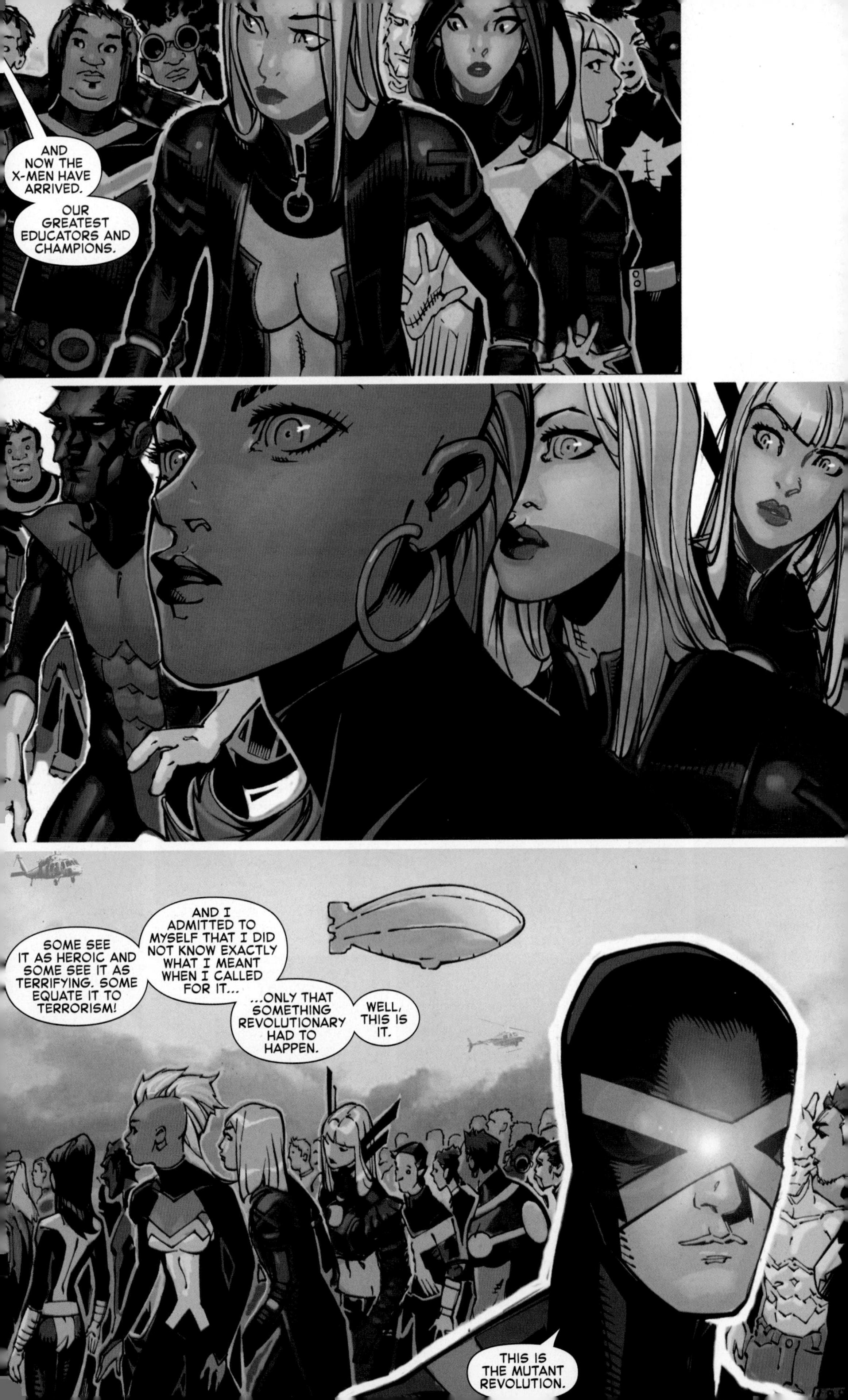
AND NOW THE X-MEN HAVE ARRIVED.
OUR GREATEST EDUCATORS AND CHAMPIONS.
SOME SEE IT AS HEROIC AND SOME SEE IT AS TERRIFYING. SOME EQUATE IT TO TERRORISM!
AND I ADMITTED TO MYSELF THAT I DID NOT KNOW EXACTLY WHAT I MEANT WHEN I CALLED FOR IT...
...ONLY THAT SOMETHING REVOLUTIONARY HAD TO HAPPEN.
WELL, THIS IS IT.
THIS IS THE MUTANT REVOLUTION.

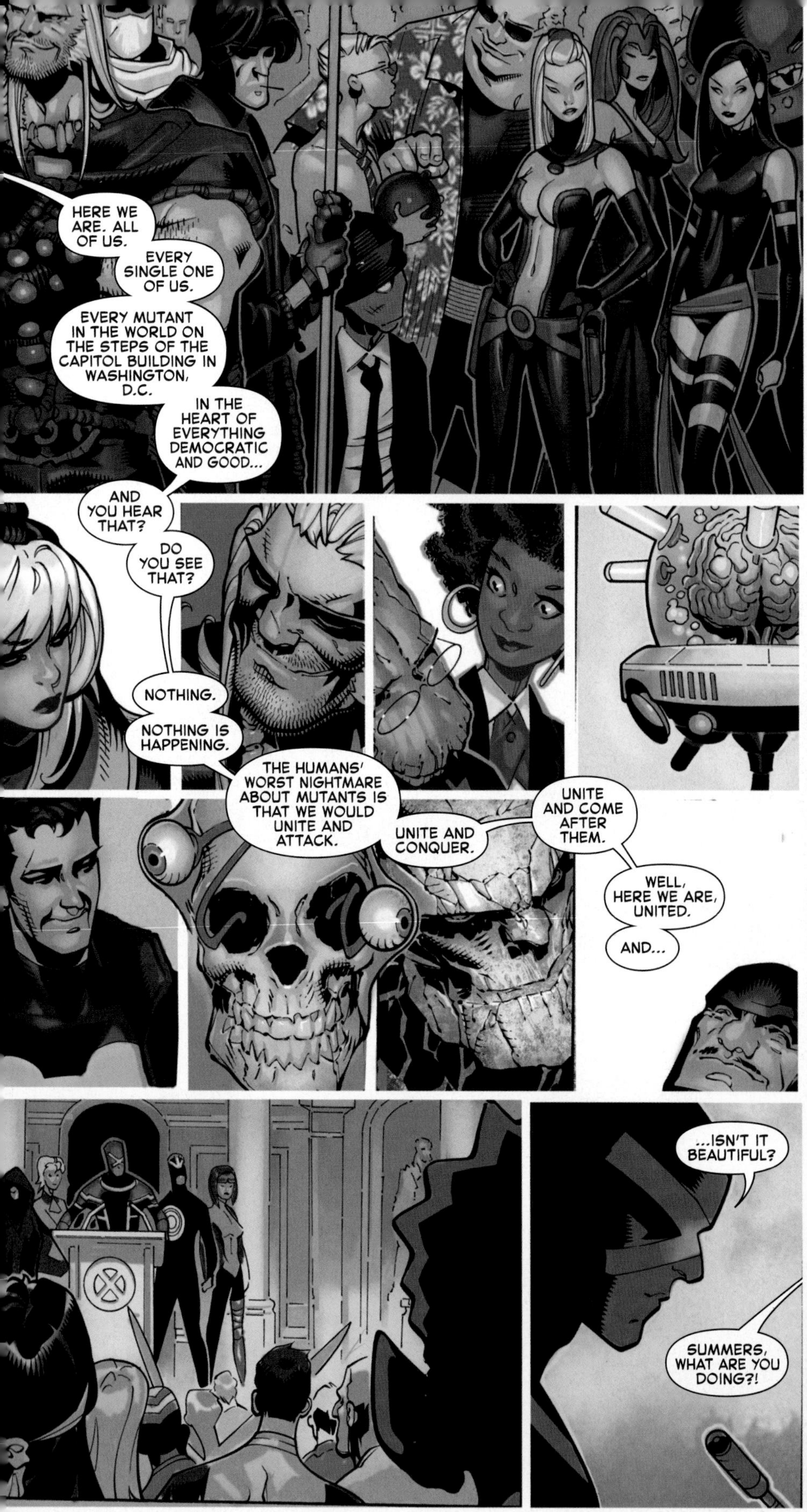
HERE WE ARE. ALL OF US.
EVERY SINGLE ONE OF US.
EVERY MUTANT IN THE WORLD ON THE STEPS OF THE CAPITOL BUILDING IN WASHINGTON, D.C.
IN THE HEART OF EVERYTHING DEMOCRATIC AND GOOD...
AND YOU HEAR THAT?
DO YOU SEE THAT?
NOTHING.
NOTHING IS HAPPENING.
THE HUMANS' WORST NIGHTMARE ABOUT MUTANTS IS THAT WE WOULD UNITE AND ATTACK.
UNITE AND CONQUER.
UNITE AND COME AFTER THEM.
WELL, HERE WE ARE, UNITED.
AND...
...ISN'T IT BEAUTIFUL?
SUMMERS, WHAT ARE YOU DOING?!
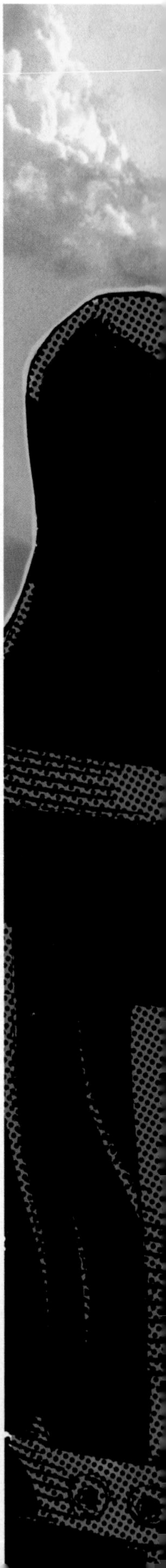

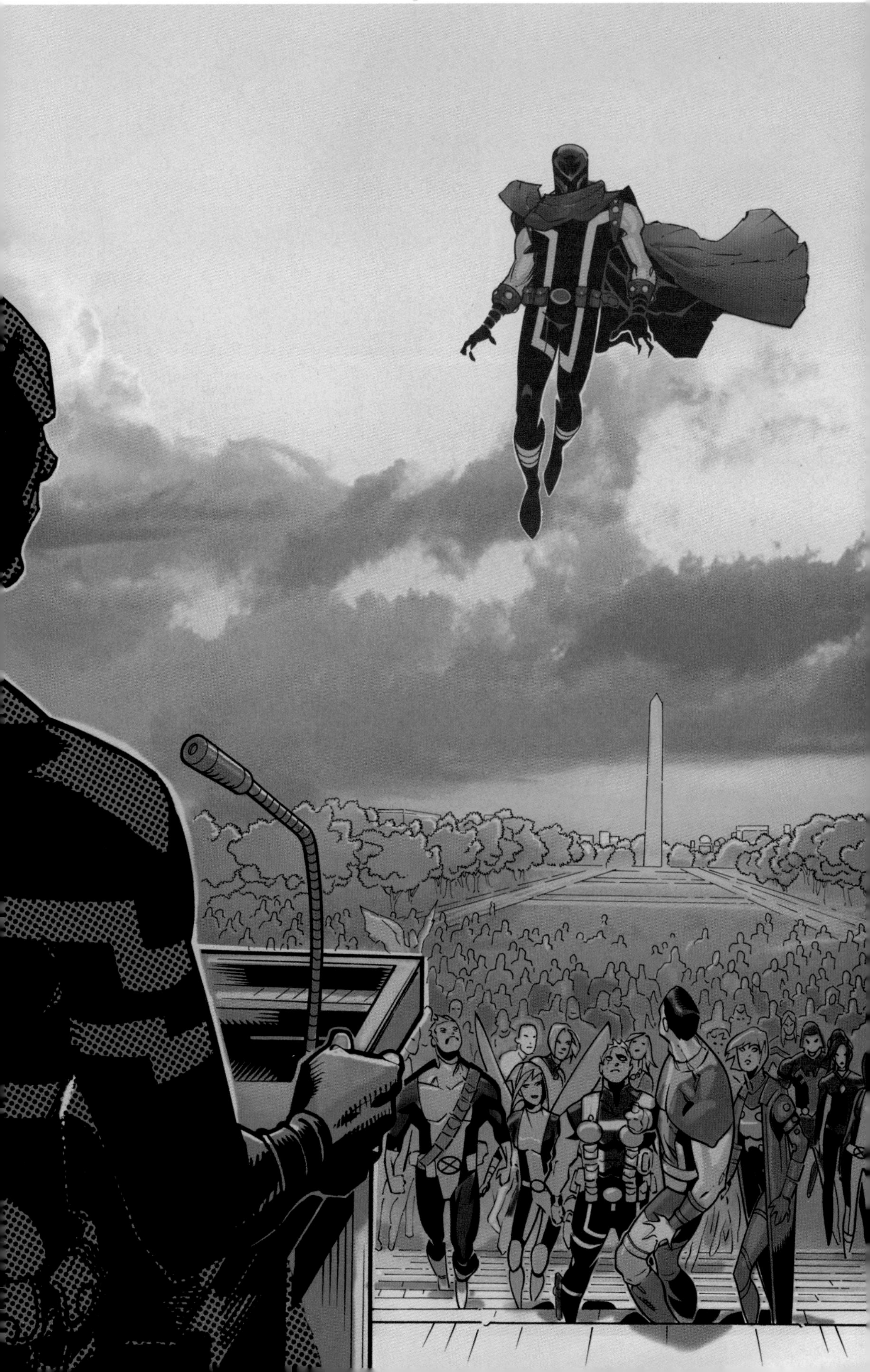

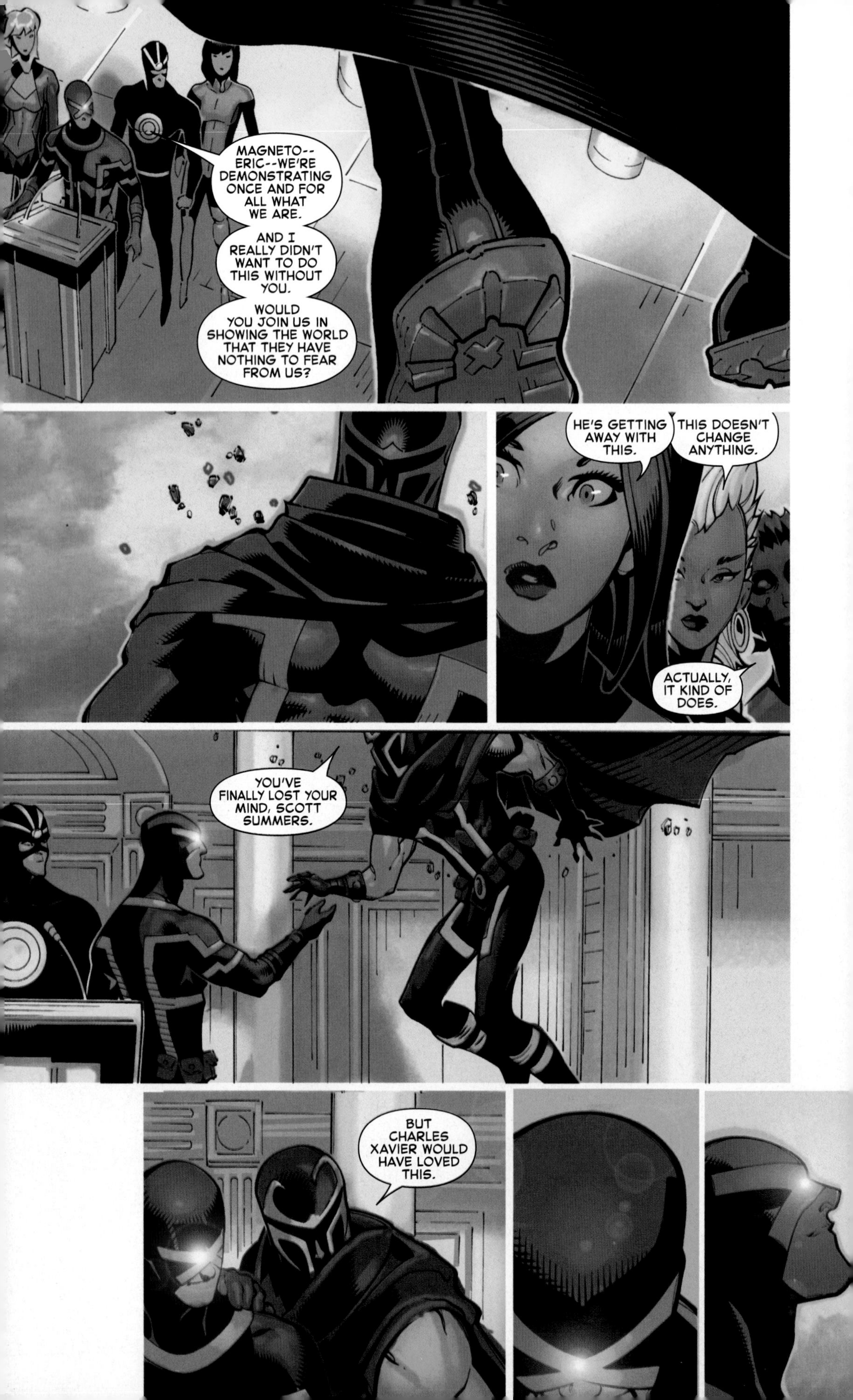
MAGNETO-- ERIC--WE'RE DEMONSTRATING ONCE AND FOR ALL WHAT WE ARE.
AND I REALLY DIDN'T WANT TO DO THIS WITHOUT YOU.
WOULD YOU JOIN US IN SHOWING THE WORLD THAT THEY HAVE NOTHING TO FEAR FROM US?
HE'S GETTING AWAY WITH THIS.
THIS DOESN'T CHANGE ANYTHING.
ACTUALLY, IT KIND OF DOES.
YOU'VE FINALLY LOST YOUR MIND, SCOTT SUMMERS.
BUT CHARLES XAVIER WOULD HAVE LOVED THIS.

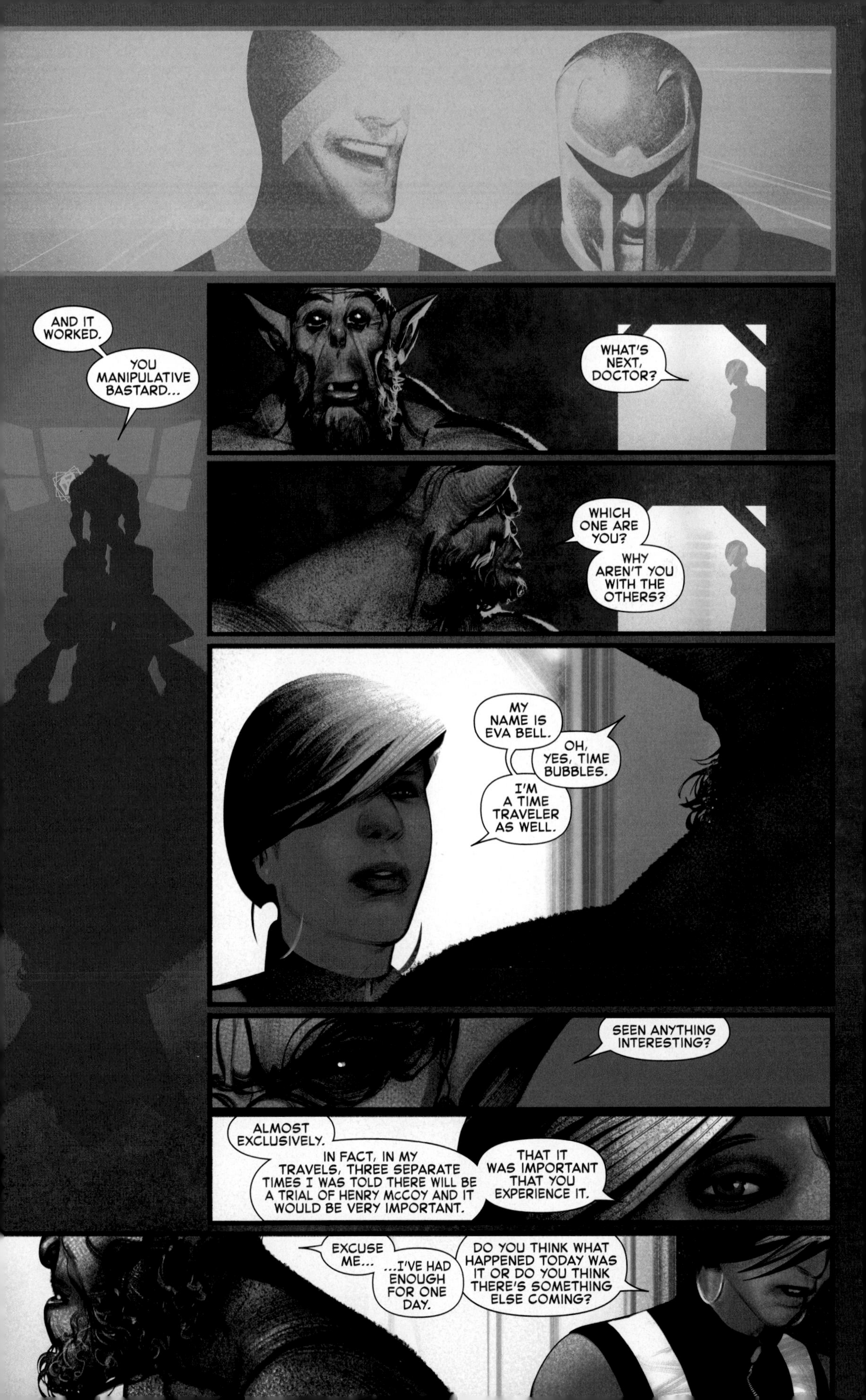
AND IT WORKED.
YOU MANIPULATIVE BASTARD...
WHAT'S NEXT, DOCTOR?
WHICH ONE ARE YOU?
WHY AREN'T YOU WITH THE OTHERS?
MY NAME IS EVA BELL.
OH, YES, TIME BUBBLES.
I'M A TIME TRAVELER AS WELL.
SEEN ANYTHING INTERESTING?
ALMOST EXCLUSIVELY.
IN FACT, IN MY TRAVELS, THREE SEPARATE TIMES I WAS TOLD THERE WILL BE A TRIAL OF HENRY McCOY AND IT WOULD BE VERY IMPORTANT.
THAT IT WAS IMPORTANT THAT YOU EXPERIENCE IT.
EXCUSE ME...
...I'VE HAD ENOUGH FOR ONE DAY.
DO YOU THINK WHAT HAPPENED TODAY WAS IT OR DO YOU THINK THERE'S SOMETHING ELSE COMING?

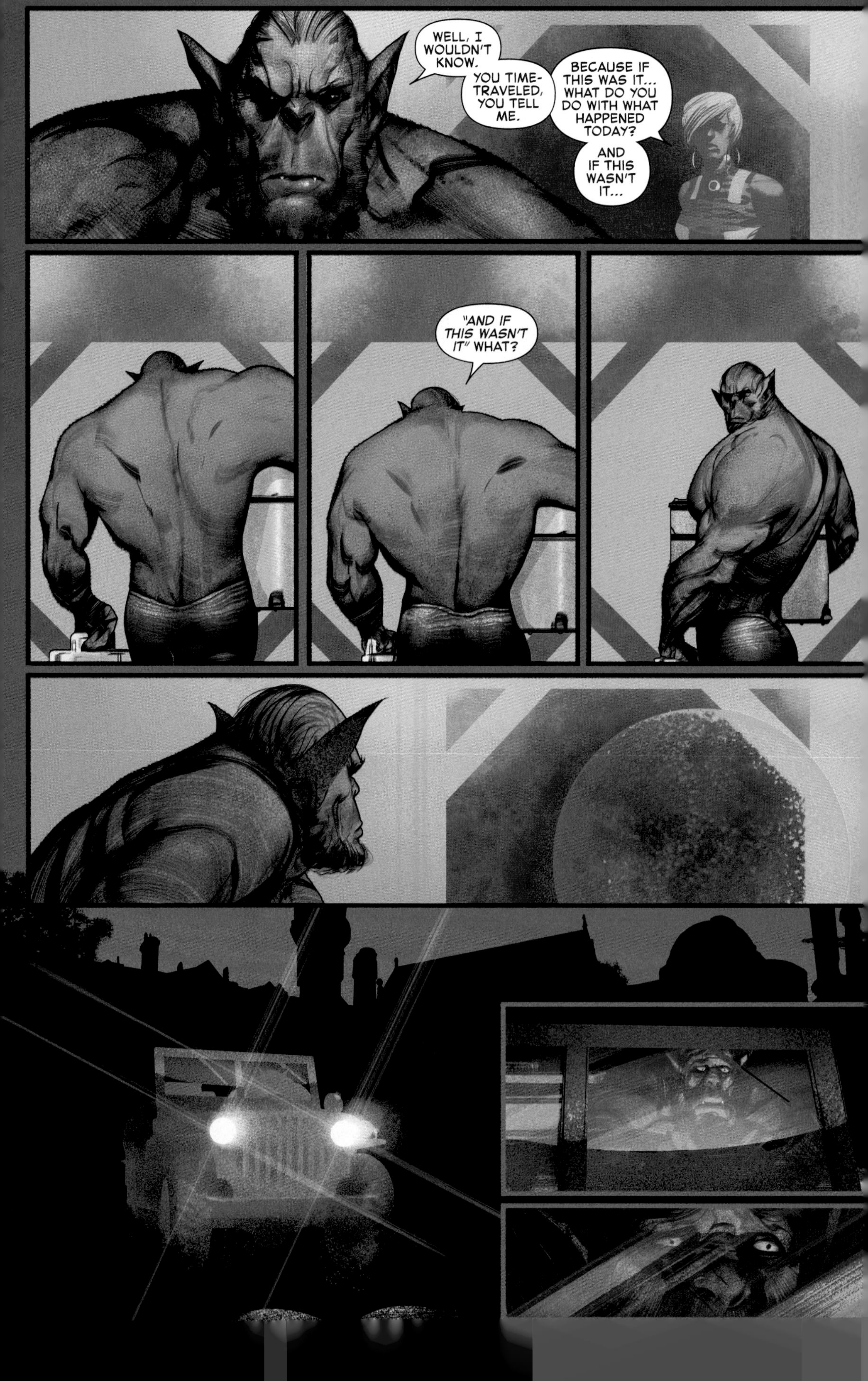
WELL, I WOULDN'T KNOW.
YOU TIME-TRAVELED, YOU TELL ME.
BECAUSE IF THIS WAS IT... WHAT DO YOU DO WITH WHAT HAPPENED TODAY?
AND IF THIS WASN'T IT...
"AND IF THIS WASN'T IT" WHAT?

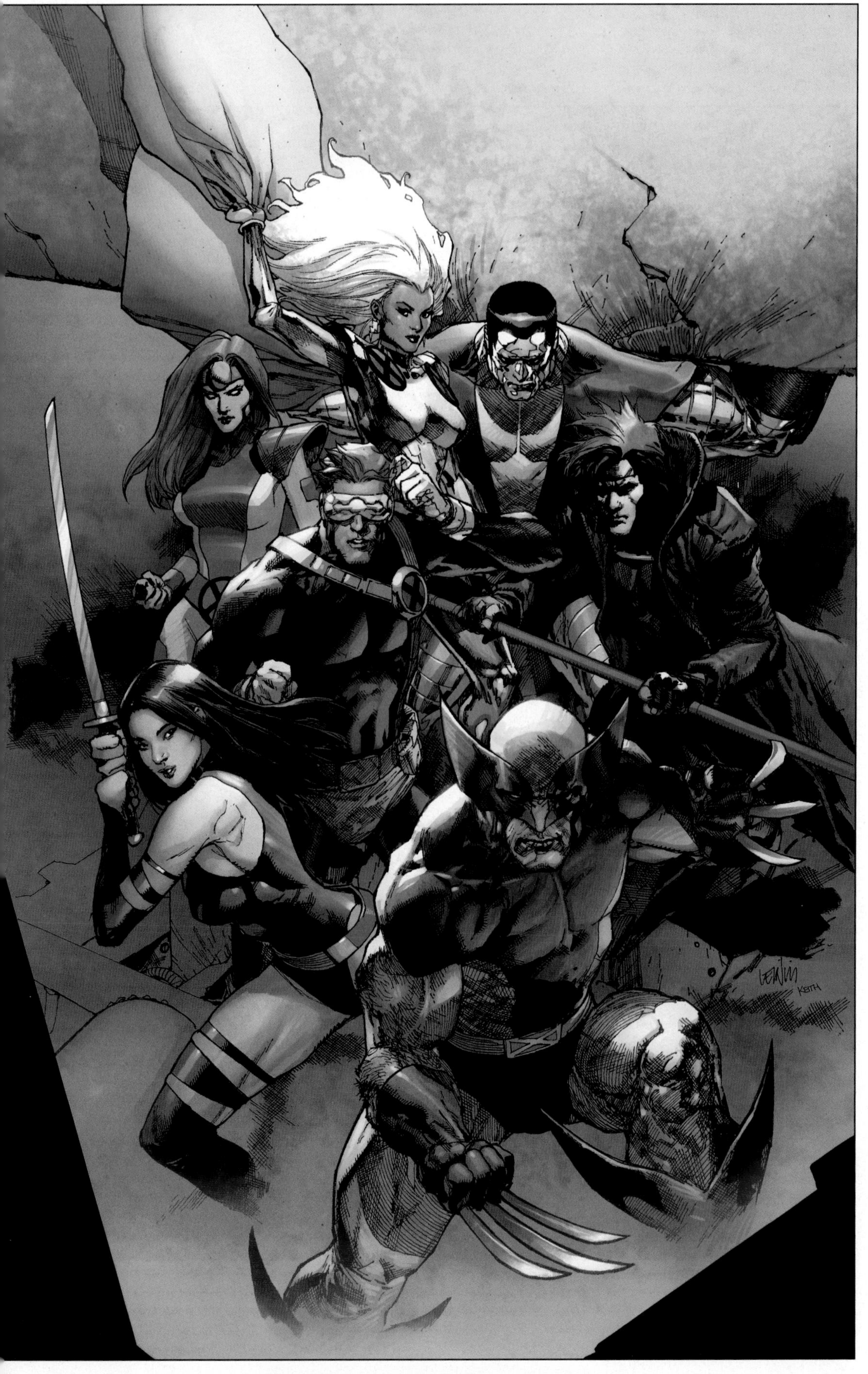

UNCANNY X-MEN #600 VARIANT

BY LEINIL YU & JASON KEITH

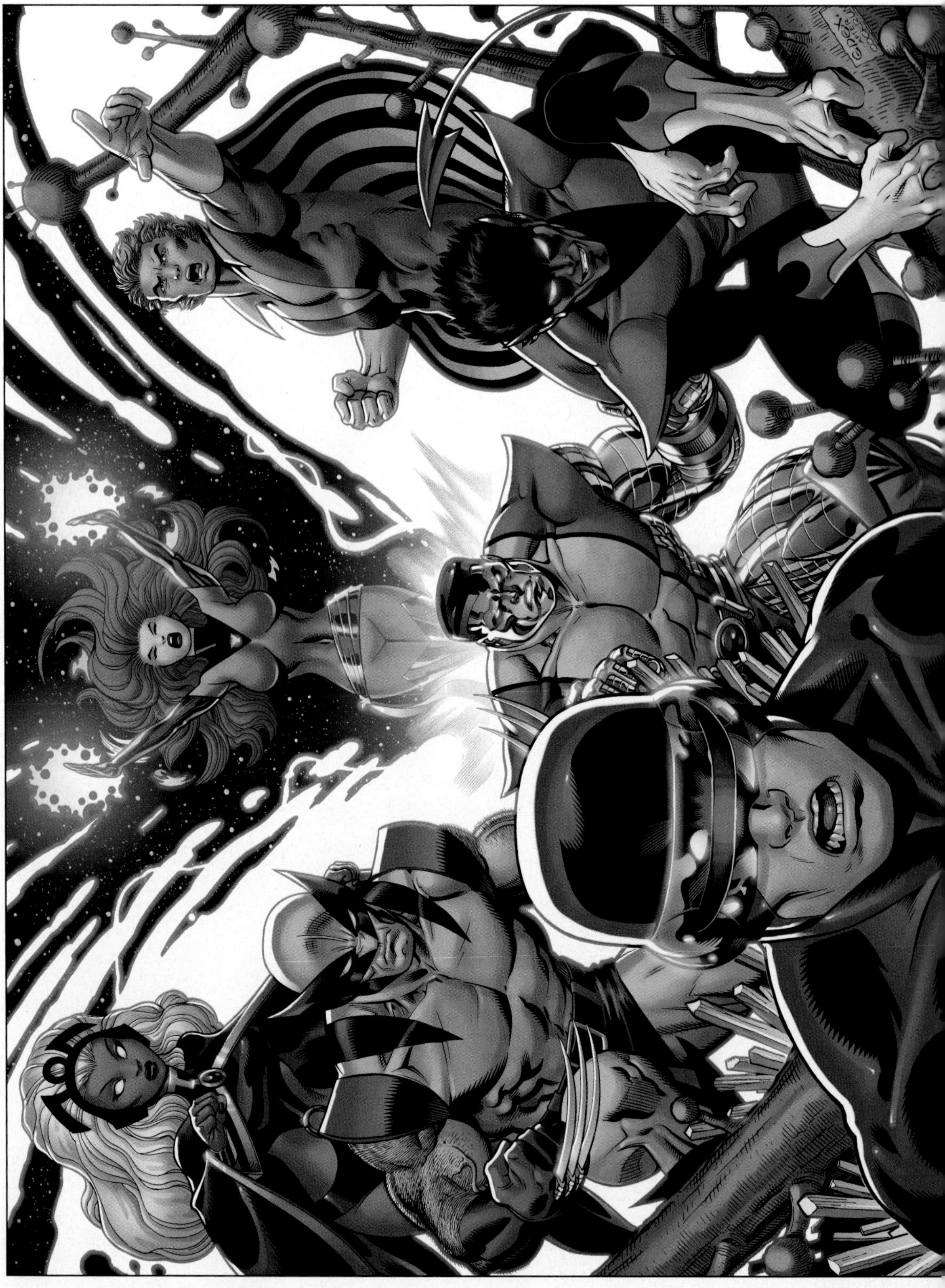

UNCANNY X-MEN #600 VARIANT
BY ED McGUINNESS, DEXTER VINES & VAL STAPLES

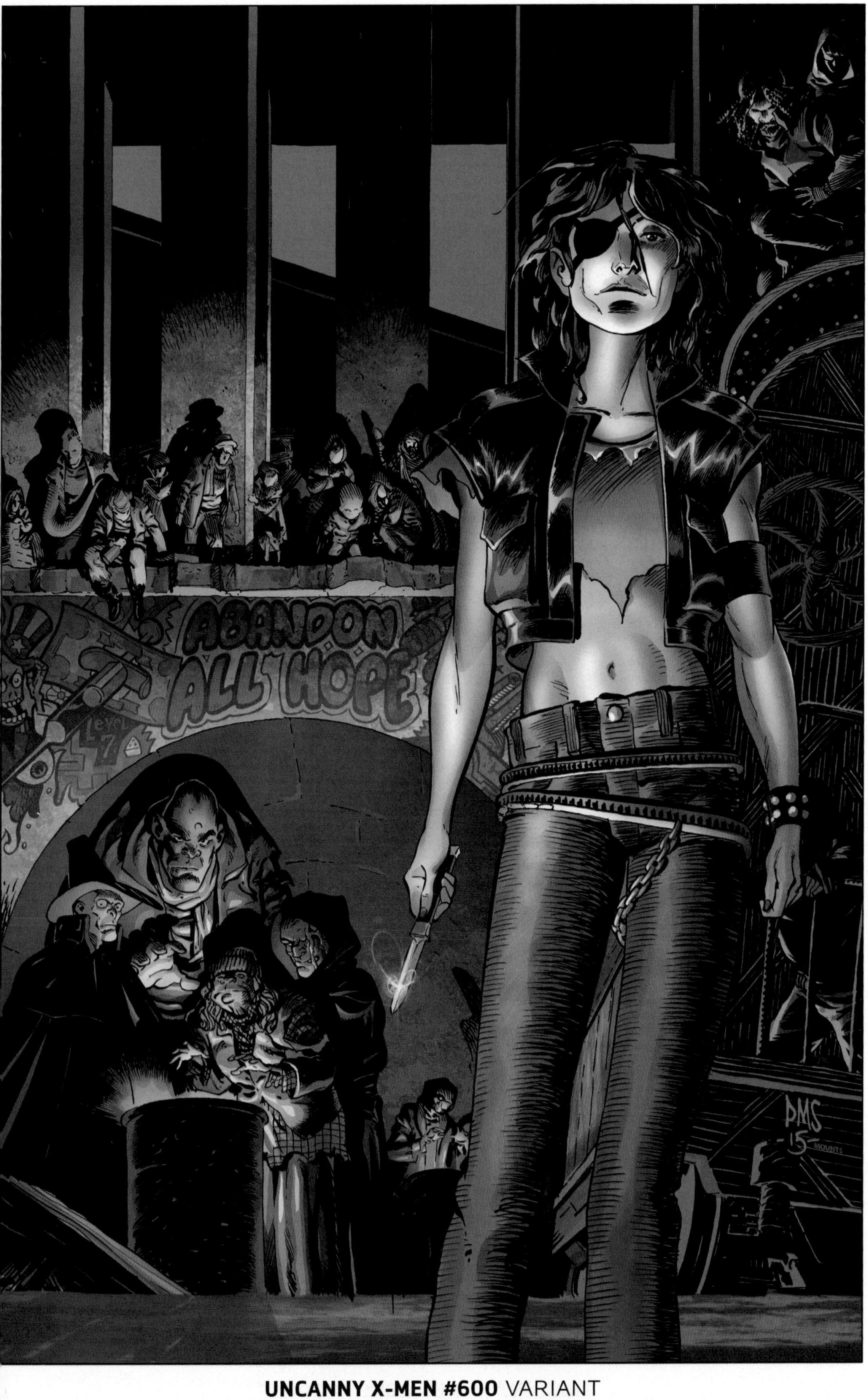
ABANDON ALL HOPE
LEVEL 7
PMS 15
MOUNTS

UNCANNY X-MEN #600 VARIANT

BY PAUL SMITH & PAUL MOUNTS

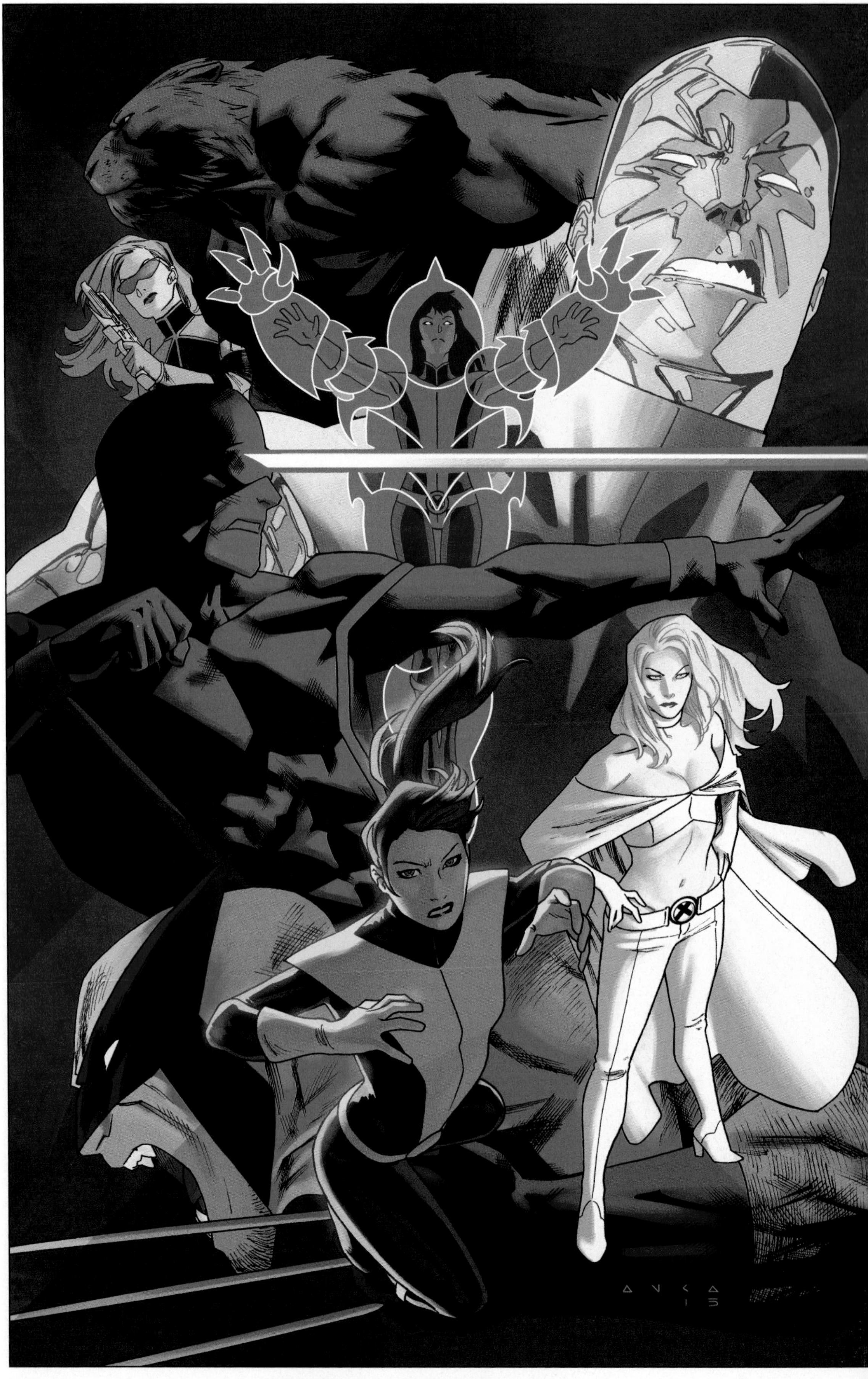

UNCANNY X-MEN #600 VARIANT

BY KRIS ANKA

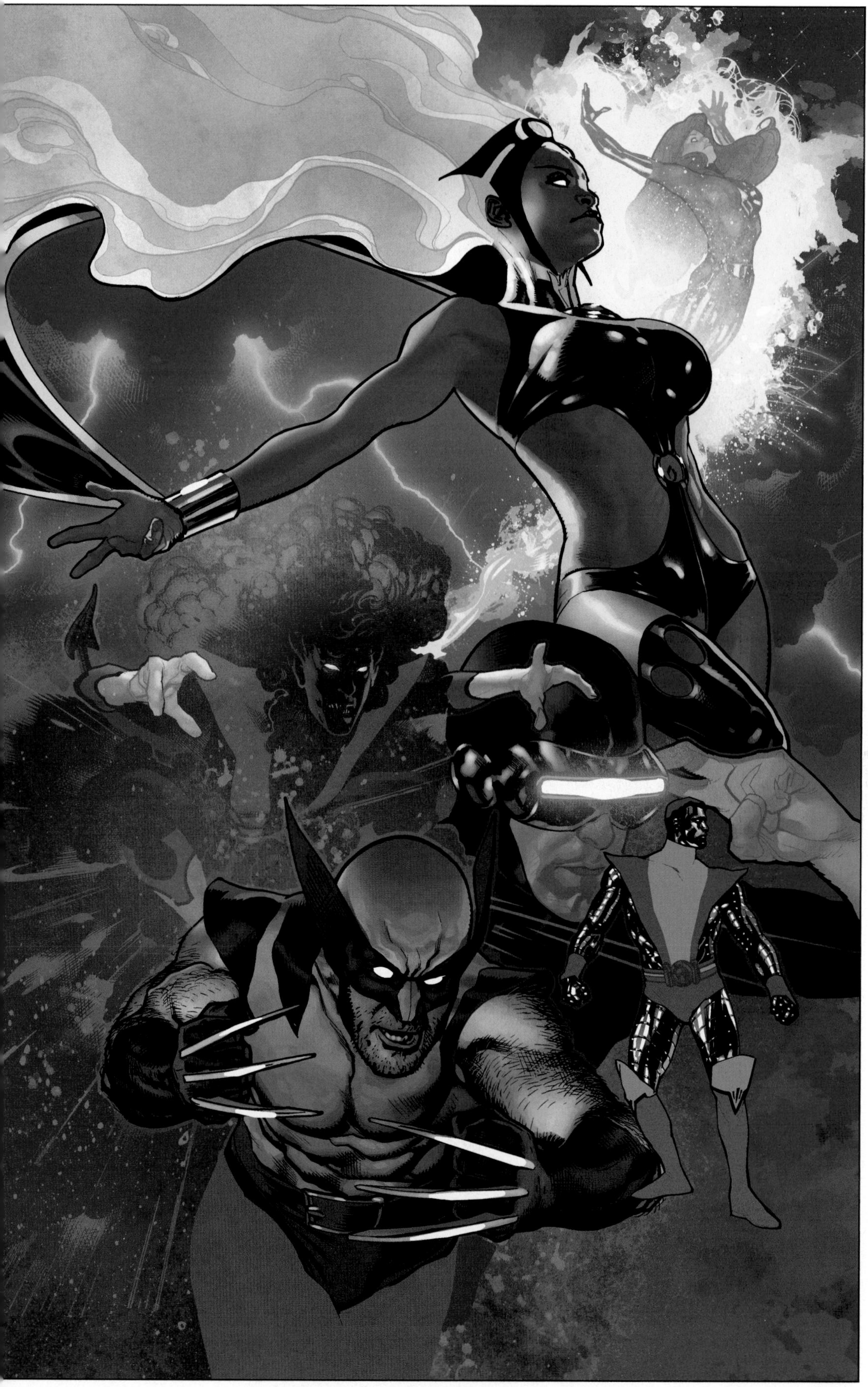

UNCANNY X-MEN #600 VARIANT

BY ADAM HUGHES

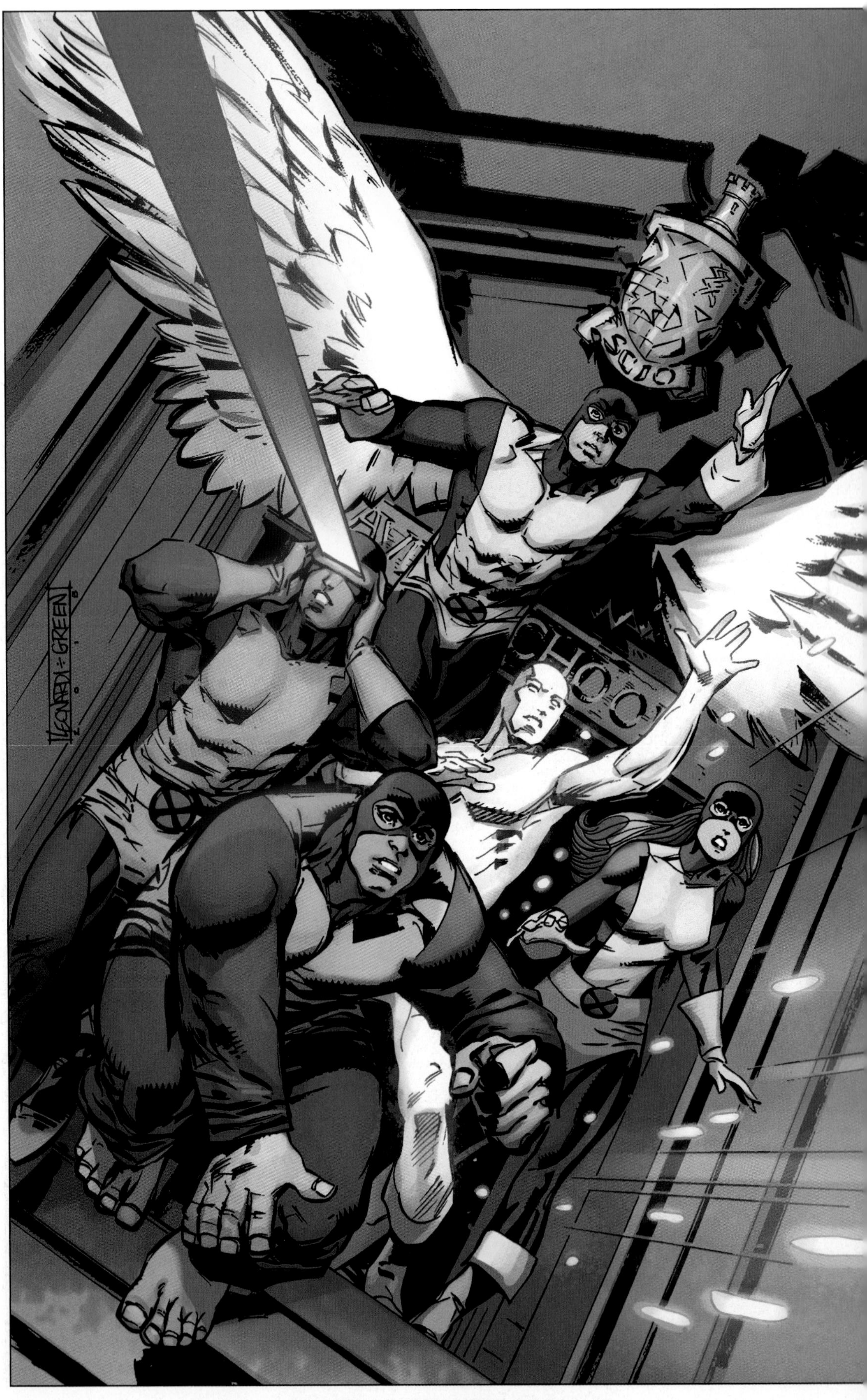

UNCANNY X-MEN #600 VARIANT

BY RICK LEONARDI, DAN GREEN & JASON KEITH

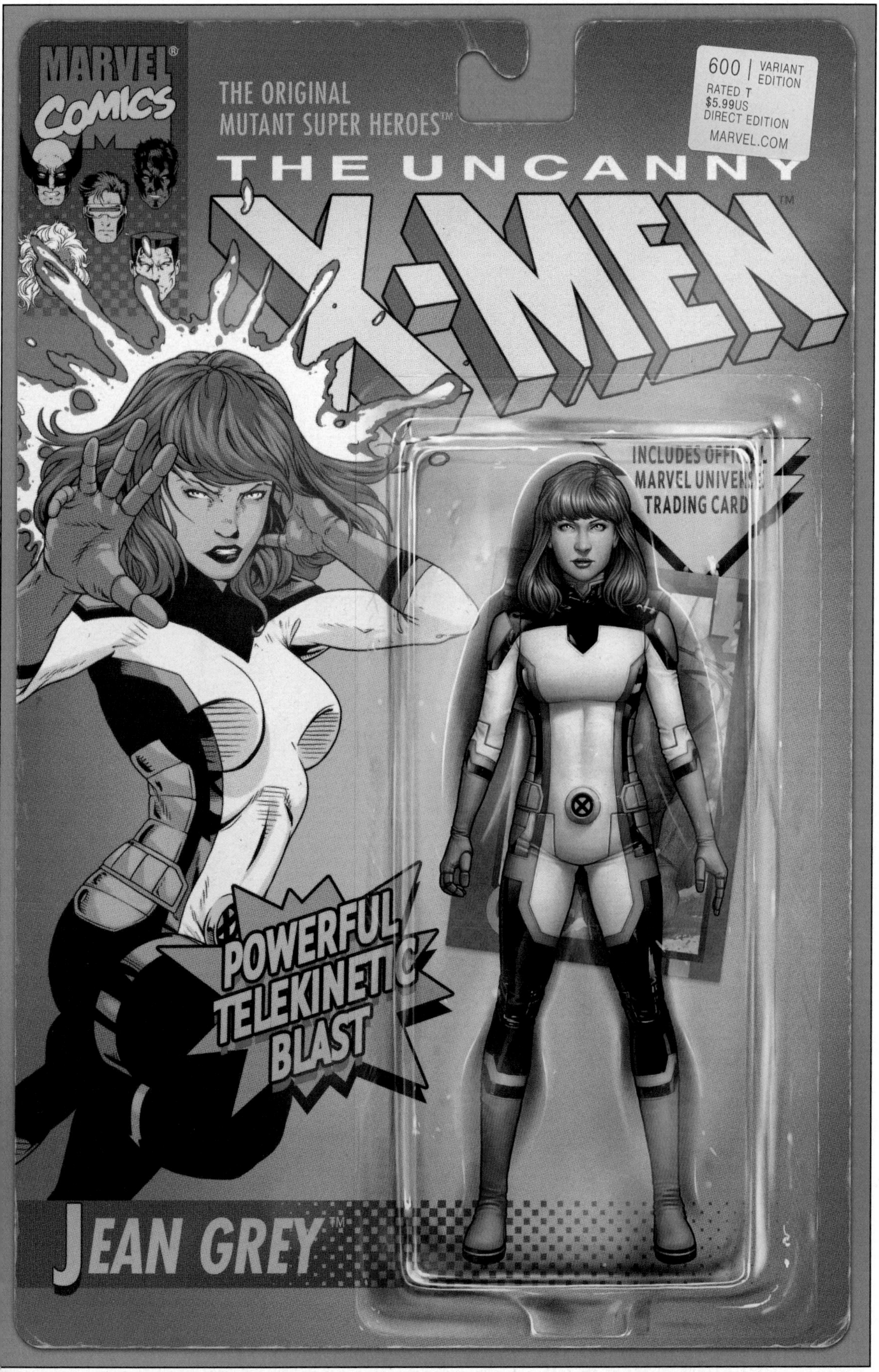
MARVEL COMICS
THE ORIGINAL
MUTANT SUPER HEROES™
600 | VARIANT EDITION
RATED T
$5.99US
DIRECT EDITION
MARVEL.COM
THE UNCANNY
X-MEN™
INCLUDES OFFICIAL MARVEL UNIVERSE TRADING CARD
POWERFUL TELEKINETIC BLAST
JEAN GREY™

UNCANNY X-MEN #600 ACTION FIGURE VARIANT

BY JOHN TYLER CHRISTOPHER

UNCANNY X-MEN #600
ACTION FIGURE VARIANTS
BY JOHN TYLER CHRISTOPHER